"I found myself in Minneota,
unemployed, divorced, unpubl.
family dead, and most of the peo,
from my childhood ancient, senile, or going fast.
I was strangely happy."

—Bill Holm

The author of the beloved *Coming Home Crazy* returns
to his hometown and investigates—through the lens of
small-town life—what community means to us and the
rigid definitions we give to "success" and "failure."

PRAISE FOR

The Heart Can Be Filled Anywhere on Earth

"The magic of this work is that Holm shares with us
people who would conventionally be thought of as obscure. . . . Luckily, Holm is able to keep these ordinary/
extraordinary people alive in his memory, and he brings
them to us in the best storytelling tradition."
—*Hungry Mind Review*

"Holm brings a world traveler's perspective to bear on
his home town, tiny Minneota, Minn., 1990 population
1,417. . . . Sometimes the best traveling can be had in
your own back yard." —*San Jose Mercury News*

The Heart Can Be Filled Anywhere on Earth

Bill Holm

MILKWEED EDITIONS

Milkweed Editions, 1011 Washington Avenue South, Suite 300
Minneapolis, MN 55415
(800) 520-6455 / www.milkweed.org

Published 2000 by Milkweed Editions
Printed in the United States of America
Cover design by Dale Cooney
Cover and author photos by B. T. Russell
Chapter-opening ornament by Wesley B. Tanner, Ann Arbor
Interior design by Will Powers
The text of this book is set in ITC Galliard
00 01 02 03 04 05   5 4 3 2 1
First Edition 2000

The essay "Music of Failure" was originally published in *The Music of Failure* (Marshall, Minn.: Plains Press, 1985) and subsequently in *Prairie Days* (Dallas: Saybrook Publishing, 1987) and *The Music of Failure* (Minneapolis: Prairie Grass Press, 1990). Reprinted with permission.

The first half of "Glad Poverty" was first published in different form in *Unexpected Fictions* (Winnipeg: Turnstone Press, 1989). The essay was published in its current form in *Beyond Borders*, edited by Mark Vinz and David Williamson (Minneapolis: New Rivers Press; Winnipeg: Turnstone Press, 1992), and was translated into Icelandic by Árny Hjaltadóttir and published in *Skírnir* magazine in Iceland. Reprinted here by permission of the author.

Milkweed Editions is a nonprofit publisher. Original publication of this book was supported in part by the Bush Foundation; Target Stores, Dayton's, and Mervyn's by the Dayton Hudson Foundation; Ecolab Foundation; General Mills Foundation; Honeywell Foundation; Jerome Foundation; John S. and James L. Knight Foundation; McKnight Foundation; Andrew W. Mellon Foundation; Kathy Stevens Dougherty and Michael E. Dougherty Fund of the Minneapolis Foundation; Minnesota State Arts Board through an appropriation by the Minnesota State Legislature; Challenge and Literature Programs of the National Endowment for the Arts; I. A. O'Shaughnessy Foundation; Piper Jaffray Companies, Inc.; John and Beverly Rollwagen Fund of the Minneapolis Foundation; St. Paul Companies, Inc.; Star Tribune/Cowles Media Foundation; Surdna Foundation; James R. Thorpe Foundation; Lila Wallace-Reader's Digest Literary Publishers Marketing Development Program, funded through a grant to the Council of Literary Magazines and Presses; and generous individuals. Additional funders for this edition are the Elmer L. and Eleanor J. Anderson Foundation; James Ford Bell Foundation; Lawrence and Elizabeth Ann O'Shaughnessy Charitable Income Trust in honor of Lawrence M. O'Shaughnessy; Oswald Family Foundation; and Ritz Foundation on behalf of Mr. and Mrs. E. J. Phelps Jr.

Library of Congress Cataloging-in-Publication Data

Holm, Bill, 1943–
    The heart can be filled anywhere on earth /
Bill Holm. — 1st ed.
        p.   cm.
    ISBN 1-57131-251-X (pbk. : alk. paper)
    1. City and town life—Minnesota—Minneota.   2. Holm, Bill, 1943–   .
    3. Minneota (Minn.)—Social life and customs.   4. Social values—United States.
    I. Title.
F614.M62H65   1996
977.6363—dc20   95-51844
                                                                                                              CIP

This book is printed on acid-free paper.

For Daren Gislason whether he wants it or not.

And: For the children of G. B. Bjornson, who kept the facts, the lore, and the stories of this small place and its immigrants alive, making them large so that others could see them, thus understanding better the pleasures and lessons of their own histories. In memory of Valdimar and Bjorn, and with love to my second mother, their sister, Helga Bjornson Brogger.

The Heart Can Be Filled Anywhere on Earth

*The Heart Can Be Filled
Anywhere on Earth*

Minneota · Much Water

Tall Grass

Americans inhabit a third of a continent, mostly in the South
Temperate Zone, but depending on elevation or proximity to
the sea, the climate provides large seasonable samples of arctic
blasts or damp tropical miasma. In the middle of the continent,
in the north of the central United States, the climate lurches
from savagery to savagery, separated by ephemeral respite. The
lowest recorded temperature in Minnesota was 60 degrees
below zero in February 1996, the highest, 114 degrees in July
1936. Each year winter and summer approach these extremes
closely enough to make the records nervous. Spring disappears
almost completely, a few days of mud and frenzied melting before insect hatch and livestock warnings. The melancholy fall,
sometimes graced with a few days of heartbreaking loveliness,
often dies abruptly, strangled by the premature arrival of blizzards whose ghosts endure in the corners of ditches for seven
months. This is not the sort of place where you would desire to
live whatever the glowing prose of nineteenth-century immigration brochures. Huge sections of several nearby states remain empty enough to justify talk of turning them into a vast
park and preserve for buffalo who, before we slaughtered most
of them, desired only grass and space, here inexhaustible com-
modities.

Minneota, Minnesota, where I live, sits close to the western
border of the state, far from forests, big lakes, or any sizable

city. It is a small dot on what geographers describe as the northern temperate tallgrass prairie. Half of Minnesota lies in that zone—the south and the west. As rainfall declines and elevation rises, not far west of Minneota, the tallgrass shrivels to a short-grass prairie of immense size and lonesomeness: the Great Plains. After about a thousand miles, the Rockies begin to rise, perking things up a bit for the scenery and real estate conscious. We cannot see them from Minneota, even on a clear day. If we desire to see anything at all in Minneota: oceans, mountains, forests, tall buildings, anything other than more of the same vast flatness rolling off toward the horizon in all directions, we must imagine, or use those necessary crutches to the mind's eye—reading or finding money for travel to see with the literal eye.

In America these days citizens imagine that they "define" themselves—that a human being or place or thing is what you say it is, what in fact you desire it to be. But however we trumpet our defining of ourselves or our fellow humans, much less nature, we allow true definition to remain where it has always lived in America: in the dependable hands of economic assessors—whether they be real estate agents, banks, investment corporations, or tax bureaucrats. The tiresome old cliché: that we know the price of everything and the value of nothing, more accurately describes our real behavior and loyalty than we can comfortably admit to ourselves. Our house, our landscape, our own history, the very centers of our lives, are worth to us only the sums we are offered for them by whatever stray power controls the purse.

Minneota is cheap. I paid five thousand dollars in 1977 for the old house where I sit writing this sentence. The market value has surely declined by now. The supply of ramshackle houses in undesirable locations overwhelms the flimsy demand—exactly as practical capitalism assures us that it should.

The tallgrass prairie is cheap, too, though fluttering booms drift over it now and again like small winds come up in the night only to expire with the sun. The 1990s are not a boom time. Should you desire a farm, now is a fine occasion to buy. You can then join the 2-percent fragment of your fellow citizens in the practice of the world's second or third oldest profession. You will neither get rich by it, nor will you have the chance to enjoy scenic vistas of tallgrass prairie. The real thing disappeared under the plow and the highway, existing now only in tiny and scattered fragments, a ghost landscape more implication than presence.

But it existed intact, untouched, virgin, only about 120 years ago, a minuscule flickering of time, perhaps three-and-a-half generations worth of humans—hardly enough corpses to fertilize a good-sized cattle ranch. What was this tallgrass prairie on which Minneota rests its buildings and nourishes its citizens? The bank with its real estate assessor's guidebook can't help us very much, except with cash numbers and they have no body, thus no real life. We are left, I'm afraid, with guides we don't trust very much: science, history, and metaphor, but you can't expect a man who lives in a five-thousand-dollar house to provide you with anything better.

David Costello's book, *The Prairie World: Plants and Animals of the Grassland Sea,* tells us: "its universal characteristic was the dominance of grasses. Even though the prairie supported a wealth of showy broad-leaved herbs and shrubs, the vegetation offered no obstruction to vision. . . . Because of the high visibility on the prairie, animal adaptations and habits were adjusted accordingly. The prairie dogs, the ground squirrels, and their enemies, the coyotes, foxes, hawks, and eagles, possessed keen eyesight as an essential part of their survival equipment." Does the same process of natural selection work for human vision or understanding? Costello goes on to say, "This prairie in the natural state was the grassland that covered one-third of the continent in the early morning of October 12, 1492, a date which marks the beginning of one of the greatest changes in history." Minneota waited almost four hundred more years to begin its part in that historic change, the eternal wallflower at the cosmic dance.

After the Civil War, the railroad crawled west from Saint
Paul bearing on its tracks the first immigrants—Norwegians
and a few Yankees in the early 1870s, then in 1878 and '79, the
bulk of the Icelanders, from whom I am descended. Three of
my great-grandfathers rode the train west from Chicago,
though none of them left a record of what they saw out
the train window. But Galiot François Edmond, Baron de
Mandat-Grancey, a conservative French nobleman in bad
water with the new Republic, came through Tracy, twenty-
five-odd miles south of Minneota in 1883. The baron's prime
mission was to explore investment opportunities in mining
and ranching in the western Dakotas. He kept his eyes open on
the train. Here's what he saw:

> About nine, we cross the Mississippi at Winona, but
> unluckily the darkness hides almost everything from our
> view. . . .
>
> When we awake the next morning we find the aspect of
> the country quite changed. We have entered into the
> prairie; not the well-cultivated prairie around Chicago, but
> the prairie in all its immensity and naked wildness. Here the
> work of colonisation is only just beginning, and in the
> vicinity of the stations only may be seen, here and there, far
> away and apart, little wooden houses with clearings around
> them. Everywhere else the eye wanders without any object
> to arrest it over an immense plain, hardly varied with a
> mound or a hill, and covered with thick grass, reflecting
> singular blue tints as it undulates under the passing breeze.
> Water is scarce: a few hollows filled with muddy pools trail-
> ing slowly their tortuous courses towards the Missouri; in
> other places the water, having no outlet, forms swamps,
> from which constantly rise long flocks of ducks.
>
> The impression produced is gloomy in the extreme; . . .

The watery blue tint of the grass comes, of course, from blue
grama grass, another metaphor of the grassland sea.

He arrives at Tracy at nine o'clock in the morning, the last stop for his Pullman car. He moves to the second-class car, sees "four or five women of very mysterious bearing occupy one corner. . . . The other places are occupied by men bespattered with mud up to their ears, habited in well-worn flannel shirts, and with their breeches tucked in great long boots. They are all inveterate tobacco-chewers." I like to imagine one of my multitude of eccentric great uncles in that car in 1883, mumbling in Icelandic, eyeing the elegant baron with a little suspicion, while spitting a long stream of black plug in his general direction. Here the baron experiences his first of many encounters with the true minister of desire in America—the real estate salesman.

> At every station men with their hands full of prospectuses rush into the carriages: they are land agents, and come up to us offering farms. One of these pushing men of business is pestering me to buy a whole quarter of a town with some sounding name, Athens or Paris, I forget which. He spreads out before me the plan. I see there grand avenues intersected by innumerable streets, and the whole well sprinkled with squares, two public gardens, seven or eight railway stations, churches and chapels by the dozen, and ten or twelve banks. When he is quite convinced I am not going to buy anything of him, he admits, pleasantly enough, that there are only one hundred and fifty inhabitants in this city, who are dwelling in about fifty wooden sheds; but he asserts that in two years there will be more than twenty thousand, and this is not at all impossible.

That real estate shark may even have been peddling Minneota, maybe my own grandfather's farm which he bought from the railroad in about 1883, or my own house in the second railway addition, not fifty yards from the old tracks. The population of Minneota in 1880 was 113. It boasted two stores and thirty or forty houses.

The baron finds a kind of rough comic poetry in the habits

of the barbarian inhabitants; he feels the "gloom" of the vast treeless landscape, but the true literature—the genuine metaphors—grew from the daily experience of settlers who came to stay.

Considered from one angle, it doesn't take long to hatch a literature in a new place. Man seems by nature a metaphor-making mammal, so much that before the ink dries on his homestead deed, or the boards seal on his first barn, he has already begun to construct images—about his geography, his daily labor, his soul life in his strange new landscape. Pound says, "Make it new!" Maybe the newness is part of the making. Maybe if we escape the siren croaks of the real estate salesman, man is more inclined by nature to poetry than to war or greed or the lust for power. Maybe . . .

Forty-four years after the baron's adventure in Tracy, Ole Rölvaag described the trip across the tallgrass prairie in his epic novel, *Giants in the Earth*. Rölvaag's wagon train moves across southern Minnesota just south of Tracy on its way to Canton, South Dakota, in the 1870s.

> Bright, clear sky over a plain so wide that the rim of the heavens cut down on it around the entire horizon. . . . Bright, clear sky, to-day, to-morrow, and for all time to come.
>
> . . . And sun! And still more sun! It set the heavens afire every morning; it grew with the day to quivering golden light—then softened into all the shades of red and purple as evening fell. . . . Pure colour everywhere. A gust of wind, sweeping across the plain, threw into life waves of yellow and blue and green. Now and then a dead black wave would race over the scene . . . a cloud's gliding shadow . . . now and then. . . .
>
> It was late afternoon. A small caravan was pushing its way through the tall grass. The track that it left behind was like the wake of a boat—except that instead of widening out astern it closed in again.

"Tish-ah!" said the grass. . . . "Tish-ah, tish-ah!" . . .
Never had it said anything else—never would it say anything else. It bent resiliently under the trampling feet; it did
not break, but it complained aloud every time—for nothing
like this had ever happened to it before. . . . "Tish-ah, tish-
ah!" it cried, and rose up in surprise to look at this rough,
hard thing that had crushed it to the ground so rudely, and
then moved on.

I live now on what not long ago was an ocean of grass so tall
that it made Per Hansa, a Norwegian probably about my size,
six and a half feet, "seem shorter than he really was." We imagine only mountains, oceans or grand canyons contain the
power to dwarf us, to taunt mankind with its own puniness.
Stars and galaxies might humble us, but to be shriveled by
grass! What indignity! Grass—commonest of things, "sprout-
ing alike in broad zones and narrow zones, / Growing among
black folks as among white. . . ." These lines live in *Leaves of
Grass,* the greatest book by an American, at whose center lies
this question:

A child said *What is the grass?* fetching it to me with full
  hands,
How could I answer the child? I do not know what it is any
  more than he.

Nor do I, nor do you. But it seems to me the right American
question. What is the grass? Where is this place I live? What is
to be learned here about my own life, about the action of
desire, about the lives of all of us, living or dead, on this
planet? Maybe only the commonest least likely of places will
ever permit us inside that question. Walt Whitman examined
grass. Henry Thoreau preferred the crow above all birds.
Emerson was intoxicated by water. Emily Dickinson lived in a
single room. I invite you to Minneota, Minnesota, a very small
dot on the ghost of a large ocean of grass.

The Information Highway

Without modesty, we call our times "The Information Age." No ironic smile plays obligato to this verbal brass band blat. With electricity—and a few sizable checks—the accumulated wisdom of mankind lies supine under our fingers on the keyboard. Move the mouse—Behold! a great mystery!

After almost fifty years citizenship in Minneota, I felt one summer afternoon a curious yearning for real information, for three simple knowable facts: Minneota's exact geographical coordinates, its elevation above the sea, and the census results from each decade from 1880 to the present, now a substantial dozen numbers. A man should know precisely where he lives, how far he has risen in the world, and how many other citizens, living and dead, have been his neighbors.

I started searching in my Luddite house, the home of many books but few machines. The house stands only a few hundred yards from Minnesota Highway 68, the single state road that bisects the town, running northwest diagonally along what once were tracks from Marshall, fifteen miles east, to Gary, South Dakota, twenty-five miles west. It fronts directly Lyon County Road 10, an asphalt road that snakes from Echo through Cottonwood and from Minneota almost to Ivanhoe. It is thousands of miles and almost a century of time away from "The Information Highway," that road on which no snow falls and whose potholes result from causes other than the freezing and melting of water and earth.

An old history of Lyon County gave me early population growth figures but stopped in 1912. My antique and imprecise atlas showed no Minneota at all. I knew where to find the exact elevation of Minneota—only a few blocks from my house. Imbedded in the brick wall of the old WPA post office from 1934 sits a bronze medallion engraved with the elevation, signed by the U.S. Geodetic Survey. Since the old post office is now a one-doctor medical clinic, you can read this plaque on your way in to be examined, discovering that whatever else might be about to carry you off the planet, you will not die from mountain sickness. The sea rumbles 1,169.204 feet under your shoes, a few thousand miles away in any direction.

From the old post office, it's a scant block's walk to the new city hall, a metal-sided shed with the architectural charm of an airplane hangar. Surely, city government would know Minneota's location on the planet; it would record in a black ledger with yellowed, brittle pages the right number of neighbors who had paid tax in any particular decade.

The new city hall sits across Highway 68 from the old one that serviced the town from before the turn of the century till the 1970s. The old city hall now houses Bubba's Bar, Minneota's only licensed saloon, once municipal and for a long time the town's chief source of revenue. It's a sturdy two-story brick building with, until recently, a bell tower, a heavy wood door and broad stairs that once led to the town library. CITY HALL is cut into the stone inlay at the top of the building, announcing in bold letters that the tallgrass prairie, after a scant generation, is now tamed, civilized, governed, connected to the larger tissue of national life and history. Midwest small towns look much alike, cobbled together fast in the turn-of-the-century real estate frenzy. They seemed anxious to resemble each other. Most towns Minneota's size boast a few blocks of imposing storefronts with the building's function, owner, and date proclaimed in stone as organic part of the structure: GEIWITZ HARDWARE, FARMERS AND MER-CHANTS BANK, MINNEOTA CO-OPERATIVE CREAMERY, CITY HALL, MASONIC TEMPLE, W.B. GISLASON BUILD-ING, OPERA HOUSE, O.G. ANDERSON AND COMPANY— BIG STORE. Sometimes the building's high and imposing front hid the embarrassing absence of a second story, or a simple timber frame putting-on-the-dog with decorative brick. If you glance quickly, downtown Minneota looks about the same now in 1995 as it did in pictures taken before World War I, an up-and-coming little town that thought highly of itself and its commercial possibilities in the great world. But depressions, bank panics, distance from markets, and aging citizens throttled its rise. Look closely down the street: business blocks are pocked with empty lots, space for wind to blow through and for snowdrifts to pile up in solitude, with dead buildings gone back to scrap lumber, leaving the streets like elderly mouths waiting to be fitted for dentures.

Betty, the City Clerk, sits on duty at her desk, armed with the weapons of an efficient modern office: a computer, copy and fax machines, a phone equipped with a call-waiting buzzer and an answering machine, and stern-looking filing cabinets presumably full of tax deadbeats and other village secrets. She looks up expectantly, maybe thinks I am about to do something serious or useful like paying a bill. Fat chance! I ask for the town's census figures and location. They must be filed away on some hard disk, I say. She's got the 1990 census. She says maybe '70 and '80 are in a file somewhere, but that there's nothing before that. She draws a blank on latitude and longitude. She rummages through a few plat maps that show ownership and zoning (real information), also revealing the curious fact that Minneota is better divided than Gaul: into eight railway additions. Jim Hill and his Chicago & Northwestern Railroad sold and pocketed the commission on every lot in Minneota. But where are we, I ask, on the planet? Are we lost? She shrugs, tells me to try the Lyon County Courthouse in Marshall. So much for "The Information Age" in Minneota. The information available at the touch of a mouse may not be what you need at all, but only what some celestial programmer decides you ought to know. Does information live only in sweating, farting humans whose job it is to pass it face-to-face to another human, making sure it gets remembered?

I walk home to look up the Lyon County official phone numbers. Which office? Clerks record and file figures, so that's my first try—the County Clerk.

"Hello, I'm calling from Minneota. I need some information . . . numbers, location . . ?"

Silence. "We don't have them. Not here."

"Where?"

More silence.

It is a serious breach of western Minnesota etiquette to ask someone a question that they might not be able to answer. Questions embarrass them. You are supposed to be embarrassed too, learning to keep questions to yourself, unless you already know the answer or are certain beyond doubt that the other party can answer without thinking. An odd question must not be introduced without long apology and disclaimer, otherwise it represents a frontal assault on the dignity and privacy of the asked. An earthquake rumbles under the face. A question turns into a social gesture, an expression neither of curiosity nor need. It is a confirmation. If the other party can't answer, the question becomes an insult. I learned this teaching school in western Minnesota for many years. This mistrust of genuine questions underlies the general fear of expressing curiosity. Parents cultivate this fear in children, teachers in students, priests and ministers in parishioners, bureaucrats in citizens. This odd fear makes for silent classrooms, silent offices, silent kitchens, silent bedrooms. All statements must be affirmative—or confirmative—thus draining the energy out of conversation well before it shows any sign of quickening.

I resume. "Where? Surely, Minneota is not lost on this planet. Someone must have an idea about where we are?"

"Try the Treasurer's office. I'll transfer you."

I repeat the question.

"We only keep records of who's on the real estate tax rolls, not the old stuff."

"Where then?"

"I'll transfer you to the Auditor's office. They might have it."

Click.

I repeat the mantra. "Where? Who? Isn't there a County Surveyor who knows our location?"

"Let me think. Yup, it's Lyle. You can call him at home. He's in the book."

"How about the census?"

"I've got figures back to '60 or '70. Will that do?"

"What do you do when you desire information like this?"

"I call the State Demographer. Want his number?"

Indeed! The Demographer himself! The high priest of statistical information who can fit you on enough graphs to transform you into a norm at last!

She gives me the number.

I thank her. She is clearly relieved to resume real county business.

I dial 1, then the Demographer's number. I smell success. A harsh voice answers — with a question!

"Are you hearing impaired or otherwise disabled?"

"Is this the State Demographer?"

"How did you get this number?"

"At the county courthouse. Is the Demographer available?"

"Are you disabled?"

"In many ways, madam. How do I find the Demographer?"

"How did you get this number?"

I register a perfunctory sign-off, think — what next?

I call an old friend who works as a professional researcher in the State Capitol. Despite a curmudgeonly middle age, he has behaved like a responsible citizen and logged onto the Internet. He finds flickering screens frequently more user-friendly than the politicians he services.

I testify to my desire for information.

"Just a minute."

I imagine the moving mouse, the images slithering over the screen, the blue science fiction light, the faint hum of electric current.

"Did you know that Minneota is not the only Minneota in Minnesota?"

"I'm not surprised. A name of that magnificence should not die without both repetition and imitation. Where's the other one?"

"Minneota Township in Jackson County. The name means 'much water' in Dakota."

"I always heard 'too much.'"

"Only 'much' in Jackson County, at any rate."

"But where is Minneota? And how many Much-water-ites were there in say—1920?"

"Here's all the raw census figures. I have no idea how to read them. Just a minute."

Click. Flicker. Buzz.

"Minneota has 104 houses built before 1939 with flush toilets, all inhabited by white citizens of Northern European extraction over sixty years old."

"Good. But where's Minneota? In relation, say, to Uzbekistan? Or Greenwich?"

"Let me monkey. Try the historical society for old census records."

I call. The grand temple of the Minnesota Historical Society sits just down the street from the Capitol. Surely here desire will be gratified, curiosity satisfied!

"Can I help you?"

I chant the mantra.

"This is not the right office. I'll transfer you."

"Mr. Coleman is on vacation. I'll connect you to the reference library."

"Do you have the census numbers for Minneota from 1880 to the present?"

"Yes."

The clouds part. Light streams through to earth. Handel arrives at the climax of his fugue—orchestra, chorus, and soloists, all join *tutti fortissimo*.

"Could I have your fax or E-mail number?"

"No."

Silence.

"Maybe you could just write them down on an old piece of paper, the back of an office memo, or a slightly grease-spotted take-out menu from a Chinese restaurant, put them in a stamped envelope and mail it to me here in Minneota. You don't really need an address, but I do have a box number. Okay?"

"That'll take a few days."

"That's fine. I'm in no hurry. I have been waiting since the foundation of the world for this consummation. Let the highway now be opened, and let information pass hither and thither, trailing clouds of bright glory and wisdom in its caravan. Thanks very much."

"Glad to be of service. If you have any further questions, please contact us again."

Two days later, envelopes begin arriving in Box 187, Minneota, Minnesota 56264. Ask and ye shall receive—the motto of a sometimes benevolent universe. Here's the census:

MINNEOTA

1880 — 113
1890 — 325
1900 — 777
1905 — 954
1910 — 819
1920 — 894
1930 — 918
1940 — 1,065
1950 —We don't have . . .
1960 — 1,297
1970 — 1,320
1980 — 1,469
1990 — 1,417

The census numbers give you the whole history of the town (and of a thousand towns like it) if you know how to read them. Numbers are like metaphors that way. You must bring everything you know and feel as a human being to reading them, otherwise they lie inert, only decorations on a page.

Here is a list of dates to illuminate the numbers:

1870—Emptiness, only tall grass, wind, and passers by: Dakota Indians, buffalo, wolf, coyote, crow.

1871—The first Norwegians settle along the south branch of the Yellow Medicine River.

1872—The tracks of the Saint Peter and Winona Railroad arrive. The first post office, called Nordland, is established— the virgin try at naming Minneota.

1875—The first Icelander arrives to take land on the river north of Minneota. The Saint Peter and Winona Railroad files the official real estate plat for Nordland Village. Now lots can be sold, commissions earned.

1878—The still unincorporated village holds an election to name itself. The post office decrees too many Nordlands. The railroad refers to their little settlement as Yellow Medicine Crossing in honor of the stone railroad bridge over the river. By this time, Minneota has two prominent businessmen, proprietors of general stores: Nils Jaeger, a Norwegian immigrant and Lutheran minister's son, and T. D. (Doc) Seals, a Yankee and self-proclaimed Civil War surgeon with a shadowy career selling "patent medicines" to the local Indians. Seals fancies the Dakota name Minneota, probably for onomatopoeia, and certainly for humor and eccentricity. The rest of the town, already sunk in pious conventionality even before incorporation, prefers Jaegersville (after Seals' competitor), or Horton (after another prominent settler), or Oslo. Minneota drops off the ballot. On election day in February, just after the voting, with Jaegersville almost certainly the winner, a cable arrives from Washington announcing that the post office has already been legally changed from Nordland to Minneota, an accomplished fact. Now the story enters the world of myth. In one version, a pal of Doc Seals steals the cigar box of uncounted ballots, trampling them into a mud puddle on Main Street. In another, Doc Seals knows somebody who knows somebody in Washington and quietly effects the name change single-handed. No one will now ever know the truth. Local scuttle-butt recounts that Doc Seals hid from the angry Norwegians for a long time afterwards, keeping a loaded revolver close at hand. I like the tissue of lies, skullduggery, and thwarted piety that led to the naming. We should all be so lucky in our handles.

1879—The bulk of the Icelanders, including two of my great-grandfathers, arrive, mostly from the district of north-east Iceland around Vopnafjörður. By implication, I suppose, I arrived, though I didn't get around to being born until sixty-four years later. The English and the Irish arrived, too. Next year, the Belgians and the Dutch. What multicultural delights in the tallgrass!

1881—The winter of 1880–81 was the worst in the history of Minneota—so far. It came early, hit hard, and stayed long. It is probably best to get a certain number of disasters out of the way early. They can fuel myth-making and give your history a little ballast and weight. On October 16, 1880, Sam Kile started off to the barn to do chores. On the way the blizzard blew off his hat. Though warned by the other men, he raged off into the whirling snow in pursuit of the hat. No one ever saw him alive again.

Minneota, now officially named, grew to the lordly popula-tion of 113 in the 1880 census—give or take Sam Kile. The citi-zens petitioned the state to become a legally incorporated village, and in January 1881, presumably in the middle of an-other howling blizzard, it was so decreed.

Any events in the next 100 years? The usual: wars, depres-sions, bank panics, droughts, floods, plagues, births, mar-riages, deaths—all the while the population advances (with a little glitch from 1905 to 1910), until the present. The 1990 population clock begins winding down a bit to 1,417. The citi-zens now average well over sixty years in age. One-by-one the nineteenth-century buildings sink back under the tangled roots of the tall grass to join the 113 corpses from the 1880 census; those from 1890 are gone, too. A few stragglers from 1900 are still above ground, not many more from 1910. No matter how much the population grows—or declines—it can't keep up with the real demography, the highway downward into the eternally beating black heart of the prairie.

So there you have them, some numbers, some dates, a tiny history, an odd christening. This freight traveled a circuitous information highway to arrive at your consciousness. What do you make of it? What use can it possibly be to a New Yorker or an Englishman or a Chinese or a Nigerian? Think twice. How different, give or take the eccentric details, is it from your own history? Aren't all histories a multitude of tributaries feeding an enormous river surging toward some still undiscovered ocean either inside the consciousness or in the universe?

But where *is* Minneota? We still don't know. Yet another letter arrives, this one from the Legislative Reference Library, which had inquired for information from the Land Management Information Center in the Minnesota Planning Agency. This gift of information renewed my faith in the state; they knew where we were all the time. Minneota was never lost.

The latitude of Minneota is 44 degrees, 33 minutes, 46 seconds north, only a few minutes south of the great invisible belt that twice encircles the globe, 45 degrees, halfway between equator and pole.

The longitude of Minneota is 95 degrees, 58 minutes, 56 seconds west, only about 6 minutes past 90 degrees, the midpoint between Greenwich and the international date line, twelve hours from yesterday, twelve hours from tomorrow.

What my father and mother told me turns out to be not only metaphorically but mathematically true. Minneota and their farm eight miles north are, in fact, the center of the universe from which all points diverge, an Omphalos of Much Water inhabited by Icelanders, inhabited by me! I had arrived at the center, when for years I thought my life had been lived at the margin. From one angle, the solipsist view of reality turned out to be literally true. In my case and in yours, too. And yours. And yours.

From Here

Someone once asked Flannery O'Connor's opinion of some new school of fashionable novelists. She offered this brisk assessment: "You know what's the matter with them? They're not from anywhere." I am of Ms. O'Connor's party—*from* somewhere. From Minneota, Minnesota, in fact. It is not the sort of place I would have selected to be *from* had I had any choice in the matter. But then, of course, I didn't. My parents were *from* here, born within three miles of each other on farms north of Minneota. Their own parents, while not born here, farmed and died here; most of them even spoke English of a kind. My great-grandparents who came here old, and who certainly spoke little English, even made a sporting try at being *from* here by dying locally, thus fertilizing patches of then still existing tallgrass.

God knows I tried to escape, to do the right American thing, making a middle-class life in a gentler, lovelier, more urbane place, some better home for an eccentric intellectual misfit; but as these essays testify, I found life without *from-ness* too desiccated for my taste. The only people who interested me when I tried living anywhere else—the East, a city, Europe, even China—were either genuine natives still mired in their own *from-ness,* or true refugees and emigrants, driven from their first *from* by some twentieth-century necessity: war, starvation, political upheaval. Their lives left them no choice but amputation without anesthetic of the old *from*, thus the genuine necessity to invent a new one. Americans who sample new places for whim, amusement, taste, or the summons of

ambition always bored the bejesus out of me. Some choices in
life we don't want to make if we intend to become entire
human beings before we die. At times I include marriage, religion, and profession among the choices we ought not to
make; but *from-ness* is always crucial. I'm afraid, considered
from one angle, this is not a very American sentiment. We
seem to believe what we are told: we can plunk our psyche
down anywhere, turn on the TV, say, "Hi, how you doin',"
order a pizza delivered, log onto the net, and be perfectly
at home.

Henry Thoreau, who represented yet another segment of
American consciousness, felt differently. I would call him a mi-
croscopic examiner, a stubborn burrower into his own *from,*
who went so deep that he came up on the other side of the
planet only to discover that the entire universe resembled
Concord. Ms. O'Connor and I join in being of Thoreau's
party. Pat Conroy, the novelist, was raised as a military brat,
drifting from post to post, changing schools, houses, pals
every year. He says, "My job was to be a stranger, to know no
one's name on the first day of school, to be ignorant of all history and flow, and that familial sense of relationship and pro-
portion that makes a town safe for a child." The intuition that
he wanted to be a writer compelled him consciously to choose
a *from*—a hometown. He chose a Minneota in South Carolina,
announcing his desire to himself in a loud inner voice: Now I
shall be *from* here. And so he has been, though in thirty years
he has not acquired a southern accent.

I was lucky enough to be born with the right accent for
Minneota, a harsh voice with flat, short vowels, heavy glottal
consonants, and a clipped inflection, probably not the sort of
English one would choose to speak, if, again, one had any
choice in the matter. But listen carefully to any consciously re-
made voice you hear. Always the ghost of the old voice lives
under it, waiting like some body buried behind a parlor wall in
a Poe story, to fall through the weakened plaster at a tea party,

revealing you for who you really are—the murderer of your own voice. What kind of truth can you tell in that false voice? What does that voice hear itself saying? What can it hear in your voice? A real Minneota voice can hear a real southern voice, or Brooklyn or Newcastle or Uganda English. I operate my life on the axiom that these voices can also hear a Minneota voice, but not the false voice of artificial cultivation. Listen to the computer voice warning you to stand away from the train door in the Atlanta airport, or the voice on your telephone telling you that Leroy Peterson's service has been disconnected. Those voices ought to give you a shiver somewhere deep inside. You ought not to trust them. They mean you more harm than simply to mislead you. A Minneota voice might be wrong, but you can trust it to come from a human being much like yourself.

I came back to Minneota fifteen years ago, half in retreat from an America I had begun to despise, half in pursuit of something inside myself I had only imperfectly or hazily started to understand. As I neared forty, I had reached, without sitting za-Zen, or any other conscious practice, a kind of Buddhist mistrust of desire. In America, the infinite possibilities of human desire shrink to two: money and sex. The first we worship and adore; the cliché: the "almighty dollar," is truer than we can comfortably admit. Money is a synonym for the only true power, military or otherwise. How much courage can you really buy? Is an army ever poor? We are justified by money; the junk it buys, whether from Wal-Mart or Tiffany's, becomes our only real confirmation that we have lived. We don't value things at all. We only want to hold them up so others can see them.

The second desire, sex, we claim to covet, but only as a disguise for our paranoid fear of the body. Americans are not sensualists at all. We are an abstract tribe, insofar as we are a tribe. We fancy ourselves libidinous, but at bottom are frightened anchorites without any conviction that we give up the sweet pleasures of our body for any higher glory or divinity. The more we work out to have "pecs of death," or "a hard body," the more times we babble "fuck" to one another or write humorless books on orgasm, the more thunderous the evidence that we haven't reached national puberty yet.

I found myself in Minneota, almost forty, broke, unemployed, divorced, unpublished, my immediate family dead, and most of the people I loved and valued from my childhood ancient, senile, or going fast. I was strangely happy and began writing affectionate essays and poems about those people, old Icelandic immigrants with odd accents, aunts, uncles, and baby-sitters who fed and praised me, faces I thought I had forgotten that came to astonishing life in the middle of hot afternoons—wide awake. These were no dreams; it was my own history, my own consciousness, knocking at an interior door, asking for coffee and a little visit. I obliged. What else could I do? I was brought up to have good manners, at least toward the old, the poor, the harmless, the generous, the eccentric, the simple (who always prove to be the most complicated of all when you take the trouble to ask them real questions), and most of all, towards the dead. My stock of rudeness—even disdain—I reserved for those who I thought deserved it: the rich, the powerful, the successful, the well-adjusted, the consciously beautiful, the fashionable, or any handy authority that tried to order me down any road that might lead to my joining any of those gangs.

What gifts had these ghosts of my childhood left inside me? I started by writing a long essay about the old lady who taught me to love music, even to sing and play. It turned out to be, among other things, an essay on politics and aesthetics. I published the essay in 1985, with some other poems and sketches about Minneota, in a book titled *The Music of Failure*. It was a small-press book but surprised me by getting a few reviews. The title proved oddly pesky for reviewers and interviewers. They announced it variously as *The Failure of Music, The Magic of Failure,* and the most surprising transformation of all: *The Failure of Magic.* Having by now grown a sense of irony about publishing in America, I only chuckled. The essay still said what it said: that to succeed in American terms meant to go straight downward into a kind of psychic limbo, and that old ladies who possessed neither education nor true talent, but were graced instead with largeness of soul and interior generosity, can sometimes teach you more about works of art or beauty and their true uses than Harvard professors.

As time passed and I neared fifty, it occurred to me that Pauline, the heroine of *The Music of Failure,* wanted company. She was by no means my only teacher. Old people had given me books, brown bread, praise, just criticism, a yard of fine white tatting, card sense, lessons in hospitality, ethical models, well-aged whiskey, a mental picture of female sensuality, a chair fit to read great books in, a piano, instruction in living an elegant life without money, thin pancakes and *Vinarterta,* boxes of mysterious old brown-toned photographs, Icelandic hymnals, God's plenty of wisdom, nourishment, and unexpectedly useful bric-a-brac. They did not burden me with pious moral warnings, whether about sex, tobacco, whiskey, gambling, or blasphemy. I think they admired spirit and courage—a willingness to live a whole life through, from beginning to end, however unconventional or unsatisfactory it might seem to others. These people knew one another in the real world of Minneota. Maybe they would keep happy company in a book together.

What in fact had I been taught in Minneota, this dot of former tallgrass prairie, 1,169.204 feet above the sea, midway between oceans, night and day, ice caps and jungles? I had been taught the possibilities of desire, how its varieties act themselves out in a human life anywhere in the universe, not only in a nondescript small town far from anything that mattered much to the general culture. The small town was of course a real place with real people, but also a *deus ex machina,* a *from-ness,* that if examined closely enough would give you enough characters to re-write Shakespeare, enough wisdom to enlarge Plato, should you exercise sufficient stubborn persistence to give it a try.

My teachers of desire, oddly enough, neglected to instruct me about money, except that it is best ignored insofar as you are lucky enough to get by with ignoring it. In Minneota, that meant living cheap, not waiting for the lottery. It did not mean "the mania of owning things." Since so many of these teachers were ancient virgins—bachelors and old maids—they didn't teach me much about sex either. Longing and imagination had to do that job, and I haven't learned much—only that sexual life is more closely connected with love, pleasure, and gaiety than with our American heavy-breathing, humorless earnestness or narrow, shrill moral judging.

These long-dead people taught me instead that humans can desire food, love, learning, children, adventure, beauty, a curiosity for their own history, and a sense of honor—even in poverty. They can desire God, though frequently not inside a church. But primarily what they taught me and what I had perhaps begun to learn unconsciously in my longing for a sense of *from-ness,* whatever its discomforts, was the desire for *connection.* In D. H. Lawrence's last book, the peculiar and touching *Apocalypse,* he argues that most of the ideas we think we live by—Christianity, individualism, democracy—were leading us to a kind of suicide. He says: "If you are taking the path of individual self-realization, you had better, like Buddha, go off and be by yourself, and give a thought to nobody." He argues that the Apocalypse, the book of Revelation, is a metaphor that "shows us what we are resisting, unnaturally . . . our connection with the cosmos, with the world, with mankind, with the nation, with the family. All these connections are, in the Apocalypse, anathema. . . . We *cannot bear connection.* That is our malady. We must break away, and be isolate. We call that being free, being individual. Beyond a certain point . . . it is suicide. Perhaps we have chosen suicide. Well and good."

I have written this book both to tell the stories of the gifts I was given by these unlicensed instructors of desire and to cast my lot with Lawrence against isolate life and the interior suicide he accuses us of choosing. Insofar as there is an "argument" underlying these essays, they try to argue first that we are sunk by greed—consumerism gone mad, a mania to acquire what we neither need nor desire; by fear—of the "stranger" who is only a disguise for fear of ourselves and our own history; by technology—which since we misuse it by trusting it too much, deracinates and abstracts us, separates us both from nature and each other; and finally, by the mad notion that we define and invent ourselves in isolation from any sense of *from-ness* or connection.

Reader, you know these old human failures, too—hardly a college education, a bank account, a love affair, or an exciting adventure among them. You live in *much water* yourself, however different the details. The only way to honor your own is to honor mine—a small favor all writers ask of all readers. Here in Minneota, the sea is below you and far away but enough water still moves under the bridge.

The Music of Failure:
Variations on an Idea

Prelude,
the Theme for the Variations

The ground bass is failure; America is the key signature; Pauline Bardal is the lyrical tune that sings at the center; Minneota, Minnesota is the staff on which the tunes are written; poverty, loneliness, alcoholism, greed, disease, insanity, war, and spiritual and political emptiness are the tempo markings; Walt Whitman and this sentence from the *Bhagavad-Gita* are the directions for expression:

> Die, and you win heaven. Conquer, and you enjoy the earth. Stand up now . . . and resolve to fight. Realize that pleasure and pain, gain and loss, victory and defeat, are all one and the same: then go into battle. Do this and you cannot commit any sin.

This true subject, the melody that counterpoints everything but is never heard, like Elgar's secret theme for the *Enigma Variations,* is my own life, and yours, and how they flow together to make the life of a community, and then a country, and then a world.

1. Another idea from Walt Whitman that no one wants to hear.

At fifteen, I could define failure fast: to die in Minneota, Minnesota. Substitute any small town in Pennsylvania, or Nebraska, or Bulgaria, and the definition held. To be an American meant to move, rise out of a mean life, make yourself new. Hadn't my own grandfathers transcended Iceland, learned at least some English, and died with a quarter section free and clear? No, I would die a famous author, a distinguished and respected professor at an old university, surrounded by beautiful women, witty talk, fine whiskey, Mozart. There were times, at fifteen, when I would have settled for central heat and less Jell-O, but I kept my mental eye on the "big picture."

Later, teaching Walt Whitman in school, I noticed that my students did not respond with fervor to the lines,

> With music strong I come, with my cornets and my drums,
> I play not marches for accepted victors only, I play
>   marches for conquer'd and slain persons.
>
> Have you heard that it was good to gain the day?
> I also say it is good to fall, battles are lost in the same spirit
>   in which they are won.
>
> I beat and pound for the dead,
> I blow through my embouchures my loudest and gayest
>   for them.
>
> Vivas to those who have fail'd!
> And to those whose war-vessels sank in the sea!
> And to those themselves who sank in the sea!
> And to all generals that lost engagements, and all overcome
>   heroes!
> And the numberless unknown heroes equal to the greatest
>   heroes known!

I left Minneota at the beginning of America's only lost war. While I traveled, got educated, married, divorced, and worldly, the national process of losing went on: a president or two shot, an economy collapsed, a man whom every mother in America warned every child against accepting rides or candy from was in the flesh overwhelmingly elected president, and then drummed into luxurious disgrace for doing the very things those mothers warned against. The water underneath America turned out to be poisoned. Cities like Denver, Los Angeles, Chicago were invisible under air that necessitated warning notices in the newspaper. A rumor flourished that the Arabs bought the entire Crazy Mountains in Montana. Oil gurgled onto gulls' backs north of San Francisco. The war finally ended in disgrace, the secretary of state mired as deep in lies as Iago. America, the realized dream of the eighteenth-century European Enlightenment, seemed to have sunk into playing out a Shakespearean tragedy, or perhaps a black comedy.

Yet as history brought us failure, it brought us no wisdom. The country wanted as little as my students to hear those lines from *Leaves of Grass*. It was not "good to fall," not good to be "sunk in the sea," not good to be among the "numberless unknown heroes." We elected, in fact, a famous actor to whom failure was incomprehensible as history itself, a man who responded to visible failure around him by ignoring it and cracking hollow jokes.

In the meantime, I aged from twenty to forty, found myself for all practical purposes a failure, and settled almost contentedly back into the same rural town which I tried so fiercely to escape. I could not help noticing that personal and professional failure were not my private bailiwick. I knew almost no one still on their first marriage; friends, too, were short of money and doing work that at twenty they would have thought demeaning or tedious; children were not such an unpremeditated joy as maiden aunts led us to expect, and for the precocious middle aged, health and physical beauty had begun to fail. It looked, as the old cliché had it, as if we were going to die after all, and the procedure would not be quite so character-building as the *Reader's Digest* and the Lutheran minister implied.

Heard from inside, the music of failure sounded not the loudest, gayest marches for cornets and drums, but a melancholy cello, strings slowly loosening, melody growing flaccid, receding toward silence. The country closed its ears against the tune; citizens denied that they had ever heard it. "Tomorrow," they said, but this was only another way of saying "yesterday," which did not exist quite as they imagined it. This continual denial gave a hollow, whining quality to conversations. Discussions of politics, work, or marriage sounded like a buzz saw speaking English.

The first settlers of America imagined paradise, God's city made visible on earth. Grand rhetoric for a pregnancy, it was, like all births, bloodier and messier than anyone imagined at the moment of conception. English Puritans who came to build a just and godly order began by trying to exterminate Indian tribes. They tried to revise the English class system of rich landowners and poor yeomen by sharing a common bounty, but this lasted only until somebody realized that true profit lay in landowning, here as in England. The same settlers who declared with Proudhon that "property is theft" wound up working as real estate agents. Old European habits of success died hard.

Hypocrisy is not unusual in human history; it is the order of the day. What has always been unusual in the United States is the high-toned rhetoric that accompanied our behavior, our fine honing of the art of sweeping contradictions under the rug with our eternal blank optimism. But if we examined, without sentimentality, the failures and contradictions of our own history, it would damage beyond repair the power of that public rhetoric, would remove the arch-brick from the structure of the false self we have built for ourselves, in Minneota as elsewhere.

I labored under the weight of that rhetoric as a boy, and when I am tired now, I labor under it still. It is the language of football, a successful high school life, earnest striving and deliberate ignoring, money, false cheerfulness, mumbling about weather. Its music is composed by the radio, commercials for helpful banks and deodorants breathing out at you between stanzas. In cities now, ghetto blasters play it at you in the street; you are serenaded by tiny orchestras hidden in elevators or in rafters above discount stores. It is the music of tomorrow and tomorrow and tomorrow. It is not what Whitman had in mind by beating and pounding for the dead. True dead, unlike false dead, hear what we sing to them.

2. The music of experience; the noise of failure.

Years ago, I traveled to Waterton, Alberta, the north end of Glacier Park, and spent a whole sunny, windy August afternoon sitting on a slope high in the mountains listening to an Aspen tree. I wrote a small poem about that experience:

> Above me, wind does its best
> to blow leaves off the Aspen
> tree a month too soon. No use,
> wind, all you succeed in doing
> is making music, the noise
> of failure growing beautiful.

I did not understand my own poem at the time.

As a small boy, I sang loudly, clearly, and as elderly ladies told me, wonderfully. I knew better, but knowledge didn't interfere with love, as it so often doesn't, and music remained the true channel to the deepest part of my feeling life.

Happiness, or at least emotion, could be described by notes with stems, and the noises of the inner life made audible by reading and sounding those marks. Though never so skilled a musician as to have made a genuine living from it, I was skilled enough to know precisely the deficiencies of every performance I ever gave. Perfection was not a gift given to many in music. Mozart may have had it. I did not.

In an odd way, this melancholy knowledge of my own musical imperfection goes on teaching me something about the wholesomeness of failure every day of my adult life. I have sometimes, like the United States, been too obtuse to remember it, but then I hear again the noise of aspen leaves.

3. *Pauline Bardal at the piano.*

I first heard a piano in the backroom of Peterson's farmhouse, three miles east of my father's place. An only child, too young and disinterested to do any real work, I was left indoors while my father was out giving Wilbur a hand with some chore, probably splitting a half-pint to make the job more pleasant. Wilbur was a bachelor, but kept his aged father, Steve, and a sort of combination housekeeper and nurse, Pauline Bardal, to look after both of them. Pauline was born in 1895 to the first generation of Icelandic immigrants in western Minnesota. When I knew her in the late forties or early fifties, she must have been nearing sixty. Age is relative to children, so I did not think of her as being particularly old. She was simply Pauline, and would remain that way until she died thirty years later.

She was almost six feet tall, without a bit of fat on her, and this made her bones visible, particularly in the hands, joints moving with large gestures as if each finger had reasoning power of its own. Her leanness was partly genetic, but partly also the result of continual work. In the cities she would have been called a domestic, though her duties at Peterson's and elsewhere always involved nursing the infirm and dying. In Minneota's more informal class labeling, she was simply Pauline.

After finishing her duties with bread, chickens, or tending to old Steve, Pauline retired to the den for a half hour of music. I was invited to listen and always delighted by the prospect. She sat herself on the bench, arranging her bones with great dignity and formality. Music was not a trifling matter even if your hands were fresh from flour bin or hen house. Pauline did not play light music; though she was conventionally religious in a Lutheran sort of way, I knew, even as a child, that music was her true spiritual exercise. She always played slowly, and I suppose, badly, but it made no difference. She transported both herself and me by the simple act of playing. Her favorite pieces were Handel's "Largo" from *Xerxes,* and a piano arrangement of the finale of Bach's *Saint Matthew Passion:* "In Deepest Grief." She had never learned true fingering, and got most of her musical experience at an old pump organ that she played for church services. She did not so much strike the keys as slide with painstaking slowness from one to the next, leaving sufficient time for the manual rearrangement of the bones in her hands. This gave all her performances a certain halting dignity, even if sometimes questionable accuracy. It was always said around Minneota that her most moving performances were at funerals, where enormously slow tempos seemed appropriate. She played the sad Bach as a postlude while mourners filed past the open coffin for the last time.

But Pauline at the keyboard was not a lugubrious spirit. Watching that joy on her bony face as her fingers slid over the yellowed keyboard of the old upright, it became clear to me even as a child that neither her nor my true life came from kneading bread or candling eggs or fluffing pillows in a sickbed, but happened in the presence of those noises, badly as they might be made by your own hands. They lived in the inner lines of that Bach, so difficult to manage cleanly with work-stiffened fingers. You felt Bach's grandeur moving under you at whatever speed. The Handel "Largo," though it has become something of a joke for sophisticated listeners through its endless bad piano transcriptions is, in fact, a glorious piece, one of the great gifts from Europe. Even on farms in rural Minnesota, you deserve the extraordinary joy of hearing it for the first time, as if composed in your presence, only for you. I heard it that way, under Pauline's hands. The Minneapolis Symphony playing Beethoven's *Ninth* in the living room could not have been so moving or wonderful as that "Largo" in Peterson's back room.

Pauline, in American terms, was a great failure: always poor, never married, lived in a shabby, small house when not installed in others' backrooms, worked as a domestic servant, formally uneducated, spoke English with the odd inflections of those who learn it as a second language, gawky and not physically beautiful, a badly trained musician whose performances would have caused laughter in the cities. She owned nothing valuable, traveled little, and died alone, the last of her family. If there were love affairs, no one will now know anything about them, and everyone involved is surely dead. Probably she died a virgin, the second most terrible fate, after dying broke, that can befall an American.

But, as the scripture bids, "Let us now praise famous men," and I mean to praise not merely Pauline, but her whole failed family, and through them the music of failure in America.

4. The history of a failed immigrant.

Minneota is a community that was born out of failure in the 1870s. By that I mean that no one ever arrived in Minneota after being a success elsewhere. It is an immigrant town, settled by European refuse, first those starved out of Ireland, then Norway, Iceland, Sweden, Holland, Belgium. Given the harshness of western Minnesota's climate and landscape, people did not come to retire or loaf. They came to farm, and had they been successful at it in the old world, would not have uprooted their families, thrown away culture and language, and braved mosquitoes and blizzards for mere pleasure. Minneota is, of course, a paradigm for the settling of the

A candid shot of an 83-year-old Icelandic woman.
Original scrawl on the back of the photo reads,
"Thiss is mother adge 83 if you looke at the pictror thrue
a inlargen glass it is verry good I snaped her feading her pet goos."

whole country. We are a nation of failures who have done all right and been lucky. Perhaps it is some ancient dark fear of repeating our own grandfathers' lives that makes us reluctant to acknowledge failure in national or private life.

Pauline's father, Frithgeir, came in 1880 in the third wave of nationalities to Minneota: the Icelanders. He likely read one of the pamphlets circulated by the American government in all Scandinavian countries, describing free and fertile land available on the Great Plains for farmers of sturdy, sufficiently Caucasian stock. The United States was always particular about the race of its failures. The pamphlet probably mentioned glowingly the bountiful harvests, rich topsoil, good drainage and pasturage, cheap rail transport, and healthful bracing climate. Frithgeir Joakimsson, who took his new last name, Bardal, from his home valley in north Iceland, arrived in 1880, found most of the best land gone, and picked perhaps the hilliest, stoniest, barest though loveliest farm acreage in that part of western Minnesota.

He was thirty-seven years old, single, and, in all likelihood, knew not a word of English when he came. Pauline, when she was old, disposed of some of her family's books to good homes, and gave me her father's first English grammar and phrase book that she said he used on the boat. It was in Danish, English, and Icelandic, well-worn though intact. Pauline clearly treasured it. Leafing through it now, I imagine rough farmer's hands, something like Pauline's, holding the book on an open deck in mid-Atlantic, sea wind rustling the pages under his thumb: *"Hvar er vegurinn vestur till Minneota?"*

For the first five years, Frithgeir farmed alone. Probably he raised sheep and hay, the only things an Icelandic farmer knew. In 1886, at age forty-three, he married Guthlaug Jonsdóttir, a new immigrant whose family came from the wildest, most remote fjord in east Iceland, Borgarfjörður, ringed with blood-red liparite mountains and precipitous scree slopes. Already thirty-five then, she was pregnant five times between 1887 and 1895 when Pauline, the last daughter, was born. One son, Pall, died an infant in 1889. Four out of five children alive was a lucky percentage then. But Frithgeir's luck did not hold for long in the new world. I give his obituary in its entirety, as I found it on a yellow, brittle page of the *Minneota Mascot* for Friday, September 8, 1899:

Last Saturday, while F.J. Bardal was mowing hay on his farm in Lincoln Co., the horses made a sudden start, jerking the mower which happened at that time to be on the slope of a hill, so that Mr. Bardal fell from his machine. His leg was caught in a wheel and he was dragged that way for a while until the horses stopped. The leg was broken above the knee and other injuries were sustained. Mr. Bardal managed to get on the mower and drive home. Dr. Thordason was sent for. He hurried out, set the bone and did all that could be done for the unfortunate man. But the injuries proved to be so serious that Mr. Bardal died last Monday morning. The funeral took place last Wednesday from the new Icelandic church in Lincoln County, Rev. B.B. Jonsson officiating.

F. Bardal was born January 13, 1843 in Bardardal Thingeyarsysla, Iceland and came to this country in 1880 and settled on his farm in Lincoln County. He leaves a wife, three children, and a stepdaughter.

Mr. Bardal was a much-liked man in the community, an active member in his church, and a general favorite among his neighbors.

Done in by his own farm. He had found the only lovely hills in a flat country, but they killed him; his widow (who knew at best minimal English) was left with four children between nine and twelve years old, and the poorest farm in the county. Nineteen years in the new world.

5. *The further history of three children, all failed.*

Perhaps a few genealogical books in Icelandic libraries, or some distant relatives might provide a bit more history of the Bardals, but not much . . . and this is after a single century in the most information-rich country on earth! It is amazing to me sometimes how little basis we have as humans on which to remember Pericles, Augustine, Charlemagne, or for that matter, Abraham Lincoln.

Four children reached adulthood. One married and left Minneota. Guthlaug, the widow, remained on the farm till she lost it in 1937, another victim of the Great Depression. She was then a very old lady and, as local report had it, not entirely in her right mind. She died in 1943, bedridden in her little house, ninety-two years old, fifty-seven years in America.

There were three Bardals left when I was a boy: Gunnar, the oldest brother, gaunt, melancholy, silent; Rose, the middle sister, not quite right in the head, with a sideways cast to her eye, as if she saw the world from a different angle than normal people, mouth half-smiling, but the unsmiling half colored by something dark and unknown; finally, Pauline, their custodian, housekeeper, surrogate mother and father. The three trooped every Sunday morning to the old wood-frame Icelandic church a block from their small house, and ascended the creaky choir loft stairs. Pauline played for services every other Sunday, and sang when she did not play.

The choir at Saint Paul's Lutheran consisted of perhaps ten to fifteen elderly Icelandic ladies, mostly unmarried and immensely dignified. They formed the foundation of singing. Only three men joined them: Gunnar, a thin cavernous bass, another equally thin but raspier baritone, and me, a small fat boy of eleven or twelve who sang soprano or tenor, depending on his semi-changed voice. I was generally the single member of Saint Paul's choir under seventy.

I sat by Gunnar who seemed always contemplating some

indefinable sadness about which nothing could be done. His voice sounded octaves below everyday life, as if it came from a well bottom. He wore a brown, itchy, wool suit, decades out of style.

Crazy Rose sat close to Pauline. After Rose's death, when I was a teenager, I heard stories of her madness, her religious mania, wandering off to preach in Icelandic in the cornfields, but as a little boy, she seemed only Rose to me, and within the range of possible normality for adults. Children judge each other harshly, but don't make nice distinctions among the grown. Sane or mad, pillar or rake, drunk or sober, adults seem merely themselves, distinguished more by age than by variations of habit, character, or physiognomy.

Rose looked like a bird ordered to continue eating despite an interesting ruckus going on in the next nest. She pecked toward the floor a few times, not paying much attention to the kernels at her feet, then raised her beak to glance furtively around, the half-smile breaking on her lips, as if what she saw was almost funny. Her face was small and thin, eyes pale and watery, almost without irises.

Rose died in 1956, in her sixties, of an embolism. Whatever was frail in the architecture of her cerebral arteries collapsed at last. Gunnar died in 1961 at seventy-four. I sang at both their funerals, and though I have no recollection of what the hymns might have been, they were surely sad and heavy-footed, perhaps "Come Ye Disconsolate," or the Icelandic hymn "Just as the Flower Withers," or "Abide With Me." Hymn singing seemed one kind of preparation for the last great mysterious failure—the funeral, when the saddest and noblest of church tunes could be done with their proper gravity.

Pauline, now alone in her little house with all the family bric-a-brac piled around her, had no one to attend to, and a social security check to keep her from having to attend others for money. Yet her habits were too strong, and having worked for fifty or sixty years, she could not stop. Now she dispensed munificence like a queen. She cared for the dying and the horribly ill with no fuss, as if she were born to it. She was a one-woman hospice movement.

She once fried steaks in a farmers' night club out in the country, an odd job for a teetotaler, and for this she was probably paid a pittance. My mother tended the bar and the two of them often drove out together. I saw them at work once; in the middle of loud country music and boisterous drinking they tended these rough farmers, not like hired help, but like indulgent great aunts looking benevolently after children having a good time. Pauline owned an old Ford which she drove with enthusiasm. Well into her eighties she took friends on vacation and shopping trips and made lunch runs for the senior citizens. Speaking of people sometimes ten or twenty years her junior, she said, "They're getting old, you know, and it's hard for them to get around." Pauline's gifts to me included more than music. She tended both my parents at their deathbeds; and when my mother, a week before she died, lost her second language, English, and spoke to me only in her first, Icelandic, which I did not understand, Pauline translated. The gifts of the unschooled are often those we did not know we would need—the right words, the right music.

Eternal though she seemed to me, age caught her. The end began with the trembling hands of Parkinson's disease, a cruel irony for a woman who took her delight in playing music, however badly. After Gunnar and Rose died, she had a bit more money, and made room in the old house by turning the spare bedrooms into storerooms. She bought a used church organ, a monster from the forties that crowded her tiny living room with speakers, pedal boards, and a gigantic brown console. The organ seemed larger and heavier than the house itself, as if even a tornado couldn't have budged it off the worn carpet. I once asked what she was playing; she looked at me sadly: "See these hands, how shaky? I can't even keep them on the keys anymore. They just shake off . . ." Soon after this she went into the nursing home, and died not long after, still peeved with the universe, I think, for taking music away from her at the end. I don't even know who was there to tend her bedside at the last. Probably she had had enough of that, and wanted to be alone. Indeed, the solitariness of her whole life prepared her for it. This was 1981, 101 years after her father left Thingeyarsysla for a new life. She had lived in America eighty-six years.

6. *Music for an old pump organ.*

Pauline was buried among the Bardals in the graveyard next to the Icelandic country church in Lincoln County. In 1922, Pauline picked out the congregation's new reed organ, and played it for services there for almost forty years, until the church, a victim of rural urbanization and of Icelanders who refused to reproduce or stay on the farm, closed its door for lack of business. While a few miles to the west, the Poles sensibly planted their Catholic Church in a hollow protected from the wind, the Icelanders defied Minnesota by building on a rise in the only ridge of hills on that flat prairie. On even a calm day at that wind-swept knoll, the church windows rattled, shingles flapped, and the black granite gravestones seemed to wobble.

Pauline and I drove out to that church a few years before her death. She carried a shopping bag full of flowers and rat poison. She had a key for the back door of the church and we went up through the minister's dressing room into the sanctuary. The room, carpentered in good oak, was furnished only with chairs, pews, organ, pulpit, and the simple altar crowned by a wood cross; no statues, paintings, bric-a-brac—nothing but that wood, goldened by afternoon light from the pale yellow windows. Wind seemed to come up from inside the church, whooshing over the fine dust that covered everything. "Nobody's cleaned it since last year. It's a shame." Pauline muttered, then went to work. First, she arranged her long legs on the organ bench, carefully folding them between two wooden knee guards below the keyboard. Thus constricted, she pumped, and while checking the stops with one hand, slid over the keys with the other, playing the chords from Handel's "Largo." "The mice have not eaten the bellows," she announced with satisfaction, then launched into an old hymn with both hands. We played for each other for a while, Pauline marveling at my clean fingering. She knew, I think, that she had some responsibility for my love of playing, and was proud of herself, and of me, but this was not the sort of thing Icelanders discussed openly with each other. Skill could be remarked on, but the heart was private and disliked language.

When we finished, she swept up the old poison in a newspaper, opened her yellow skull-and-crossboned boxes, and laid down a fresh lunch for any rodents who might presume to make a meal of God's own organ bellows. Even though the church would never likely be opened, nor the organ publicly played there again, such things ought to be attended to for their own sake. Who knew? Perhaps the dead a few feet away liked an occasional sad tune and didn't fancy the idea of rats interfering with their music.

Pauline locked the church carefully, looking back at it with a sort of melancholy nostalgia. She proceeded to the graveyard with the rest of the contents of her shopping bag, and there performed her next errand. She swept off the graves, then put a flower or two on all of them. The row read:

PALL	FRIDGEIR	GUDLAUG
7/25–8/2 1889	1843–1899	1851–1943
ROSE		GUNNAR
1890–1956		1887–1961

"And I will be between Rose and Gunnar," she said, "in not too long."

Indeed, within a few years the row was full; six dead in the graveyard of a dead church, no progeny, no empire following them, only the dry wind of a new world that promised them and all of us so much.

7. Pack-rat houses, and what they tell.

The opening of the Bardal house was not greeted with amazement and that is, in itself, amazing. Traditionally in Minneota, as in villages all across the world, pack rats, generally unmarried, die in houses stuffed to the ceiling with moldy newspapers, rusted coffee cans full of money, and an overpopulation of bored cats.

The first astonishing fact about the house was the sheer amount inside it. Though tiny, it held the combined goods for a family of six who threw nothing away. It was neither dirty nor disorderly. The piles had been dusted and the narrow crevices between them vacuumed and scrubbed, but within some mounds, nothing had moved for forty years. Papers were stacked neatly in order, probably put there the week they arrived, from 1937 onward. The Bardals were schooled historically and genetically by a thousand years of Icelandic poverty of the meanest, most abject variety. They moved to a poor farm in the poorest county of Minnesota, and when the Depression reduced penury to catastrophe, moved into a poor, small house in Minneota. While their storage space shrank, their goods expanded, and the double beds became single beds after the floor space filled up to the bedsprings. They were a family on whom nothing was lost, not even the useless doodads that arrived from answering every "free special offer" ad for over a half-century.

They accumulated no coffee cans full of bank notes, no hidden treasure, nothing of any genuine monetary value; the Bardals were in that regard truly poor. But not poor in mind and spirit! They owned books in three or four languages: Plato, Homer, Bjornson in Norwegian, Snorri Sturlusson in Icelandic, Whitman, Darwin, Dickens, Ingersoll, Elbert Hubbard; piles of scores by Handel, Bach, Mozart, George Beverly Shea, and Björgvin Guðmundsson, old cylinders of Caruso, Galla-Curci, Schumann-Heink, John McCormack; cheap books reproducing paintings and sculpture from great European museums. There was an organ, a piano, violin, and trumpet; manuals for gardening, cooking, and home remedies; the best magazines of political commentary and art criticism next to *Capper's Farmer,* the *Minneota Mascot,* and the *Plain Truth;* dictionaries and grammar books in three or four languages; books of scientific marvels, Richard Burton's travel adventures, old text books for speech and mathematics, Bibles and hymn books in every Scandinavian language; *Faust, Reader's Digest,* and *Sweet Hour of Prayer.* That tiny house was a space ship stocked to leave the planet after collecting the best we have done for each other for the last four thousand years of human consciousness. And none of it worth ten cents in the real world of free enterprise! The executors might as well have torched the house, thus saving the labor of sorting it, giving mementos to friends and peddling the rest at a garage sale on a sweltering summer afternoon. What one realized with genuine astonishment was that the Bardals piled this extraordinary junk not only inside their cramped house; that house was a metaphor for their interior life that they stocked with the greatest beauty and intelligence they understood. They read the books, played the instruments, carried the contents of that house in their heads, and took it with them at last into their neat row in the Lincoln County graveyard.

But not entirely. . . . Anyone who carries a whole civilization around inside gives it to everyone they meet in conversations and public acts. Pauline gave me music; Gunnar, the model of a man who read and thought; literally he gave me a first edition of Arthur Waley, an Epictetus, and the *Heimskringla;* Rose, in her odd way, gave me her crazed longing for God. Not one of them had so much as a high school diploma. They gave what teachers hired for it so often fail to give.

8. The idea of failure noted in literature, both old and new.

Having introduced you to Pauline and the rest of the Bardals, I reiterate the question I posed at the beginning of this essay: What is failure, and what is its use in our lives, either as private humans resident in our own Minneota of the soul, or as Americans, public citizens of the richest, most successful nation in history?

At the beginning of human consciousness, men seem not to have appreciated the virtues of failure either. The Gilgamesh epic, at least a thousand years older than Homer or Genesis, and thus the first record of what troubled us as humans, contains the following scene: Gilgamesh, the king, is unhappy in his willful solitude, satisfying his sexual whims, living a materially splendid life, and thoughtlessly brutalizing his subjects. He feels a part of himself missing. One night he wakes from a disturbing dream, which he tells his mother, Ninsun, a goddess who has power to read dream symbols:

> I saw a star
> Fall from the sky, and the people
> Of Uruk stood around and admired it,
> And I was zealous and tried to carry it away
> But I was too weak and I failed.
> What does it mean? I have not dreamed
> Like this before.

She explains that the star symbolizes his equal—something too heavy that he will "try to lift and drive away, and fail." This worries Gilgamesh:

> But I have never failed before, he interrupted
> Her, surprised himself at his anxiety.
> It will be a person, she continued . . .
> A companion who is your equal
> In strength, a person loyal to a friend
> Who will not forsake you and whom you
> Will never wish to leave.

Gilgamesh thinks this over quietly, and soon after dreams again, this time of an ax: "When I tried to lift it, I failed." She consoles him:

> This ax is a man
> Who is your friend and equal.
> He will come.

Enkidu comes. Gilgamesh falls from godly solitude into friendship, and when Enkidu dies, falls again through grief into true humanity. The failure that so disturbs his dreams is, in fact, the longing for full consciousness as a human, and this is learned when "A man sees death in things. That is what it is to be a man." Only by failure can Gilgamesh find this wisdom, and before he does, the whole country suffers from his thoughtlessness. There is surely a lesson here, even thousands of years later, for countries that insist on being led by those who have never gone through the failure and grief necessary to see this "death in things."

Forty or fifty centuries after *Gilgamesh,* E. M. Forster imagined a similar scene in *A Passage to India,* though now there is no Enkidu to come. Mrs. Moore and her thick-headed boy, Ronny, a British civil servant, are arguing about the behavior of the English in India. Ronny trots out all the clichés about God's work and the white man's burden, but his mother surveys him with an ironic eye:

> His words without his voice might have impressed her, but when she heard the self-satisfied lilt of them, when she saw

the mouth moving so complacently and competently beneath the little red nose, she felt, quite illogically, that this
was not the last word on India. One touch of regret—not
the canny substitute but the true regret from the heart—
would have made him a different man, and the British
Empire a different institution.

The argument goes on, not a trace of regret penetrating
into Ronny. Finally, exasperated, she says:

> "The desire to behave pleasantly satisfies God. . . . I
> think everyone fails, but there are so many kinds of failure.
> Good will and more good will and more good will."

Forster's point, like that of the Gilgamesh poet, is that human
beings learn goodwill by coming to a consciousness of the
"death in things," the failure that moves Whitman to praise,
and so disgusts and terrifies us as a culture.

9. A fortissimo *blast from Walt Whitman,* *swelled by the author's indignation.*

I try, again and again, through literature, music, history, and
experience, to get at the point of failure—but I fail. Perhaps
that is my point. Clear logical structures, much as I love them
myself, are not so germane as the "touch of regret that comes
from the heart" in understanding what I am trying to
penetrate.

This idea began with an image, a comparison, really.
Disgusted with my whole country after the 1984 election, with
its bludgeoning rhetoric of business success, military victory,
and contempt for the failures and oddballs of America who
have tried to ask difficult questions, I tried to imagine what it
would be like to be in a room with my own leaders, perhaps
inviting the current administration over to my house for

drinks. Aside from their withering scorn that someone so obviously able and white would choose to live in a shabby house in an obscure backwater like Minneota (this would provoke only angry sputtering fulmination from me), I realized that they would bore the bejesus out of not only me, but of everyone I valued and a great many of those I didn't.

I would rather have spent an evening with Pauline Bardal, playing music and listening to her Icelandic stories. This poor, presumably ignorant and obscure woman would even have taken the fun out of the drinks, since she disapproved of them; yet she was more fit to organize society than the most exalted leaders on the planet. She was not empty as a human, and therefore, however ordinary, gave off love, and could not be boring in quite the same way. Since she had a genuine feeling for beauty, though little skill at making it, "good will" and some richness of soul would enter a room with her and grace it. And yet she was one of millions in a culture that had been bamboozled, for reasons no one quite understands, into accepting a cheap destructive idea of success and publicly worshipping it in the most demeaning and mindless way. That success idea surfaced like a hydra after every American disaster that ought to have taught us something about ourselves, history, and love—the Vietnam War, the Depression, the imperialist fiascoes with Spain and the Philippines at the turn of the century, the Civil War. Here is Whitman, the poet of boisterous optimism, as high schools teach him, describing the spiritual life of America in 1870 in his sad essay, "Democratic Vistas":

> I say we had best look our times and lands searchingly in the face, like a physician diagnosing some deep disease. Never was there, perhaps, more hollowness at heart than at present, and here in the United States. Genuine belief seems to have left us. The underlying principles of the States are not honestly believed in (for all this hectic glow,

and these melodramatic screamings), nor is humanity itself believed in. What penetrating eye does not everywhere see through the mask? The spectacle is appalling. We live in an atmosphere of hypocrisy throughout. The men believe not in the women, nor the women in the men. A scornful superciliousness rules in literature. The aim of all the *littérateurs* is to find something to make fun of. A lot of churches, sects, etc., the most dismal phantasms I know, usurp the name of religion. Conversation is a mass of badinage. From deceit in the spirit, the mother of all false deeds, the offspring is already incalculable. An acute and candid person, in the revenue department in Washington, who is led by the course of his employment to regularly visit the cities, north, south, and west, to investigate frauds, has talked much with me about his discoveries. The depravity of the business classes of our country is not less than has been supposed, but infinitely greater. The official services of America, national, state, and municipal, in all their branches and departments, except the judiciary, are saturated in corruption, bribery, falsehood, maladministration; and the judiciary is tainted. The great cities reek with respectable as much as non-respectable robbery and scoundrelism. In fashionable life, flippancy, tepid amours, weak infidelism, small aims, or no aims at all, only to kill time. In business (this all-devouring modern word, business), the one sole object is, by any means, pecuniary gain. The magician's serpent in the fable ate up all the other serpents; and moneymaking is our magician's serpent, remaining today sole master of the field. The best class we show, is but a mob of fashionably dressed speculators and vulgarians. True, indeed, behind this fantastic farce, enacted on the visible stage of society, solid things and stupendous labors are to be discovered, existing crudely and going on in the background, to advance and tell themselves in time. Yet the truths are none the less terrible. I say that our New World democracy, however great a success in uplifting the masses out of their sloughs, in materialistic development, products, and in a certain highly deceptive superficial popular intellectuality, is, so far, an almost complete failure in its social aspects, and in really grand religious, moral, literary, and aesthetic results. In vain do we march with unprecedented strides to empire so colossal, outvying the antique, beyond Alexander's, beyond the proudest sway of Rome. In vain have we annexed Texas, California, Alaska, and reach north for Canada and south for Cuba. It is as if we were somehow being endowed with a vast and more and more thoroughly appointed body, and then left with little or no soul.

It could as well have been written in 1985. This is the failure you get if you begin and proceed with a phony notion of success. This failure, which the culture calls "success," is a true spiritual death, not the "death in things," but hell, as Milton conceived it: death in the midst of life, because the world itself, the universe, is dead from inside out, and we carry the corpse with us into every conversation and act.

10. *The poor and the drunk: two more kinds of failure.*

Two failures we teach children to fear are poverty and alcoholism. We state them positively: work hard and stay sober. Yet Christianity, to which we give public lip service, praises glad poverty; many alcoholics date the birth of their true humanity from the realization of booze's awful power in their lives.

James Agee, in the course of spending a summer writing about some poor, ignorant Alabama tenant farmers in the thirties, discovered that their small, failed lives could not quite be described by normal American power values. He calls his book about them *Let Us Now Praise Famous Men* and comes to this conclusion about the poor and failed: they are human in precisely the same manner as ourselves, and therefore bottomless. It takes him hundreds of pages of thundering prose to grab the scruff of the reader's neck, and shake him to the same conclusion. Money earned, suit brand, car model, school degree, powerful army, big bombs, bootstrap rhetoric, make no difference. Everything the success culture takes for granted turns to fog that burns off when you put light on it. At the bottom of everything is skin: under that, blood and bone. This simple fact shocked Agee and gave him a case of ecstasy.

We feel it even more in the simple, direct photographs Walker Evans took as pendant to Agee's prose. Those, for god's sake, he seems to say, are children, real children, and that is a shoe, and that is a table, even though so badly carpentered of rough wood that it stands on a short leg. What should we tell that child to succeed at, since it is already demonstrably a child? Should we tell it to wash and put on a good shirt? What should we say to the shoe? Make yourself new, close up your cracked sole, polish yourself, grow into a boot?

Like poverty, alcoholism is a failure hard to deny, for denial leads to suicide. The ideas that Alcoholics Anonymous proposes to help alcoholics recover have in them the "true regret from the heart" that Forster speaks about, and staying sober requires "good will and more good will." An alcoholic must confess to his fellows: All greetings begin, "My name is Joe and I'm a drunk." Substitute your own name in that sentence and the music of failure sounds in earshot. Drunks black out, remember nothing; A.A. requires memory, the acknowledgment of actions' effects on self and others, then apology and atonement. You must make right what you have put wrong with your drinking; pay just debts. Imagine America coming up from one of its blackouts to apologize to Cambodia, Nicaragua, the Sioux, interned Japanese, or the blacklisted. Imagine yourself. . . .

The Serenity Prayer, spoken at every A.A. meeting, is the true national anthem of the country of failure Gilgamesh dreamed about when his conscience tired of brutalizing Uruk, and longed for the true failure in humanity:

> God, grant me the serenity to accept the things I cannot change; the courage to change the things I can; and the wisdom to know the difference.

No bombs bursting in air in that one.

11. Failure in national life: a little history of Iceland.

What, then, shall we say in praise of the Bardals, all dead in a hundred years in America, and failed miserably by almost every definition our culture offers us? In my judgment, our false language of power and success, and its consequent notion of sweeping genuine failure harmful to other humans and ourselves under the rug, has left us no true language (except perhaps poetry or song) to describe or think about their lives and thus absorb their history into our own. Without that acknowledgment of failure, memory disappears, history ceases to exist accurately and is of no use to us. We drive by the cemetery a thousand times and cannot see or remember the names written on the stones.

The Bardals came out of an immigrant culture that had succeeded at failure. They were Icelanders, and conscious of it, and though none of Frithgeir's children ever saw their ancestral home, they called themselves "western Icelanders," and could observe by looking at any television set that they were not quite American in the manner conceived in commercials and soap operas.

The Icelandic immigration at the end of the nineteenth century took place, as did so many such movements, largely because of grinding poverty. The Icelanders, historically, showed talent for surviving near-starvation; but, by 1875, an escape opened to them that was like none other in history. Free land was not an offer taken lightly.

At thirty-six I went off to live in Iceland for a year or two and had a look at the farms the ancestors of Minneota Icelanders left, including my own grandfather's and the Bardals'. In 1875 the houses must have been dank turf-covered hovels, smelling of chamber pots and boiled fish, with ceilings so low that generally tall Icelanders must have developed hunches stooping under their own roofline. In 1875 there were no roads, only horse tracks; no sophisticated machines, only scythes and hand rakes; almost no light, heat, sanitation, or plumbing. Aside from a handful of Christmas raisins or prunes, and daily rutabagas and potatoes, their whole diet consisted of boiled dried cod, boiled salt mutton, rotted shark, and a pudding made out of sour milk. They had never seen an orange, an apple, or corn, much less an avocado. They had little topsoil, a minuscule growing season sufficient for almost no food crops, interminable winters and gray, cold, drizzly summers, frosts in June, snow in August, and icy sea fogs in between. They raised hardy old Viking sheep, a cow or two for milk, and hay that was really only native grass, to feed the animals. They moved around on small sturdy horses who coped with endless frost heaves, bogholes, cliffs, and gravelly, cold, glacial rivers that separated one remote farm from the next. Icelandic farmers lived, for all practical purposes, in the twelfth century until well into the twentieth. It is almost impossible for us to conceive the meanness and isolation of their lives. They occupied the outer edge of an island on the outer edge of Europe in poverty worthy of the most dismal backwater in Africa or Asia.

Iceland also had a history of losing, both geological and political. Settled by ninth-century Vikings who organized the world's first genuine Parliament, they were the only kingless Europeans, but lost that prize through their own quarrelsome squabbling. Birch trees held in their loose but fertile volcanic soil, which they squandered by denuding the countryside for firewood. Even the elements conspired against them. They built up new areas into fertile farmland by painstaking labor, only to have a neighborhood volcano blow up and bury the field under burning ash. The climate, temperate when they came, soon returned to its true arctic disposition and froze out their hay. Polar ice hugged the shore, as if trying to finish the poor Icelanders off for being impetuous and foolish enough to try to settle this unlikely island and make a civilization out of it.

And yet they did indeed make a great, though curiously austere, civilization. With no usable building stone, no musical instruments, no minable metals, and a paucity of food and shelter, they built the most substantial European literature of the Middle Ages by using the only equipment left to them on this barren rockpile: language, not Latin, but their own beloved vernacular Icelandic.

What is the heroic subject of the greatest of that literature? Failure. *The Sturlunga Saga* chronicles with bloody detail the venial civil quarrels that led to the breakdown of political structures and ensuing loss of independence. Snorri's *Prose Edda* consisted partly of a versification manual for a kind of poetry (a few hundred years obsolete when Snorri wrote it) that no one would ever write again except as a literary exercise, and partly a history of the old Norse mythology that was by that time utterly obliterated by Christianity and forgotten in the rest of Europe. *Laxdaela Saga* records a willful woman's successive failed marriages and loves that make *Anna Karenina* or *Madame Bovary* seem cheerful by comparison. The gods themselves, in Viking mythology, were doomed to perish, and Valhalla is a temple of failure. In *Njal's Saga* (a worthy companion to Homer) almost all the main characters are swept up in a violent tide that culminates in the deliberate burning to death of Njal's whole family, including aged wife and grandchildren, inside his own house. It is surely a caution-ary story, designed to be told to an audience themselves afflicted with a quarrelsome nature and a taste for recrimina-tion and revenge. The book ends in spent vengeance, and a surfeit of charred, beheaded, stabbed, chopped, impaled corpses that exceeds the final scenes of *Hamlet* or *Lear*. The human failure in *Njal's Saga* is of such size it attains majesty, but the gods are not blamed for any of it.

The Icelanders, by facing the drastic failures of their history and nature, created a literature that held the national ego to-gether through six hundred years of colonial domination, black plague, leprosy, volcanic eruption, and famine that by 1750 reduced this already half-starved population to half the size it had been when it was settled. The most wretched Icelandic household had those books and read them; Gunnar, Njal, Gudrun, Egil, and Grettir were the ballast every Ice-lander carried through the long centuries of failure.

A saga reader visiting Iceland now, expecting blood-thirstiness or violence from the population, is in for disap-pointment. He finds instead a mild, harmonious, democratic welfare state, just and literate, almost without murder, theft, or any violent crime. Doors are left unlocked and lost billfolds returned to strangers.

Poverty in any sense an American might understand is un-known. It struck me while I lived there, and must equally strike many American tourists, that Iceland is what America says it is and is, in fact, not. Our literature, too, is full of fail-ure—the sunk *Pequod* and the dead crew in *Moby Dick,* Hawthorne's vision of failed love in an icy community, Huck Finn on the raft, choosing evil, and Whitman's great poems in praise of death—but we do not carry these books around in-side our public life as Icelanders carry theirs.

What distinguishes Icelandic from American failure is the sense of responsibility. It was neither Norwegian, Dane, black plague, nor polar ice who wrecked Iceland's independence, fertility, and prosperity; their literature makes absolutely clear that it was Icelanders themselves who did these things. We make terrible mistakes and we alone are responsible for them, they say to one another in books. Viewing their history generously, you might think they could share blame for their troubles with Norway, Denmark, or at least chalk it up to bad luck, but Icelanders will have none of it. It is a matter of national pride to have behaved so stupidly in the past and survived as a nation to learn something from it. Alteration is possible if you stop in time; this is one of the clear lessons both of A. A. and of history. In addition, there is a certain pleasure that comes from swallowing your own failure. A great deal of Icelandic humor grows out of these indigestible lumps of history.

Nothing that is *itself* can conceivably be termed a failure by the transcendental definition. But things must acknowledge and live up to their selfness. This is fairly effortless for a horse or a cow, more difficult for a human being, and judging by the evidence of history, almost impossible for a community or a country. When it happens occasionally, as I argue that it did in the case of the Icelanders, it creates a rare wonder, a community that has eaten its own failures so completely that it has no need to be other than itself. Iceland has no army, because an army cannot defend anything genuinely worth defending. In my more melancholy utopian moments, I think America would be better defended without one, too.

The Bardals came out of that failure tradition, and it schooled them well for their hundred years in America. Friends of mine meeting Pauline for the first time would remark on her aristocratic bearing. There was no bowing and scraping in her; she met bank presidents and failed farmers with the same straightforward kindness. And why, given the Declaration of Independence, the Constitution, and the rhetoric of American history, should she not? Her soul was not tied to a bank account or elegant clothes, and whatever difficulties life dealt her, she remained Pauline and that was sufficient. No one can steal the self while you are sleeping if it is sufficiently large in your body. A country with a sufficient ego casts off paranoia about plots to steal its factories and merchandise, and behaves with grace and mildness toward its neighbors.

But an alcoholic protects that weak self by filling it with whiskey. A stock speculator in the twenties filled it with Dusenbergs, ermines, Waterford chandeliers, and Newport villas. When these toys disappeared abruptly, the now defenseless self stepped to the window and, taking advantage of the fact that it lived inside a heavy body, dropped out. Some alcoholics drive off cliffs if you take whiskey away. An empty country, then, protects itself at all costs against the idea of its own failure, lest some part of its weak psyche understand that it must commit a sort of suicide whenever it is tempted to feel the "true regret." A hundred years ago, this was serious, but not final. A country more or less blown off the map, even a large one, would still be populated by deer, muskrats, fox, weeds, and grass. Since 1945, self-building has become a matter of life and death for the whole planet. We have now reached the point in human history where some cure is absolutely necessary, some embracing of wholesome failure.

12. A reprise of Walt Whitman: real and transcendental failure.

I return now to Whitman, who had two ideas about failure: the first transcendental, and the second political. The "natural facts" as Emerson defines them in *Nature*, were not revealing cheerful news about the "spiritual facts" of American life after the Civil War. I argue that the news is no better now, maybe worse, since more time, more evidence, and more material progress have passed our way. Whitman wrote his first joyful hymn to failure in 1855, in the first edition of *Leaves of Grass;* his attack on "hollowness of heart" came sixteen years later, in 1871. Those years were, prior to our own generation, the most rendingly violent and tempestuous time in American history, but I think we have surpassed them.

Think first of our own conventional notion of failure, and how it differs from either of Whitman's. Success involves the acquisition of power, money, position, sensual gratification, and acquiring the attendant public symbols for these things. Not to acquire them, but to be schooled in a culture that wants you to want them, is our idea of failure.

Think next of "hollowness of heart" as Whitman's language for what we, living in an age of psychology, call the weak ego, or the empty self. How do you fill an ego, make a self strong? The ego requires first the power to sympathetically imagine something outside itself: the lives of other human beings, perhaps enormously different from your own; second, the capacity to love something outside the self in the world of nature, art, or human beings. True symbols of fullness of heart exist only in nature, and cannot be put on credit cards: rocks, weeds, animals, air, water, weather, and other people.

Whitman had experienced profound conventional failure in his own life by the time of his great attack: he saw the horrors of a Civil War hospital as a volunteer nurse for the dying; he lost a government job for writing obscene poetry; he suffered strokes that eventually crippled him; he found no true audience for *Leaves of Grass;* he endured the most corrupt national administration before Nixon's. Yet still he beats and pounds for the failed generals with his transcendental notion of failure. Something succeeds if it is itself: victor and defeated, living and dead, are not separate states but a continuum; success and failure are only different faces of the same thing.

Music is a good metaphor for this idea, since it also is a tissue, a continuum, a process. How heavy is music's body? Does it own much land? What sound investments can it make? Does music slice vegetables with a knife or electricity? Does music like sunny climates and lovely cities or is it willing to endure Minneota? Is music bored with the "Largo" from *Xerxes*? Do old ladies' wrong notes offend music's ears? What hymns should you sing at music's funeral? Would music prefer quiche lorraine or boiled potatoes? What is the gross national product of music? Does music worship Jesus, or the other way around?

When is music ever finally done? Basho (translated by Robert Bly) says:

> The temple bell stops
> But the sound keeps coming
> Out of the flowers

Even Minneota flowers . . .

13. A coda: the still small voice of Minneota.

This has been a long incoherent journey toward this idea. The reader must perhaps exercise "good will" and remember that the whole culture, perhaps the whole weight of western civilization, is against it. The English language even denies it, as one tries to bulldoze a word from one definition to another. And yet, I know it's true. What proof have I offered? The life of Pauline Bardal and her family, a poor tiny country on the edge of the arctic, a half-dozen books, experience, some music, finally only a feeling . . . not much. Yet in every artery in my body, and in yours too, that music of failure plays—continually. It sounds like Bach to me, and you must make up your mind what it sounds like to you.

Should you not hear it where you are now, let me remind you that it plays in Minneota, Minnesota daily, under the water tower, or deep inside the grain elevator bins. You do not need the price of a bus ticket to arrive here, since it is where you are now, wherever that is. You must simply decide to be here, and then you will be.

Always remember, though, that it is a real place in both senses of that word, though not much of a place in American terms. It will never make it on television, though it has ground, water, sky, weather, all the ingredients of placeness. It has pianos, clarinets, and songs, though it wants violins, and the wind that blows over it comes from Prague and Nairobi and Auckland and brings part of them to live in it. Its humans are often tedious, but sometimes astonishing, here as elsewhere, and the endless weather talk once had a piece of poetry under it. The Bardals lived here, still do in a way, under stones with their names, but in air, too, that comes into the house when you take off the storm windows in spring. I live here now, and plan to always, wherever I am.

Whatever failure is, Minneota is not it. Nothing can be done about living here. Nor should it be. The heart can be filled anywhere on earth.

Smile—Hold Still!

The Chinese hold one kind of right idea about the uses of photography. Pure landscape, the scenic view, does not interest them. A mountain is a mountain is a mountain, they might have said if Gertrude Stein had been Chinese, but your girlfriend is something else entirely. When I lived in China in the mid '80s, every tourist site of great antiquity or beauty that I visited swarmed with photographic entrepreneurs who had set up little stands next to the right spot for a snapshot. Most ordinary Chinese still couldn't afford cameras, film, or developing, so these small tails of capitalism provided vacationers with posed mementos. And such posing! More than half the fun at these tourist spots came from watching the Chinese arrange themselves to be memorialized, brushing dust off shabby clothes, fixing makeup, combing hair, adding colorful scarves brought fresh for just this precious moment, then striking postures either (if male) of heroic strength and resolution, or (if female) the coquettish poses of old Chinese courtesans from Ming screens. The beautiful Miss Wang gazes wistfully into the misty distances falling away from Mount Huashan; the eyes of sturdy Mr. Wu follow the sinuous curves of the Great Wall like some time-traveled soldier in the emperor's guard. The difference between the Chinese notion of a photograph and our candid camera snapshots must be something like the difference between the heroic nineteenth-century acting style of Henry Irving or Sarah Bernhardt and the new method realist acting that mumbles like real everyday folks in real everyday kitchens. For a Chinese tourist, that photograph is an event; if you've taken the trouble to arrive at a landscape or a monument, you want a record that says Kilroy Xiaoyu was here. You already know the mountain is there, and won't go anyplace, so why bother to look at pictures of it? But people you know come and go—and age. See how lovely and happy they looked on our journey to the great Buddha with giant feet? A friend of mine walked up Mount Emei, a 10,000-foot sacred temple mountain in Sichuan on a foggy drizzly day in January. She was alone, nobody to take pictures. Just before she reached the peak, when the drizzle had turned to ice, fog, and sleet, she came on two Chinese couples. The men bided their time, loading film into their cheap Shanghai camera. The women sat in the middle of the trail, passing the mirror back and forth, adjusting their eyeliner and lipstick, putting hair in its proper place. She waited on the narrow trail for them to finish—a leisurely and exacting process. Finally, they rose, brushed the dirt from their jeans, fluffed their jackets, pursed their lips to even the color, grabbed umbrellas, and proceeded to the top, ready to be recorded on negative in fog and sleet, beauty making its way into history.

While my mother, Jona, didn't look Chinese with her flaming red hair and green eyes, she shared their prejudice about the just content of photographs. Whatever was human interested her, but whatever wasn't didn't. Preferably the humans were specimens you knew and loved, but if that variety wasn't available, any handy biped would do. When she was over sixty, I took her, my wife, and my mother-in-law on a trip to Iceland and Scandinavia. She had traveled to a few places in America and had been to Winnipeg—not for scenery, climate, or gravy on french fries, but to track down relatives and old friends. This was her maiden transcontinental adventure. Her father had left Iceland at twenty, her mother at thirty-two, and she herself hadn't spoken a word of English till she went to a country school at about six. I was curious to watch her in

Iceland, to see if the first look at her parents' landscape moved her. Having been acquainted with her since my birth, I ought to have known better.

She took a quick look out the window of a tourist bus on its way to see Thingvellir—the old Parliament plains and canyons, and then to Gullfoss, one of the myriad Icelandic thundering, grand waterfalls. The bus moved past rugged lava fields, a black and pale green treeless wilderness, circled with black slab mountains and ice blue glaciers. Now this was scenery! Jona turned her head back into the bus and said, "My God, the farm in Westerheim must have looked like paradise to him," and resumed practicing her Icelandic with complete strangers whom she clearly found more entertaining than the landscape. Icelanders were the real Icelandic scenery; they could talk and had faces that registered what you said to them. No glacier ever made a remark, so far as Jona was concerned.

I don't suppose it's necessary to tell you that her tourist snapshots were somewhat unusual; she invariably faced away from the scenic view so that she could get all the heads clearly. If you missed Thingvellir, you could always buy a postcard, and if you wanted Gullfoss, you could fill up a bathtub quickly to enjoy the thunder of cascading water. Of course water is going to fall down if you stick a canyon in its way! Besides, if you have a full tub, you can always take a bath. She took my favorite of her snapshots in Norway. We had ridden a ferry through Oslo Harbor to Bygdøy, a wonderful little island full of ship museums: the old Viking ship *Öseberg,* Frithjof Nansen's icebreaker *Fram,* Thor Heyerdahl's rafts. It was raining so the light was gray in every direction. From the ferry dock you could look back over water at the interior mountains and the colorful roofs and skyline of Oslo. Jona instructed her three traveling companions to line up on the end of the dock next to a couple of fuel tanks. One of us pointed out to her that a fuel depot might be a less interesting backdrop than sea, mountains, and Oslo. Useless. She thought we all looked better standing between two rusty tanks. Less distraction when you looked at the faces and bodies later.

The democracy of the cheap automatic camera brought the making of images into the power of anyone interested in making them. Before 1839, when the daguerreotype and the callotype entered history, hanging a portrait on your wall to memorialize a face or a place meant hiring a painter, thus having money. The factory owner had paintings; the factory worker had his memory—as long as it lasted. But as photographs became progressively cheaper and the technology less complex, we could all have "albums" and save the images of faces we loved or felt obligation toward. I sometimes think the refrigerator was invented not to cool food, but to move "Baby Suzy" and "Uncle Carl" out of the parlor and back into the kitchen to keep you company, a vertical exposed family album with leftovers in Tupperware hiding behind the gallery wall.

The immigrants who settled Minneota at the end of the nineteenth century were beneficiaries of that artistic and technological revolution. Unless completely destitute, (a not uncommon but not universal condition), many brought onto the boat a few brown-toned portraits, even tintypes, to remind them of the humans they left and would never see again. They did not bring pictures of landscape—however picturesque or beautiful Ireland, Iceland, Norway, or Belgium might have been. That landscape betrayed them, impoverished them, humiliated them, sometimes even tried to kill them. They liked the flat, bland plainness of the Minneota prairie where they now owned farms and houses with heat and furniture, though they didn't intend to take snapshots of the prairie either. That was right outside your window where it belonged. Instead, they framed the ancestors—a dour, scowly, and mostly toothless lot—and hung them in curlicued frames in the parlor, to be examined only on state occasions.

I always loved those gloomy pictures, and as a child tried to imagine how those bewhiskered and bound-haired heads were connected to my pink, plump, but entirely alive body. At about twenty-five, I wrote a little comical poem about what I thought were my Gislason great-great-grandparents, the original land-takers who came from Iceland in 1879, already in their sixties.

Old Family Pictures

I

Great-great-grandmother Gislason
looks fiercely out
under her Icelandic bonnet,
an owl who just discovered
she is a mathematical prodigy—
This is not a woman
to be monkeyed with!

II

Great-great-grandfather Gislason
points toward the earth
with his whole body;
his long white beard,
a sad Old Testament prophet's
who no longer believes in God,
seems made of lead, not hair.
The farmer's shoulders,
the great heavy nose
droop . . .

He has accepted the unfairness
of the universe with good humor.
He lives with
Great-great-grandmother Gislason.

At about thirty, I discovered I had my facts wrong, and that while Bjorn was indeed my great-grandfather, Athalborg, his third wife, was not only unconnected to me, but she would probably not much fancy the idea of my existing. My great-grandmother was Sigridur Sigfusdóttir, a hired girl on the farm Grimstadir. I was only half a Gislason after all! I rummaged through the old brown-toned pictures and interrogated relatives until I found her face, too. She didn't look so different from Athalborg, the mistress of the house—same black dress, same wound white hair, same shrunken mouth. It's odd how much the dead begin to look alike, how faces become archetypal in the old pictures. I decided not to revise the poem, but to leave metaphorical truth to triumph over literal.

Edward Lucie-Smith, the English poet, writes in his book about the first century of photography, *The Invented Eye,* that "the camera presented men with a new way of seeing the world. The invention of photography changed men's attitude toward what they saw, and changed it in a fundamental manner. For the first time it was possible to bring time itself to a halt, to freeze the stream of moments, to choose one instant and keep it on record forever." He argues that in a photograph we are not seduced by the sensuous texture of the medium itself as we are with paint, but rather that we "look at what they represent more directly; we concern ourselves with the subject, and not with the way the subject is rendered." Content arm wrestles form to the table—once and for all. Lucie-Smith uses the curious word "rawness" to describe the content of photographs and then goes on: "The subject appears uncooked and unmasticated. The whole digestive process, whereby visual elements are transformed and subordinated to the purposes of the picture, has not yet taken place; the spectator has to undertake it for himself." He argues that this "rawness" of photographs, this aesthetic impurity, "is not a defect, but an important part of their interest. Not only must accident play at least a minor role in the creation of every image, but it is impossible to prevent mixed motives from creeping in. Photography is larger than aesthetics in the way that written language is larger than literature." Beauty, of landscape, of the houses and bodies of the rich and beautiful—is only a part of the purpose of a photograph, and even that is mixed and blended by accident, by unconscious irony, by the intrusions of nature, or by the technical process itself. Photographers want to record images for "a wide variety of reasons . . . scientific curiosity . . . social reform . . . the wish to record a fact . . . private obsessions. But the photograph is an image and not a description, not an approach to reality but in some sense a counterfeit of it, and this means that it alters our consciousness as well as adding to our knowledge of what is shown."

There's a kind of rough, straightforward honesty in the Chinese tourist's and my mother's attitude toward the photograph—to lay on the interior table with a loud bang the counterfeit notion of the experience itself, and to proceed from there. This is fake. Of course it is. Partly. Say cheese. Move in closer so I can get everybody. The hell with the Eiffel Tower. What was interesting was not snapshot as artifact, but snapshot as history—of a face, of an occasion, of an image clearly intended to alter "consciousness," to court "impurity," even to seduce it. Be altered or else—the photograph orders anyone chancing to look at it.

Photographs, like music, are a language we learn to read. Old photographs can speak to us, give us news of our history as private humans, as community, as civilization, that we couldn't possibly get in any other way. But we sometimes need a little help with the grammar of a photograph—as with Albanian or Sanskrit; maybe we need a visual Oxford English Dictionary to show us the history of usage, the alteration of meaning with time. Or maybe even the shadowing of meaning itself. After all, we see a frozen moment that floats in moving water—a visual iceberg nine-tenths hidden under the surface of time past.

I will try to give you a translation of a few images of Minneota and of my own life so that you can see something of what I see in them. Don't be deceived into imagining that I see them whole, or even with true understanding. I can't even see my own face clearly, and neither can you see yours. That's one of the maddening charms of history—or photography or poetry. Anatole France takes a sly and ironic view of that when he says: "It is extremely difficult to write history . . . . When a fact is only known by a single testimony, one accepts it without much hesitation. The troubles begin as soon as events are recorded by two or more witnesses, for their testimony will always be contradictory and always be incompatible."

Here, then, is a single vision of some counterfeit images. Your job is to be contradictory.

I

Here's a pair just off the boat: Jóhannes Sveinsson, farmer from Korekstaðir, Hjaltastaðaþingá, and his wife Soffia Vilhjálmsdóttir, born a few miles away. They left that farm, sometime after 1880 and took the road south passing Soffia's birthplace, following the largest lake in Iceland, Lagarfljót, a long, skinny glacial cut that opens into Arctic salt marshes before disappearing into the North Atlantic Ocean. Straight north of those marshes—called Hérað—there is nothing, no land till you arrive at the other side of your globe, only the polar ice pack, and that is not so far away. In bad years, drift ice seals off the northeast fjords in Iceland, isolating them even more than usual—from the rest of Iceland, much less Europe, New York, or Tahiti—and there have been a lot of bad years in the 1870s.

At Egilstaðir, now a small town, then not even a village, the horses turn east and begin climbing a steep mountain ridge to a pass called Fjarðarheiði—sheep pasture wasteland. The pass,

Jóhannes Sveinsson and his wife, Soffía Vilhjálmsdóttir,
farmers at Korekstaðir in Hjaltastaðaþingá. Bill Holm's
great-grandparents. They look fresh off the boat.

well over one thousand meters, is still the highest a traveler
must cross to arrive at any of the fjord towns along the Iceland

coast. The top is flat and bleak, gray boulders, puddles of ice melt, only a few insane mosses and lichens risking life at this altitude this far north. Suddenly the flat ends and the dirt path (now a gravel road) plunges abruptly down to the sea and to the distant town of Seyðisfjörður. In 1979 a sign warned motorists that the grade was 17 percent, leading almost straight downhill. A thousand meters is about thirty-five hundred feet, two-thirds of a vertical mile. The fjord, narrow as a snake, walled by steep basalt mountains, frequently fills with fog and gray mist. The water, most days, has an oily cold sheen—almost black. The town of Seyðisfjörður is full of Danish merchants and bureaucrats who have painted their wooden houses, and best of all their roofs, in gay, bright colors—orange, red, pale blue, gold. Jóhannes and Soffia must look two-thirds of a mile down at the only spot of brilliant color in sight; but being by genetics and necessity stoic, they probably either say nothing or "watch the horses—be careful!" The road keeps plunging down past a half-dozen waterfalls catapulting from everywhere off ridges, out of cracks in the rock, and rushing faster than the small, sturdy careful Icelandic horses down toward the Atlantic, to join the last gasp of the Gulf Stream.

Seyðisfjörður was a busy town in the nineteenth century, the third largest in Iceland and the shipping center for the whole east coast. Fish, mutton, hides, and wool move out from here toward Denmark, while sugar, coffee, flour, bolts of cotton, lumber, dried fruits, books, hardware, and the mail arrive for distribution to the district farmers. Probably Jóhannes and Soffia mutter about the outrageous price and low quality of coffee and hope it will be cheaper in the New World. They probably want a cup now, but can't afford it at town prices. What little cash they could muster went for six tickets on the steamship *Camoens* now docked in the harbor, overwhelming the small fishing boats. They have four sons ranging in age from twenty to thirteen: Gunnar, Vilhjálmur, Sveinn, and

Guðjón. Jóhannes and Soffia are in their fifties, spring chickens these days; but after the hard, poor life on the farm in the nineteenth century, they are almost old, teeth gone, a little bent and stiff in the joints.

They carry their goods in a couple of wooden chests with holes in the handles so they can be strapped to the side of a horse. They've never owned much, had to leave most of that, and now are down to a couple of medium-sized boxes. Inside the boxes are a few articles of clothing homespun out of wool from their own sheep (even wool underwear), a few Icelandic-style dresses, homemade from Danish cotton, with a few hand-made silver ornaments to decorate them; loaves of heavy dense black bread that will last for months; some dried fish and mutton, a jar of butter, and a block of hard white cheese, both from their last now-dead cow; and maybe a last big splurge on a bag of prunes that never made their way into *Vinarterta,* an Icelandic prune cake popular in the nineteenth century. Soffia has brought her knitting, her loom, and crocheting needles, her spindles and combs to card wool, and maybe a wood butter churn or a cheese mold. Jóhannes has brought a few primitive farm tools unchanged from their twelfth-century ancestors. And books—most of the sagas, a few collections of poems, Hallgrímur Pétursson's *Passion Hymns,* but probably fewer religious books (the Icelanders weren't much afflicted with piety—then or now). Maybe there were a couple of dictionaries: Danish and English, and maybe a picture book in Danish about their new western home. I imagine Jóhannes and Soffia were literate even in the lowest malebolge of their poverty and misery; the Icelanders never quite gave that up. One of their four sons will graduate from a university at the turn of the century and go to New York to have a career as a writer and journalist.

There's a swarm of neighbors and a lot of cousins on the dock waiting to board the *Camoens.* This is the high season for emigration, the biggest movement of Icelanders since their ancestors settled the country in the tenth century. For a thousand years they have endured poverty, disease, isolation, a nasty climate, and hostile geography. But they can't blame themselves for not giving it a try. Here they made a real civilization, a live culture out of almost nothing, and it lasted. It still lasts, for that matter. What will they make in the New World? That thought must stick in their minds like one of the heavy gray stones back on the pass. They board the *Camoens,* are assigned to their space in steerage, take out a piece of black bread to chew, and go back on deck for one last look as the ship's moorings are cast off and it begins moving out on the black tide past rock walls rising a couple of thousand feet straight up from the water. The ship's horn blasts. The Icelanders waving good-bye from the dock disappear in the gray mist. The *Camoens* turns an elbow in the fjord and Seyðisfjörður itself disappears. Now Europe lies in front of them, straight east and a little south. They go the wrong direction to get to Minneota! But first they dock in Glasgow, then Liverpool, to pick up more immigrants, process papers, and wait. Then the ship sails straight back across the Atlantic and up the mouth of the Saint Lawrence River to Quebec where the family disembarks, listening to French this time, not English—still another language they don't understand. They were seasick for a month on board *Camoens.* I say that with confidence, though, of course, I can't ask them. Despite living next to the sea, none of them had likely ever been in a boat pitching and rolling in the big Atlantic swells, tossed around by northeasterly gales. They are almost out of black bread, jerked mutton, and cheese, anxious to walk on dry land again, to let the interior pitching and rolling fade and disappear from inside their bodies. That will take a week or so.

At this point they face a large choice and must decide. Icelanders on board have already been quarreling—as Icelanders so successfully and steadily do. Will it be Canada or

Minneota? Canada has an Icelandic republic, New Iceland, in the harsh brush interlake country north of Winnipeg. Here, by Canadian law, Icelandic is spoken and Icelanders run their own show, settling next to each other. In Minneota you settle next to Irish, Norwegians, Germans, some Icelanders, and Yankees. Life goes on only in a language you don't yet speak. The land is a little more fertile, the climate a little easier. In a generation or two your descendants will stop speaking Icelandic or being Icelanders; your culture will go "poof" and disappear. What to do!? The hell with the cultural nationalists! You book a train for Chicago, then west to New Ulm, finally getting to Minneota where a few of your neighbors—and a couple of Soffia's sisters—have already settled. The good homestead land is gone when you get there, so you borrow money to buy a stony farm on the only hill in Swede Prairie Township in Yellow Medicine County just north of Minneota. You buy it from the Saint Peter and Winona Railroad acting as land agent. They swindle you just a little so you are in debt beyond anything imaginable in Iceland. You stake a homestead claim on a neighboring eighty acres, making 280 in total. You, Jóhannes, are a land baron for the first time in history! But you borrowed money to buy the land, then more to buy sheep, a cow, seed, and a few tools. You begin asking your neighbors: What grows here besides hay and potatoes? You have never seen corn, wheat, flax, barley, rye, or oats in a field. You have never seen an undried fruit—not an apple or a pear or an orange. You have never seen a pig and now you rather like them—to eat at least. You plant a dozen trees to keep the lone cottonwood and boxelder company on your hilltop. You have never seen a tree taller than your own body in Iceland. At night frogs ribet, crickets hum, a coyote eats a couple of your sheep, you step on a garter snake walking through a field. You've neither seen nor imagined any of these creatures. You listen to English every time you go to town and still can't make out more than a few words of it. Your boys, though, seem to be doing well at mastering it, particularly the youngest, Guðjon, later John G. Holme, who shows signs of great cleverness, hiding all day with his nose buried in American books, scribbling in a tablet. For sealing your homestead claim, you need to take citizenship, and the damn fool Americans demand that you have a last name. You are the son of Sveinn, your sons the sons of Jóhannes, your wife the daughter of Vilhjálmur. And on back into the generations. Isn't that enough? No, the county office must have an unchanging tax roll name. What to be? Holm! That's it, a simple Icelandic word that means almost nothing at all—an island or a sandbar. You shall be Holm for the county's sake.

You tell Soffia, "We should have our picture taken so the boys can remember us. We're getting old now, maybe dead soon. The neighbors have been to Marshall where there's a photographer. Maybe this week, if the road isn't muddy." So you harness the horses and travel fifteen miles cross-country to Marshall. Your old suit that Soffia wove from Mulesysla wool is still good. And so is the plaid dress made from the material the Danish merchant sold you. The exposure takes a long time; Soffia sits, you stand immobile, your huge meat-hook hand hanging on your right side. It's somewhere around 1885 or 1890 now and soon you will be too old to farm. Your boy Sveinn will marry a Gislason girl and stay on the hilltop. Young Guðjon will go off to university and change his name and that will be almost the last you see of him. The climate is hard here, even nastier than Iceland, and your other two boys Gunnar and Villi decide to move west to Bellingham, Washington, another little Icelandic colony in a gentler place. There fruit grows, the sea is full of fish and doesn't freeze, and there are even volcanoes just outside the door. So you and Soffia move for the last time—to Washington, next to the sea once more. Your two boys buy a little farm with an orchard and you wait for the first decade of the new century to die, both nearing eighty—a long, hard life, but no different from that of your neighbors or from that of most humans anywhere on the planet. Only one of your grandsons, Bjorn, was born in 1896 before you left. You never saw the rest, nor did you imagine a great-grandson sitting in a kitchen only a few miles from your Minneota farm, looking at the old brown-tone picture of the two of you, now a little over a century old, and seeing his own face almost uncannily reproduced in yours—the same thick body, sloping shoulders, hairline, bristly beard. His hand holding this pen is smaller than yours, more delicate. It never did any serious farm work. It plays the piano and writes words on paper like your son, Guðjón Gunnlaugur Jóhannesson— John G. Holme. Whatever the name, there's no mistaking the face and body. They're ours! You and Soffia never managed to become Americans, even though you signed the papers in your own awkward hand. Your suit, your dress, and the cast of your eyes say it: you are Icelanders adrift. But then, if we think twice, we are all adrift.

II

For these two Icelanders the process of "melting" worked. The pictures, taken just after the turn of the century, show them ready to meet the new century head on. Ninety years later, these two would be the first on their block on the Internet. They are real Americans. By being somebody, they could be anybody. There is not a whiff of Mulesysla or the farm drifting off them—only good perfume (eau de toilette), Bay Rum, Milwaukee cigars.

Barney Jones was born Bjarni Jónsson on a farm in Vopnafjörður, northeast Iceland, in 1859. Stefania Árngrimsdóttir was born two miles away in 1860. They arrived in North America in 1879, twenty and nineteen, respectively, looking presumably much like a younger version of the old couple in the first portrait. But look at them now—maybe a quarter century later in their forties. He slouches at ease in an oak arm-chair, quality suit and overcoat casually unbuttoned and askew. His hat sits back at a jaunty angle, Walt Whitman style. His black leather gloves might be for motoring—he probably owns one of the first horseless carriages in town. His right hand holds a half-smoked cigar. He's got a few wrinkles around the eyes but looks at you with an expression of wry confidence and good humor—ain't life grand?, and ain't the world a swell place, says that face in the down-home American slang he's learned to sling around by now. Under his bushy mustache is a cocky open-mouthed grin. That's a bully Teddy Roosevelt head. It lives a vigorous life, shoots game, takes

Barney Jones, born Bjarni Jónsson, all dressed up
for the recently begun twentieth century.

no guff from small countries, looks the future bolt in the eye—confident and optimistic. Twentieth century, here we come—watch our smoke!

Stefania Jones—she's got a real last name now, just like everybody else—could be a lady straight out of a Henry James or an Edith Wharton novel, dressed for a day's shopping in the city or an opera matinee: feathered hat, embroidered bag, mink boa, chic fur coat, a big toothy smile, (note that the Jones's show real teeth; there's a dentist down the street, and

Stefania Árngrimsdóttir, dressed up even more elegantly than her husband, Barney.

even the middle-aged now chew meat with wild abandon). Her right hand touches the belt of her fur coat. Is she a little dazzled at the grandeur of owning it, or is she lovingly petting her fine coat, singing silently to it: nice coat, soft coat, sweet coat of the new world?

She and Barney live in the finest house in Minneota, as fine as any in the state, a huge wooden Victorian castle with an octagonal tower-room, medieval lead glass windows, a carriage house in back, a large roofed side porch to park the horses or the Model A so that when it's raining you can enter and leave without soaking the majestic ostrich feathers on your hat. Local rumor has it that the house was designed in 1895 by Cass Gilbert, architect of the state capital in Saint Paul and of mammoth skyscrapers like the Woolworth building in New York, most famous and expensive of the turn-of-the century architects. How did Barney amass the money for this grand mansion while learning English, taking citizenship, and being fitted for his suit? He opened B. Jones Meat Market in 1892, advertising that he "sells fresh and salted meats and buys hides from local farmers." Which probably accounted for some of it. But Stefania is related to the merchant family of Andersons (Arngrimsson) who opened the Big Store, Minneota's Dayton's or Saks Fifth Avenue. Rumors float locally that one of her uncles invested in an oil boom, made a killing, and later, like a good American, lost it all. The house still stands a century later across the street from the Icelandic Church where the two were pillars of the choir, Barney a bass and Stefania an alto. That house is material proof in wood and stone of the promise, the mad optimism of America.

Stefania's reputation as a fastidious and exacting housekeeper survives her by a half-century. The grand central staircase in the house ascended three floors—all the way to the octagon turret. A Minneota woman who died in 1994, almost a century old, remembered cleaning for Mrs. Jones, dusting each spindle of the varnished banister of the stairs with a soft cloth—daily. The Jones's had no children of their own; they adopted a daughter, Marja Gudrun, who died at sixteen of "consumption" in 1902, either just before or just after these handsome photos were taken. Some things even the prosperity and promise of the New World couldn't make right. The Jones's themselves lived to such ripe ages that I probably saw them as a baby. Barney and Stefania may have patted my fat, little pink head before they died as they were born, a year apart, he in 1944, she in 1945, eighty-four years old apiece, sixty-four in the New World. The suit, driving gloves, fur coat, boa, ostrich hat, must have been packed in moth balls in the back closet.

I once asked my mother how Barney Jones could have been an Icelander; that was the name of a baseball player or a rail-road engineer, a real American. Just a name they took, she said, that sounded a little like his real name, one that customers (foreigners—*utlendingar*—out-country persons) could pro-nounce. Try it now in its original incarnation. Bjarni is a form of the Norse word for bear. Put a *y* after the *b* and trill the *r* with all the ferocity your mouth can muster. Make a harsh buzz. Let the second syllable—the long *e* sound—drift off to nothing like a long sigh. Put a long round *o* in Jónsson, son of Jón Rafnson—the raven. There—you're getting it! Keep prac-ticing and it will come.

III

It's the turn of the century. An old Icelandic lady sits on her porch at the north end of Minneota, spinning wool, probably sheared from sheep raised in Westerheim Township by immi-grant farmers who still haven't gotten the point that real money comes only from row crops, hogs, and cattle. The tree-less prairies stretch off mistily on the right side of the picture. Her barrel waits patiently for rain to come down the spout.

She leans forward on her wood rocker, the plaid ruffle on the cushions spread out under her black old lady dress and gingham apron. Her big black bonnet is tied securely under her chin; only a few white wisps of hair escape it. From her dress, wrinkles, and shrunken mouth, we can tell she was no spring chicken when she left Mulesysla twenty-odd years ago. Her spinning wheel probably traveled here in a wooden chest over the Atlantic. It shows no signs of wearing out yet—good for another century, four more generations of yarn. Her black shoe works the treadle; her gnarled hands string the wool strands onto the spindle. From the shadows cast by spinning wheel and barrel, we can see that this is a sunny day in the midwest almost a century ago, maybe the first fine day of spring—no snow visible on the prairie. I'll bet even money that this old lady will not answer your questions in English. That porch is still Iceland to her, the location changed several thousand miles south and west, but wool still wool, sun still sun. She is

An immigrant grandmother, spinning wool on her
sunny porch at the turn of the century.

the great-grandmother of us all, but everyone has forgotten her name.

This is a "candid" picture of everyday life, but it has visual poetry inside it too. A premature cultural anthropologist must have thought this picture would say something to us in a hundred years. So it does.

IV

These are the first four of Thórvaldur Gislason's six children dressed in their Victorian best about 1907 or 1908. After Thórvaldur became Walter, he moved off the Gislason farm to Minneota and opened a hardware store, which his grandson still runs to this day. He and his wife, Effie Griffing of Gary, South Dakota (a genuine WASP!), were readers. They named these four children, left to right: Virgil Voltaire, for a Latin poet and the French satirist; Waldo, for Emerson; Melba, for Nellie the famous prima donna; and Io, for the Greek muse. No more old country names with odd letters and trilled *r*'s for these handsome and stylish children. They could be taken anywhere without the smell of the boondocks trailing behind them, and, in fact, they all did become travelers. Three died in Cleveland, Ohio, and vacationed in Europe (the Continent, not Iceland) and Florida.

Virgil Voltaire (V.V. as he was called), had an adventurous youth, but came home in his late twenties to take over the hardware store. He was the handsomest, best-traveled, most worldly man in Minneota until his death at well over ninety. He stood six foot three with black hair and a deep stentorian voice, a voice used to giving orders. He was a dandy who fancied finely tailored suits, handmade monogrammed shirts, Nunn-Bush cordovans always polished to a military gloss, a razor crease in his gabardine trousers. He was a dead shot with his large collection of expensive shotguns, played the stock

market, and kept a basement full of fine whiskey and brandy—
even through Prohibition. He was a famous host who delighted in serving proper martinis and quality whiskey in

*Left to right: Virgil Voltaire, Waldo, Melba, and Io Gislason,
the four oldest of W. B. Gislason's six children,
dressed up in their best Edwardian finery.*

heavy-bottomed glasses. Each glass arrived with its own swizzle stick from a famous resort or nightclub Virgil had visited. He had immensely courtly manners and flirted in the grand nineteenth-century manner. My mother said no woman could resist him, and by rumor, many didn't, though he was also a devoted and loving husband for sixty-odd years to his wife Mary Helen, a Cleveland girl with class.

When I was a boy my parents always dropped me off at Saint Paul's to sing in the choir and attend Sunday school. No churchgoers themselves, they continued a half-block down the street to Virgil's solid old mansion, full of brass and marble and great slabs of varnished oak. Jona, my mother, and Mary gossiped and chatted while Virgil and my father had a few eye-openers in the gun room. I was to meet them at eleven-thirty for the next round of Sunday morning visiting where I would score Icelandic pancakes stuffed with cream and jam in the kitchen of an old lady named Borga. One Sunday morning when I was about six I announced that scripture had gone on long enough; I was late and had to meet my parents at Virg'n Mary's. First the Sunday school teacher, then the whole assembly of children started giggling.

On a morning in May, 1975, after my mother had died at about 4:30 A.M., I stumbled out of the nursing home into a blood-red spring dawn. After the undertaker took her body downtown for the next rigmarole, I walked around Minneota for an hour or two, listening to roosters waking up, the first firing of car engines, thinking about what needed to be done next. Pallbearers—you can't have a funeral without pallbearers! I walked to Virgil's house. He was a widower living alone now, and at seventy-five still got up early in the morning. I knocked on the door some time after six. He opened it, dressed in an elegant burgundy dressing gown, still erect, iron gray and handsome. "Jona died a few hours ago," I said. "I was wondering if you'd be a pallbearer." Since he was a little deaf I spoke loudly. The neighbors were still asleep. "Come in," he said in his *basso profundo*. "You've been up all night?" I confessed that I had, sitting by the bed alone, waiting. He said, "You need a drink." It was a statement, not a question. "Sit down." He disappeared down the stairs to his crypt full of whiskey—the private stock, the secret bottles. He came up dusting an ornate old flask, loosened the cork, set it on the table, and came back with two crystal shot glasses ringed with gold leaf, embossed with a gold *G*.

"I bought this whiskey in Canada in the thirties. It was bottled before Prohibition and aged twenty-five years before that in oak. I think it will be all right." He poured two shots, raised his glass, looked me in the eye and said, "She was a lovely woman, your mother. To Jona."

We drank. And then another. The whiskey was, as Virgil suspected, all right.

Look again at the proud imperious face of the seven-year-old Virgil Voltaire. It was the same face that toasted my mother. In some odd way, we never change at all in the tiny flickering of energy between birth and death. Old photographs sometimes make that fact clear to us.

V

Is this Bonnie and Clyde, or Etta and Butch, getting a big hug from Al Capone and friends just before going off to do a railroad heist? No, it's four Icelanders and a Norwegian, four lovers and a lonesome widower on a summer day in 1929 standing in front of a car parked next to a farm grove in Westerheim Township north of Minneota. I'll give you their real names and ages, though you'll never meet four of them; the fifth is eighty-five and in sound health, but don't dawdle forever.

From left to right, Bill Holm, Sr., my father, twenty-three-years old and neck-tied for probably one of a dozen times in

*Left to right: Bill Holm Sr., Jónina Sigurborg Josephson,
Abo Bjornson, Agnes Rafnson, and Sam Severson.
This photo was snapped in 1929.*

his life; Jónina Sigurborg Josephson, his nineteen-year-old
girlfriend whom he has been chasing since she was eleven and
he first saw her in her father's farm kitchen, (she will keep him
chasing until 1932); Eyólfur (Abo) Bjornson, at forty-one my
father's oldest first cousin, Bjorn Gislason's grandson by the
first of his three marriages. Abo married a Hallgrimsson girl,
Gudrun, in 1919; she died in childbirth in 1920. He will remain
alone until his death in 1968. Next to him is Agnes Rafnson,

also nineteen, Jónina's high school classmate and best friend. She is a rare raven-haired Icelander (her last name, Rafn, means raven). Shall we blame wind or design for that wonderful black hair falling over her eye? Sam (Selmer) Severson, only eighteen, is chasing an older woman, the nineteen-year-old Agnes. They will get married in a few months and stay that way till Sam's death in 1994, sixty-five years later. Sam, my father's next-door neighbor from Swede Prairie Township, is the oddball in this picture—a Norwegian. Sam and Abo wear matching wool caps; my father shows off his reddish, sandy-colored hair. It will be gray by the time I meet him. Jónina is a flaming redhead.

Someone snapped this frozen moment in time before the stock market crash, before marriages, foreclosures, children, quarrels, before the Dust Bowl, before the Big War and rationing, before Franklin Roosevelt rose from his wheelchair to tell all five of them not to be afraid, before Prohibition finally ended (though my father certainly had a jug of moonshine under the front seat of that car), before gray hair and dentures and hearing aids, before the world had quite started its real business with four of them. When I first knew them, four were middle-aged and Abo was old. He stayed in his farmhouse all of his life but retired from farming early and left the working of the land to one of his younger cousins who lived with him in the big house. Abo sat in a wooden rocker by a sunny window filling his omnipresent pipe and emptying it into a brass ashtray, reading endless newspapers, magazines, books, punctuated with coffee and ginger snaps a few times each day. He said little. As a child, I thought him a kind, sad man who lived behind a wall of privacy, lonesomeness, and pipe smoke, quietly, even serenely, waiting for this business of living to be over and done. He died, almost eighty, the year of the Chicago convention, of the assassinations of King and Robert Kennedy, and the shooting of George Wallace.

Sam and Agnes and Bill and Jona stayed friends for the next half-century, going to dances together—Jona and Agnes complaining about their husbands, Bill and Sam probably just having a nip and talking politics and hog prices. Agnes's beautiful daughters and her mother, Grandma Rafnson, baby-sat little Billy when he arrived eleven years after Jona and Bill's marriage. I went to the funerals of Abo, Jona, Bill, and Sam, and sang at three of them.

When I found this old snapshot in 1990, I had an enlargement made and took a copy to Sam and Agnes. Agnes glanced at it briefly and said, "Look how young we all were," before resuming her coffee. Sam, though, was transfixed—maybe transfigured would be the right word. By this time he was almost eighty, old, sick, bored, full of complaints—a normal human his age in every regard. But the sight of that picture struck him speechless, and he gave off some kind of odd light and heat I can't quite describe to you. After a minute of holding the picture, staring at it, he said, reverting to a name few still called me, "Make me more copies of this for the grandchildren, Billy." In the usual middle-aged chaos of obligations, promises, duties, I think I forgot to do it, and a few years later he died, too, but at least I take some credit for having unearthed that picture and given him a copy. It gave him some pleasure to be eighteen again for a while on a fine summer afternoon before almost anything had happened.

VI

The Big Store, O.G. Anderson and Company, was for three-quarters of a century the glory of mercantile Minneota as it would have been in your town had you been lucky enough to have it. It was Harrods, Macy's, Marshall-Field, and Dayton's rolled into one. This big brick box was dedicated in 1901, with an addition half this size added on to the left at about the time of World War I. Only twenty years before this, Minneota had been an unincorporated whistle-stop on the virgin tallgrass prairie.

Ólafur Guðjón Arngrimson—in America, Anderson—was, like Barney Jones, born in 1859 on a Vopnafjörður farm. He tried farming here but because he was a wise man, soon gave it up and came to town to clerk for the Icelandic cooperative store. Like so many Scandinavians, Icelanders arrived here with proper socialist-leftist-cooperative notions, but capitalist temptation defeated them, and they adjusted as best they could. In 1896, Olafur opened O.G. Anderson's Cash Store "with bargains in dry goods, shoes, notions, 'Boston' or

The Big Store, Minneota's famous Icelandic business.
The building was erected in 1900 and is now on the
Minnesota State Register of Historic Buildings.

'Trilby' bicycles, dresses in exchange for eggs, and cashmeres for 25 cents." He prospered, moved to a bigger building, and finally, behaving like a genuine old-line entrepreneurial American, borrowed more money to build this huge state-of-the-turn-of-the-century-art behemoth. The Opera House upstairs was equipped with a grand piano, theatrical backdrops, velvet curtain, and gas chandeliers. Mark Twain would have lectured there had he arrived on the Chataqua circuit, but alas. . . . The main floor boasted a commodious freight elevator, spring-loaded money tubes running on wires from every department to an ornate teller's cage, a painted silver tin ceiling, oak and glass-doored cabinets, huge mirrors where women could admire their new ostrich hats.

In 1916, the Big Store with the new men's department addition.
Note the "opera house" above. Vilhjálmur Stefansson
(among other eminent Icelanders) lectured there,
bringing his Arctic travels to Minneota.

The Big Store sold everything you could want; no need to take the train to Minneapolis. When it finally closed in 1975, some of the clerks had been working there since 1910—at the same posts. Anna Anderson, the buyer for young ladies dresses, was then over ninety. When the family sold off the accumulated stock from the vast crypts under the building, they unearthed unopened cases of stiff-wing collars, spats, high-button boots, Icelandic books, wool knickers, and silk bloomers.

The Big Store was so complete and accomplished a time warp that even as a boy I imagined it as a vast museum, the clerks waiting around at their various stations for imminent taxidermy. Yet it remained the biggest dry goods store between Mankato and Sioux Falls—a vast stretch of prairie—for its seventy-five years of life. These photographs remind me that all

Interior of the Big Store, sometime before 1920. O. G. Anderson's store was a descendant of the Icelandic commercial co-op of the 1880s and 90s. It was the biggest dry-goods store west of Mankato. "State of the art" in 1900, it stayed pickled in that condition until it closed in 1975.

the old were once young and frisky, that everything on earth was once brand spanking new. That's one of the joys of reading Homer: watching civilization so clear, bright, shiny, a newly minted consciousness.

In these photographs, the Big Store wears its patriotic mantilla of flags for July 4th, sometime in the first decade of the century. Quite a building for a prairie town of under a thousand in population. The interior shot comes from the same decade, a last supper of thirteen clerks, suited up and ready to serve you. Barney Jones, the meat cutter with the mustache, stands fourth from the left. The two floats, crepe paper touring sedan and land-locked battleship manned by underage sailors remind us of World War I patriotic fervor. Ain't America grand, buddy?

The Big Store float sometime around the First World War.
A roadster bedecked with tissue, roses, and a gala pennant.
Even Icelanders were once guilty of whimsy!

*The annual Big Store float, this time with a naval motif—
young Icelanders at play sometime around America's
entry into World War I.*

VII

My mother would not have liked this snapshot, though she
was as fond of the cat, Bootsocker, as she could be of any creature not human. It was taken some time in the late 30's and can
be dated by two facts: first, a tornado that almost picked the
Holm hill clean of trees and of Holms in 1937 or 1938, as if the
Great Depression and the Dust Bowl were not enough to cap-
ture a citizen's attention. My cousin Clifford remembers that
after the big whirlwind neatly de-shingled the house and removed the glass from every window, the yard filled with blind
birds, caught in the great maelstrom of wind and doomed to
fly afterwards through eternal darkness. One-and-a-half trees
survived, a boxelder just under the cat's tail and the cottonwood on the right, its top neatly sheared of leaves and left to
dry in the sun.

The house faces east; the old loose walls of the right half, built in 1885, were filled with bees. Honey oozed out between the painted siding. The "new part" on the left was built in 1900 when Sveinn and Emma, my grandparents, had their third child. The house boasted no central heat, only an oil stove in

Bootsocker the cat held hostage on the post by Peggy the Labrador, both having just survived a Minnesota tornado.

the dining room with wrought-iron ceiling grates to let heat rise, maybe protecting you from frostbite in the upstairs bedrooms. In 1940 the house still had no electricity, no running water, no flush toilet, no telephone. These niceties arrived in the late '40's and early '50's when I was a little boy. In my bedroom, facing west on the other side of the "new part," a bedside glass of water froze solid for three months of every year.

The second fact dating the picture is the presence of the cat and the shadow below of the black Labrador, Peggy, who has 'treed' Bootsocker on the fence post and waits anxiously to lick him to death with her wet red tongue. Both these animals survived long enough for me to make their acquaintance, to pull their respective tails, to try to sneak them under the covers as bed partners on winter nights. No luck. In my mother's house, the orderliness of the great chain of being prevailed; humans lived indoors, animals visited now and again, but kept their permanent address elsewhere—in barn or granary.

The house and pets are flanked by machinery, a '36 Chevy to the left, an iron hay rake to the right. There is a nice symmetry in this old and unselfconscious snapshot. The human world, the mechanical world, the animal world, the forest—all there, but noted with a proper thrift in the eye, a kind of elegant bareness that sees objects singly and in just order with a little space between each other for civility and clarity. If I had been alive when this photograph was taken, my mother would have ruined it by putting me at the center.

VIII

This picture can be precisely dated. It is the fall of 1954, just before Election Day. Valdimar Bjornson, the Minnesota State Treasurer and a Minneota Icelander of immense local fame and repute, was drafted by the Republicans to run as a sacrificial lamb against Hubert Humphrey, in those days so impregnable

that if Christ himself had returned in glory to run for the
Senate, the old farmers might have said, "Well, Jesus is a wonderful fella, but I believe Hubert would still be the better senator." Although I was still ten years away from voting, this race
created a great conflict for me.

At eleven, I met Hubert at a Farmer's Union meeting at the

*Young Bill Holm with senatorial candidate and famous local
Icelander, Valdimar Bjornson. It is autumn, 1954.*

Swede Prairie township hall, and shook his hand while getting his autograph for my little red book. I still own it. I saw him working the crowd of local farmers, smiling, affable, confident, remembering every name and some small detail from everyone's life. He climaxed the night with a fine tub-thumping speech, ending with a unison chanted chorus of "Parity! Parity! Parity!" At eleven, I thought him a great man.

But I thought Valdimar an even greater man, despite his being a Republican. I inherited from my father and still nourish the notion that Republicans are those who have acquired enough money, often by inheritance and blind luck, to entertain the opinion that their fellow citizens should work harder and be more grateful to the moneyed class while they refrain from work themselves and sit in clean rooms with folded soft hands examining their bank statements and brokerage reports. But not Valdimar; he was a man famous for his eloquent oratory, his quick wit, and his orotund and distinguished prose—in both Icelandic and English. He was a writer, a talker, a word man. I had something in that line in mind for myself. And he was an Icelander, to boot, son of the famous Gunnar Bjornson, an Icelandic foundling who became one of Minnesota's most highly regarded journalists and editors, in his second language. Valdimar had just given one of his smoothly elegant—and often improvised—campaign speeches in his old hometown, Minneota, where he didn't need any votes to begin with. The *Minneapolis Star* sent a photographer to cover this piece of political nostalgia. I came into Valdimar's presence with my mother, an old friend of his, safely behind me. As he wrote his autograph, the photographer got both of us and my mother's right eye and beringed left hand. But I meant that moment seriously, took it seriously then and still do. I saw it, I suppose, as a kind of passing of the torch of language to a plump, nerdy, eleven-year-old, spoiled boy who loved words and saved his deepest respect for those who made themselves servants of language.

I still keep Valdimar's autograph from 1954 and every letter he ever sent me after I grew up and we became friends.

Valdimar lost that election, of course, and soon returned to his old State Treasurer's job. I think, in retrospect, that he might have been a better senator than Hubert, more willing to call Joe McCarthy a venal fool, less willing to toady during the Vietnam War; but who among us can second-guess history? But though he failed to win that election—an election so calm, dignified, literate, full of content, and completely without personal attacks on the part of either man—my memory of its honor and eloquence is one foundation of the energy I've spent as a writer praising failure in America. I want to fail exactly as Valdimar did and so do we all, if we think about it.

I had forgotten that picture. The photo librarian at the *Minneapolis Star,* cleaning out old files, found this shot and sent it to me. I treasure it, not least because of the admirable shirt this four-eyed orange-haired nerd of a boy wears on his lucky back.

The Long Craziness

Every morning at about nine, I walk two hundred yards from my back door to pick up mail at the Minneota Post Office. Six months ago, a new poster went up next to the Wanted notices and the commemorative stamp announcements. It's a crude picture of a dog wearing a trench coat; the caption reads: McGruff Says: Don't Speak to Strangers. I thought to myself: What a repulsive order! Who else would you speak to? You already know what your neighbors are going to say! "Cold enough for you? . . . Get enough rain yet? . . . Back to work then?" And you've already rehearsed your answer: Yup, yup, and yup. I mean no disrespect to my neighbors, since their job in this world is not to surprise and delight me daily—nor is it my job to reciprocate. We make small grunts to acknowledge each other's presence, and that is a fine thing to do—a civil courteous gesture among fellow citizens. "Don't Speak to Strangers" comes from some other world. Once yearly from every pulpit in town, Lutheran or Catholic, a priest reads the parable of the Good Samaritan from Saint Luke. Christ answers the question: "Who is my neighbor?"—only another form of "Who is a stranger?" The tale Christ tells of the man fallen among thieves on a strange road is a direct slap on the snout of the dog, McGruff, a sort of canine Levite.

I told a friend about this unsavory poster and asked her, "Who the hell is McGruff?" "A sort of watchdog to protect children," she said. "McGruff houses are safe houses for children when they find themselves in trouble." "And children are not to speak to strangers?" I asked. "Not if they're too friendly," she answered.

At this point in an essay, most readers feel a fulmination coming on, some sort of angry nostalgia about the collapse of civil life in America and a roseate description of the writer's pastoral childhood. If they are sensible, they stop reading. That's not quite what I intend to say, though for a while it will seem to veer in that direction. Be patient.

What astonished me most about the McGruff poster was the implication that adults represent danger—the necessity for caution, even suspicion. As a child I perceived exactly the opposite. Danger lurked in other children; they would pelt you with snowballs, trip you, hide snakes in your bed, take your precious books and rip them or throw them into manure piles, and generally humiliate and terrify you. I can list to this day which Minneota children of 1955 I learned to beware of, hide from, avoid. I often thought then that if they could make it through their childhood without killing someone or being jailed, they might improve as they aged. Mostly they are now kindly and respectable middle-aged citizens. One has now even become a successful lawyer for the poor.

I suppose I was a better-than-average target for town bullies—the Draconian enforcers of childhood conformity. I was an oversized, plump, soft, bookish, nearsighted, piano-playing boy with flaming orange hair, a multitude of cowlicks, and conversation decorated with polysyllabic quotations from nineteenth-century poetry. A perfect target! Irresistible! If I hadn't in fact been one, I would have probably enjoyed humiliating and terrifying such a character myself. Adults were my haven, refuge, and protection from this bullying; every house was a safe house if someone old lived there. From adults I got praise, food, and courtesy. They even left me alone to read or do whatever I pleased.

I was lucky, I suppose, to have grown up on a farm close to a small town where everyone knew everyone else and a third of the citizens were related to another third. To such a place, however, a stranger brought relief. You could throw away the prerehearsed conversational script and actually listen with attention and curiosity to what others said. "You're from where?" "How did you get here?" "What's it like there?" If you were lucky, and the stranger were not a Scandinavian Lutheran, he might even be an entertaining storyteller or have new jokes to tell.

Is this confidence in the decency of adults gone from the United States? Are we all now to become Levites, crossing to the other side of the road to avoid suspicious strangers? I hope not. I am afraid that such an attitude might be the death blow to civil life among us.

What gives any of us the confidence to assume that others will love us or at least treat us civilly? How can we give a humane answer to Christ's question? Who is the stranger?

In Minneota, and in your neighborhood, too, that confidence often was born of the experience of unconditional love from the old—the ones who valued us and fed us simply because we were children, not because we lived or failed to live up to our peers' standards.

I was an only child born to parents who by early middle age had given up any hope of having one. They were affectionate people who had been until that time deprived, by luck and circumstance, of at least one avenue for that affection. My arrival provided it. A vague aura of gratitude filled the house, and since children are no fools, I felt it immediately without entirely understanding it. My presence excused whatever I did or said. If I made a mistake, forgiveness was available and forthcoming. If I did something intelligent, or showed some small ability, praise arrived punctually. My duty consisted only of existing, and that was easy.

Not only did baby-sitters inspire no fear, I longed for my parents to go off to poker games, or dances at ballrooms with names like Showboat, Fiesta, Blue Moon, Valhalla, or to any adult occasion that offered them an excuse to drop me in new territory. The world seemed full of kind old ladies, often born in Iceland, who baked cakes and bread, kept Depression glass bowls well-stocked with peppermints or chocolates, and lived in houses that smelled of mothballs, powdered sugar, cold cream, and medicine.

My favorite was Sigurjóna Eyjólfsdóttir, though I neither called her that nor had at the time any idea that it was her name. She was Grandma Rafnson. I thought "Grandma" her first and only name and couldn't imagine anyone calling her anything else. She had nine children of her own, and though none were so prolific as their mother, they nevertheless managed to provide her with fifty or sixty blood grandchildren by the end of the forties. But she was insatiable for grand-motherhood, and every child in town called her Grandma whether they were Icelanders or relatives or not. Albanians, Ugandans, and Trobrianders who might have found their way to Minneota would soon have been adopted into her clan. Whether consciously or not she had been publicly transformed into her function—indeed into an archetype. She was Grandmother, not only of the Rafnsons, but of the universe.

She seemed ancient and simultaneously ageless to me, yet when I was six or seven in 1950, she was a mere child of seventy-two. Like so many old people in Minneota when I was a boy, she had been born in the countryside around Vopnafjörður, a fjord on the northeast coast of Iceland that opened its rocky arms north to the polar ice and the Arctic Ocean. It was then, and still is, the outer limit of the habitable world. Just before her birth in 1878, a volcanic explosion buried the local sheep pastures in ash; so, as a child of two, she joined half the district that emigrated to western Minnesota. She must have taken a ship from east Iceland to Liverpool to Quebec, come by train to Chicago, then west to Minnesota; but she was too young to remember the journey, and whatever she knew of Iceland, she never troubled children by telling them anything about it. She existed out of time or place or process, seemingly unchanged from the foundation of the world, as Scripture has it.

Just before the turn of the century, she married a local farmer, Ólafur Rafnson, born in her district of Iceland, and began her own brood of seven daughters and two sons. In a sea of blondes and redheads, she improved the look of Minneota by raising black-haired children. I have no idea whether she or Ole had black hair, because by the time I arrived, Ole was long dead and she was a gray-haired widow. When, years later, I learned a little Icelandic and thought of her married name, I laughed. The universe let down its guard a little to show some humor. Grandma's children were sons and daughters of the raven—*rafn*—in Icelandic, looking every hair the part. At gatherings of Icelanders, they provided the pepper to liven the pale Norse salt. I thought her daughters the most beautiful women in Minneota. One daughter, Agnes, born in 1910, was one of my mother's high school classmates and best friends. In a snapshot of her taken in 1929 her raven hair falls over one eye—turning her into a Minneota Hedy Lamar or Ava Gardner.

Whenever my parents, along with Agnes and her husband Sam, went dancing or visiting, it was often my good luck to be dropped off at Grandma's little apartment, occupying half an old house on the highway through town. She was a small round woman, and though I suppose she owned dentures, she never wore them. With her O-shaped mouth, she hummed and whistled to herself continually, sometimes sucking in her breath for a *yow,* the Icelandic "yes." I remember asking her now and then what she was humming, but the only answer I ever got was, "Oh, it's nothing," followed by another meditative in-sucking of breath, a *yow* or two, then a resumption of the tune. Even then a little deaf, she was selective in choosing either to hear or not to be pestered about something so unimportant as the name of the tune. Her internal and automatic humming functioned like the purring of a cat to calm both the hummer and any child nervous or silly enough to pay much attention to it. That hum seemed not so much music as noises the sun makes coming up and going down, or the planet turning on its axis in space.

While she hummed, she knitted, crocheted, or tatted. Her hands were never without needles or hooks in them, or her lap uncovered by a half-finished piece of something. Back and forth, knit and pearl, in and out, was automatic as the tune. The rhythm never varied in speed or energy; she seemed in no hurry to finish whatever project half-filled her basket. Perhaps, like Penelope, she took out her stitches each night, crocheting them back into existence by daylight. Or maybe those stitches were the warp and woof of her life—which went on years after my boyhood to her death at well over 103. With her humming, crocheting, and Buddha-like calm imperturbableness, she seemed eternal to me—and in fact came as close as humans ever come to true eternity. You can't last much longer than 103.

I knew even as a small boy that Grandma did not think in English, and when you asked her anything which needed some response, the question disappeared first down into the dark well of Icelandic, then, as the language bucket rolled back up toward daylight, picking up enough English for an answer. This hesitation seemed normal to me as a child; everyone Grandma's age was born somewhere unimaginably far away and part of their consciousness hadn't moved all the way to Minneota yet. Probably I thought that was what it meant to be old in America: to translate every sentence twice, to hum in a foreign language. What did I know? I had never even seen a television set.

When I went to live in Iceland for a while in my thirties, I met real Icelandic old ladies—toothless hummers and tatters in baggy dresses, older than greenstone, patting children on the head as they sucked in their breath for a *"yow, yow, elskan"* ("yes, yes, love"), rocking back and forth to their own music, as if singing a lullaby to their own so-long-arriving death.

Grandma Rafnson was one of them. In one way, she never left her icy farm next to the weapon fjord in the old country, living for over a century in western Minnesota without entirely moving here. How ironic the hysteria about bilingualism, illegal immigrants, and the intransigence of some groups at adapting to the television life of modern America. Since we are all the children of "wetbacks," it would do us some good to remember it now and then—with even a little affection, if we could muster it up amidst the welter of our opinions.

Grandma Rafnson neither spoke about nor made a point of being an Icelander to the children dropped off at her house. That would have been ridiculous as a bear regaling you with the pleasures and mysteries of "bearness." Some things simply are; they needn't be fussed about. By 1950 most of her grandchildren were half something else—German, Belgian, Polish, Norwegian, God's plenty of varieties, but whatever the mixture, they shared this common denominator: they were children, therefore in need of being fed, amused, calmed, tucked in, hummed at, trained to join the eternal procession of parenthood themselves. She was a genius at keeping children quiet, with endless tricks and games tucked into the sleeves of her old-lady print dresses. Every child who passed through her house at bedtime learned the Lord's Prayer in Icelandic—*Faðir vor, þu sem ert á himnin.* I suspect most of them thought it the real and original form of that prayer, spoken in Jesus's own language, all translations being only spiritual cribsheets. Surely Jesus rolled his *r*'s with the best of them.

She was born into poverty, raised in it, married in it, widowed in it, and died in it after more than a century. I imagine she owned only half a closet of clothes, a few books, some shabby furniture, her knitting and crocheting supplies. Viewed from one angle, she endured poverty so long she became used to it. Her children lived to adulthood, married, had children of their own, so she had no further use for more than what little she possessed. What more did anyone need?

You didn't need toys. She taught children the usefulness of

their own bodies as sources of pleasure and humor. Think of it! Ten toes and ten fingers, all capable of wiggling! And noses—and ears! All free! Imagine the aristocratic generosity of nature. Children needed neither Nintendo nor any other expensive electronic gadgetry as long as they had a body, an imagination, and a sense of humor. The exact games have slid away from my memory. They involved counting, naming, patting, touching, and chuckling. I remember only the pleasure and the names of the fingers. Hold up your hand. Begin with the thumb. Now repeat after me: *Thermotut, Slakey Pot, Lángi Mann, Stalkey Jóhann, Litla Joi Á Endan.* Those are your fingers. Enjoy them. What do the names mean? I'm not sure anymore. Grandma may have made them up; they might have been an Icelandic children's game, or the names of Christmas trolls (part of the twelve *Jolasveinar*). They might have been the purest nonsense with Icelandic phonemes. Does it make a difference? Make up your own names for your own children, and may you live to be 103, though all your gadgets and machines break down and fail, leaving you only fingers, toes, and a brain.

I do remember the rules for *Lángavitleysa*—the Long Craziness—an Icelandic card game for children whose name is an understatement, as you will see. Icelanders, unlike Norwegians, suffered little from Lutheran piety, not regarding card-playing as an instrument for your personal delivery into the devil's clutches. Civilized people passed their time by playing cards, waiting for winter to end or political arguments to begin, whichever came first. Children learned rudimentary card sense: suits, tricks, counting, and a little strategy, so that if adults were drunk or indisposed, they could be summoned without fuss to fill a fourth chair.

With a dime-store pack of cards, you could defeat boredom: solitaire for introverts, rummy or cribbage for couples, whist or pinochle after dinner at family gatherings, and *Lángavitleysa* for children, the crazy, and the feeble minded.

Here are the rules: Take a bunch of cards, preferably from old decks with fewer than fifty-two cards that would be otherwise thrown away. The more cards the better—or worse depending on your patience for the long craziness. Divide the cards in half. Show a card. It's a seven. Here's mine; it's a ten. I win the trick. Put the pair on the bottom of your pile. Show another card. The queen. Here's mine; a deuce. You win. Continue. The game ends when one player has all the cards. There is some difference of opinion as to whether any game of *Lángavitleysa* played anywhere on earth has ever, in fact, ended. Usually sleep calls a truce. Past the age of four or five, *Lángavitleysa* loses its charm for children of normal intelligence; they feel a longing to move on in the general direction of bridge, chess, or auto racing. But Grandma Rafnson tirelessly played it with an inexhaustible supply of children. There is a kind of genius in the game—a few little flurries of moderate excitement when you win a few tricks, followed by the gradual realization that true progress is impossible. By this time, Grandma's humming and the vast stretches of eternity opened to you by *Lángavitleysa* have heavied your eyelids. Time for the last cookie and the Lord's Prayer: *Faðir vor, þu sem ert á himnin . . .*

Before climbing alongside her under the warm quilts, to be once and for all hummed into the world of dreams, I saw two more wonders that fascinated me as a child and whose image remains bolted in my memory—her hump and her hair. Part of her roundness came from an enormous cyst or tumor on her back. I thought it simply a necessary part of being an old lady, the inescapable weight of a long life made visible in flesh. As an adult, I asked my mother, who knew the secret answer to every question in Minneota, the explanation for the hump. Only a benign cyst, Jona said, but by the time Grandma consulted a doctor, it had grown to such size that he was afraid it would kill her to have it removed. I suspect that aside from remodeling her dresses to accommodate its size, it never troubled her.

She seemed without vanity and if, in fact, it finally killed her at only 103, it was certainly a poky and kind-hearted cyst. It provided a warm pillow for little boys to curl against on winter nights.

Just before the last prayers, she took down her hair to comb it. Like most women of her generation from the old country, I think she died without ever having had a haircut, instead piling her long gray hair on top of her head every morning, taking it down every night, combing it while she hummed. It fell all the way to the linoleum. I first saw her hair in its seventies; by the time of her death, it was over a century long.

I always left Grandma Rafnson with regret, though my own house was equally full of affection and attention. She seemed to inhabit another world—without school, farm work, newspapers, or even weather, a timeless world of enormous age and virgin innocence, without the complications of middle-aged adult life. However much the middle-aged loved you, they still lived in a world made sticky by money, labor, marriages, politics, gossip, the necessity of adult privacy. Grandma aged past all of that, her whole world inhabited by children, grandchildren, great-grandchildren. Aside from knitting and humming, I think nothing else interested her. Wars, depressions, scandals, elections, catastrophes seemed not of much grand consequence so long as her numberless brood stayed safe from danger.

Yet she kept an exact census of that brood, her own blood generation plus any of the countless, like me, who crossed her path and shared her bed. She memorized their birthdays, hundreds of them, reminding everyone of their exact age when they visited her. No computer ever paid you such exact and affectionate attention, nor could it play cards, name fingers, or hum. Her mind remained alert to the end, though by the time she reached 100, she was almost blind and deaf. I went to visit her at her last little apartment in her daughter Agnes's house. She sat in a straight wooden chair by the window warming her body in the sun like an old cat, using whatever power was in the light to help her see. Though her eyesight was slight, she could tat by feel, her lap still full of her project, a basket of thread still sitting by the chair. She leaned forward favoring her by now gigantic hump, rocking and humming the same tuneless song, her gnarled fingers busy tatting. I wondered if she would know me. My mother warned me to speak loudly in her ear, in Icelandic if I could manage it, since the hard consonants of her first language seemed easier for her to hear. Her century of hair, now almost, though not completely white, and still uncut, was piled safely on her head.

"Billy, is that you?" she asked when I walked into her room.

"It's me, Grandma. How are you?" She ignored the question.

"So, you're going to be thirty-seven on the 25th of August. That's only a month. Don't you have any children yet?"

"No, Grandma."

"Well, that's terrible. You should get busy." Having covered the subjects that meant anything to her, she resumed her tatting, sucking her breath in while "yow-yowing" a bit.

"It's been a long time since I've seen you, Grandma. How old are you now?" Her memory was better than mine.

"Too old." More tatting.

"Don't be silly, Grandma. There's no such thing as too old. You're over a hundred now, aren't you?"

How naive and foolish the young are to imagine that they understand the loneliness of great age, the outliving of your contemporaries, anyone to whom your century of memory might make any sense.

"Too old," she repeated. "Parents shouldn't live longer than their children."

Her youngest boy, Harvey, probably the apple of her eye, had died in his sixties, shortly before my visit. I could think of nothing to say. Instead, I thought of handing her a pack of cards to see if we could finish a game of *Lángavitleysa*.

"I see you're still knitting, Grandma."

"Tatting," she said, a little short with male ignorance. "I can't see anything anymore. I'm too old."

"It's lovely work," I told her.

"Here, it's for you, Billy. Save it for your first child." Now that yard of fine tatting hangs over the dresser mirror in the bedroom where I sleep.

Within a year of that visit, Sigurjóna Eyjolfsdóttir, Sara Rafnson, Grandma, slipped peacefully into death, presumably still counting her hundreds of grandchildren reminding them of birthdays, scolding them to get busy—to have more children. The long craziness ended after one hundred-three years, three months, twenty days.

What did I learn from Sigurjóna Rafnson? What do any of us learn from her by whatever name we have known her? The rules of a silly card game whose secret end is boredom and oblivion. A childhood prayer in a foreign language understood by almost nobody still alive. An aural memory of an unnamed tune—hummed into the ear as if through a half-century of gauze. Most important, we inherit the interior confidence that the universe itself is a safe house for us. That if we don't close ourselves away through fear, the currents of simple love, kindness, civility, will find us out, feed us cookies, and tuck us in. In Grandma Rafnson's world, no child was a stranger. Those were two mutually contradictory states of being. Even if years of simply staying alive in a sometimes difficult, brutal world try to poison us with fear and suspicion of our neighbors and the world itself, some core of our inner life remains safe—even buoyant. That core will not go away. It is tied to the soul with a yard of fine tatting, a gift we receive without deserving that cannot be refused without some interior death. It speaks to all strangers.

Glad Poverty

I come to the garden alone,
While the dew is still on the roses;
And the voice I hear, Falling on my ear;
The Son of God discloses.

Chorus:
And he walks with me, and he talks with me,
And he tells me I am his own,
And the joy we share as we tarry there,
None other has ever known.

C. Austin Miles,
"In the Garden" from *Jubilate*

I

Sara Kline was the most visibly poor woman in Minneota when I was a boy. Old, small, shriveled, hunched over, almost toothless, she wore the same black rags for years on end, her stringy, greasy gray hair covered with the same black scarf, the same black high-tops with a dozen frayed knots in the laces. Her stoop probably came from scouring the gutters with her poor eyesight, looking for serviceable cigarette butts that she liberated from the cement or from under the sidewalk gratings into her filthy cloth bag—a Minneota "bag lady," years before that term became fashionable.

But the strongest image of her poverty arrived not so much

to the eyes as to the nose. Within twenty or thirty feet, her presence announced itself: a stale smell of unwashed damp rags, sweat, urine-soaked underwear, rotting food in rotted teeth, old cigarettes, the fetor that rises off a mattress that should have been thrown away decades ago, the smell of the old and poor who have ceased to be able to care—whose vanity has atrophied out from under them.

I came from a family of big men, making my judgment of human size untrustworthy; but I remember Sara as half the size I thought right for a normal human. She was closer to the earth than she should have been—not a bad metaphor for her whole life.

In the forties and fifties, Saturday was the night for late hours in the stores. It was the night for shopping, visiting, cleaning up after a week of farm work, driving the pickup down the gravel road to town, for getting haircuts, buying groceries and beer, bolts of material, oyster shells for the chickens, and Velveeta for the humans. Saturday was for gossiping while you sat on the warm car hood, going to Medart Debbaut's Joy Theatre for Hopalong Cassidy, popcorn, and Mr. Nibs. The town crinkled with crisp, new bib overalls and smelled of sticky hair spray. This was the midwest version of bright lights and urbanity.

But Sara Kline was always there to remind you that this was not Norman Rockwell's America, not a Farm Bureau poster of contented, prosperous rural family life, that God, even if he were on duty at the moment in heaven, had not quite yet managed to make all things right with the world.

The Saturday night division of labor in the Holm house was this: my father said his obligatory in-town hellos to whomever my mother thought necessary, and then disappeared into the Round-Up Tavern for whist, rummy, buckeuchre, beer, Camels, swearing, and male privacy; my mother investigated whatever bargains might have surfaced during the week at the Big Store or Johnson's Red Owl, exchanging her ritual information with other ladies who liked Saturday night chumminess; I tried to disappear into the Hopalong Cassidy movie as quickly as possible, or find some gang of under-age street marauders setting off to engineer themselves into parentless, thus more interesting, situations.

Before these rituals began, though, there came another, sterner test. My father parked his dirty brown Dodge as close as possible to the Round-Up. This meant we passed Sara's light pole. She lived in the back room of a crumbling frame building on an alley behind the Round-Up. Minneota was then a town of broad front porches, picture windows facing the street, unshaded and unhedged front lawns with chairs sitting on them. An alley meant a place to hide something, a place to throw garbage, to piss, to be drunk, to quarrel, to smoke (if you were a teenager), to tell low jokes, a place for shame, for the poor, for strangers, for what did not want to be seen.

Children are constitutional xenophobes; it is their natural instinct to humiliate and abuse the crippled, the old, the ugly, the peculiar, the grotesque. Children love their own beauty and energy so much that they excoriate others for lacking it. Neither my contemporaries in Minneota nor I were unusual in that regard. The process of being made to feel guilt and shame for that xenophobia, thus stopping its progress, is called civilization. It is the first teaching duty of parents.

Mine took their responsibility with what, at the time, I thought an uncommon severity. They instructed me that I was never to pass Sara Kline without shaking her hand, greeting her courteously in Icelandic, and, worst of all, bending down to kiss her on the cheek. Even as a young boy, I towered over her shrunken black figure. My mother coached me in proper Icelandic grammar, so that I would not commit the awful sin of using a male ending to address a lady. *Komdu sæl og blessuð, Sara,* I would mumble, preparing myself for the smelly, humiliating ordeal.

She was always there, waiting on the sidewalk in front of the old barbershop and workboot store that shared the front of the ramshackle building. My father greeted her on his way to the Round-Up; my mother chatted a bit in Icelandic, probably inquiring after Sara's health, and then it was my turn. With a feigned courtliness, I greeted, shook hands, kissed, all the time hoping that none of my classmates watched this ordeal. Sara would tell me that I was a nice boy and getting so big with such fine red hair just like my mother's and then reach up to pat my cheek with her leathery, grimy hand. Then it was over for perhaps another week.

I had not, at that time, read the story of Jonathan Swift and the beggar woman outside Saint Paul's Cathedral in Dublin. After preaching one Sunday on the subject of charity and humanity to the poor, he made his way down the steps of his cathedral still dressed in his ecclesiastical robes when an old beggar reached up her hand for alms. Swift looked down at the hand, then turned away in disgust. "She might at least have washed that hand," he is reported to have said, and so might I have said, if my parents would not have disowned me for saying it.

Indeed, Guttormur Guttormsson, the Icelandic minister in Minneota for almost fifty years, did not say it either. Like Swift, he was dean of a Saint Paul's, but this smaller one was built of oak in 1895. He greeted Sara each Sunday at the door of the church with the same courtesy and, of course, the same impeccable Icelandic that he used for his most elegant parishioners. She was a regular churchgoer, always arriving a bit late and sitting alone at the back of the church. She had, without intention, a private pew, and her fellow Icelandic Lutherans should be forgiven for not wanting to crowd her too closely. Guttormur's sermons were heroically long and the church stuffy.

By the time I was a teenager, I had become a sporadic church organist, with a perch in the balcony where I surveyed the congregation, read D. H. Lawrence novels, and otherwise avoided being improved by lengthy discourses on the theology of sanctification and grace. I carefully watched Sara while the collection was taken; she never failed to put her coin or two into the velvet dish full of silent paper, always letting go of them with a little regret, turning her head to follow the plate of money as it made its way down the aisle toward the pink painted Jesus.

Like many other old ladies, both rich and poor, she asked me to sing at her funeral, and I did. For Sara, I sang "Come, Ye Disconsolate" and "I Walk in the Garden Alone." She was cleaner in her coffin, brighter, paler, though even smaller, and I think, happier. There was, as I remember, no family to sit in the mourners' pews, but, instead, a good many of the congregation who had known her well for three-quarters of a century.

My mother was a great repository of stories and local history, a sort of village gleewoman, but she was always close-mouthed when I asked for the history of Sara Kline. "She was a poor woman, and her life was full of suffering," Jona said, "and children were always mean to her because she was dirty and odd-looking. You mustn't add to that; and when you see Sara always go out of your way to greet her respectfully in Icelandic and kiss her hello. She deserves . . ."

"Yes, yes, yes," I would interrupt this often chanted mantra, "but what happened to the poor woman that reduced her to such a god-awful life?"

"Her life was full of suffering, and you must always . . . ," Jona started again, making no progress in giving me the details of Sara's obviously dark, checkered past.

I found out something of that past almost accidentally, long after both she and my parents were dead. Sara was buried in the Icelandic town graveyard a half-mile south of Minneota. Most of the names on the stones there were normal, everyday names like Gislason, Hallgrimsson, Bjornson, Guttormsson, Rafnson, Jokull, but there were a few odd ones like Schram and Kline. Their oddness never occurred to me as a boy; I assumed that God had made certain that only Icelanders wound up in such a favored spot and could be trusted to dispose of others elsewhere. But one day, I was walking through the cemetery with a family of distinguished and elderly Icelanders who knew everyone in the place and addressed them by name as they stepped over their stones.

"Look at that," said Bjorn. "Someone mowed Skunk's grave and planted flowers on it. It's better than the son-of-a-bitch deserves."

"Skunk?"

He pointed down to the grave of a man dead in 1945. "Why is his grave next to Sara's?" I asked.

"Didn't you know? Sara was his mother. She was a hired girl brought over from Iceland by old Schram. His name was German, not Icelandic. One of his brothers got Sara pregnant, and then gave her nothing. The brother went back to Iceland. Sara, a poor ignorant girl, raised her boy alone. He grew up to be a drunk, stole from his mother, abused her, finally died drunk."

"And his nickname was Skunk because . . ."

"It suited him."

The poor, withered, unwashed body of Sara rose up inside me; I smelled the stale half-smoked butts in her bag, felt her leathery paw on my cheek again. This was the story my mother never told, the reason I was so punctiliously trained to treat Sara as if she were a countess. Quite enough had happened to her in this world, thank-you very much, and she needed no more indignity on her way out of it. Civilization often consists not so much in knowing what to do the first time around, as in being intelligent and humane enough to try, without much hope, to repair the damages, or at least to offer some honest consolation on the second go.

Sara's poverty and misery were of the kind that could not be hidden. She had no resources to hide them anyway. She was not beautiful, she was not educated, and she was not endowed with the arrogant bravado and self-possession that sometimes gets you through this world without either gift.

I I

Just as Sara Kline could never hide her poverty, so my Aunt Olympia Vilborg Sveinnsdóttir Holm Amundson Quamen could never show it. My father was the baby of a family mostly of sisters, and despite the fact that by the time I knew him he was a rough-spoken, gray-haired, burly man, he was pampered and bossed like a small boy by his three older sisters: Sophie, Dora, and Olympia (Ole). I loved them dearly as a boy, those three big kindly women, but Ole had me entirely in her thrall, as she had all men.

She was born in 1904, and I own a photo of her as a teenager, taken in 1922. It shows her dressed in a gauzy light-colored dress that whips around her knees in the wind. She grins coquettishly straight into the camera. She is standing in front of the old Round-Up, a few Model T's parked in the background. She loved having her picture taken; she loved being watched and admired; she loved men, like Oscar Wilde, not wisely but too well; she probably loved the unknown cameraman taking the snapshot on the main street of Minneota, and flirted with him both before and after, and clearly during the picture. I would bet my last dollar that it was not a woman holding that camera, and no one who knew Ole would bet against me.

She was not, I suppose, a beautiful woman by conventional standards; she looked like a Scandinavian archetype. But then, how am I to judge? She was my aunt, and from the age of perhaps three I was in love with her. Others always found her attractive, and when she walked into a room full of strangers, she never failed to get her fair share of their attention. For a good part of her life a beauty parlor operator, she never allowed any-one to see her less than well-turned out. Her hair, elegantly snow white for the last fifty years of her life, was always "done"; her makeup in place; her fingers ringed, not expensively, but splendidly and gaudily like a Viking gypsy; her clothes were bright and silky, lavender and cream. Ole was no Puritan. And her Emeraude! It was, I imagine, dime-store perfume, but I smell it as I write this sentence, redolent of attar of roses, of ambrosia, of lavender, not of women but of movie goddesses, not of reality but of memory. After Ole sat in a room, Emeraude held her ghost in the curtains, in the cushions of the sofa and the chair, in the crocheted tablecloth, for hours, for days, I think even for years afterwards.

Probably much to her own daughters' chagrin, she loved little boys much more than little girls. My first memories of Auntie Ole were her visits to my father's farm. She swept into the small cold parlor, Emeraude trailing her, rings clanking like Cleopatra's tambourines, and hoisted her small, fat, bespecta-cled nephew into her lap. "And how's little Bill? You've got dimples just like your father used to have; and you're getting so big and strong! And how much do you love your old Auntie Ole today?"

How do you answer a question like this? I rashly promised to get rich when I grew up, so that I could buy my dear Auntie Ole a fur coat. Her not entirely whimsical complaint to the universe and to any adult within earshot was that her old Persian lamb was moth-eaten and bare, and she could afford only fake fur coats, an unsatisfactory substitute.

The offer of the coat delighted her, and she then plunged into her second perennial request. "And you have such a beautiful voice, little Bill, you must promise me that you will sing 'I walk in the garden alone, while the dew is still on the roses . . .' at my funeral."

With violent protestation that she was never going to die, I would promise it and then shift subjects as fast as possible.

One of my small gratitudes to the divinities of luck remains that I had to wait a very long time to make good on that second promise.

On the first, the fur coat, I failed. But then Ole never really expected men to get rich or to make good on their promises of wonderful gifts. Experience in that regard had been too unkind to her.

Her father, my grandfather, died of pneumonia when Ole was five, and her widowed mother raised five children with next to nothing, partly on the charity of better-off relatives. Ole married young, a handsome though none-too-prosperous local Norwegian farmer, and had her three children during the Depression. Just when times might have improved for her, her husband died of epilepsy, and left her, like her mother, a poor widow with young children.

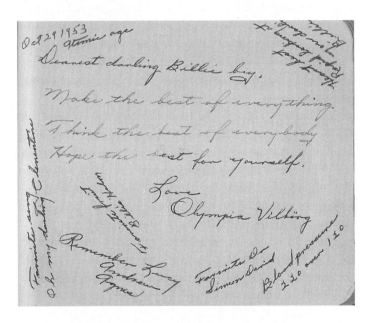

Words of wisdom from the author's aunt, preserved in his childhood autograph book, from 1953.

She moved to South Dakota to open a beauty parlor, as-suming, I suppose, that beauty was the only money-making skill that nature had given her. But her bad luck continued. She turned out to be allergic to the chemicals she had to use; her Icelandic skin burst into fiery rashes, her blood pressure went up, and her temporary trade was finished. By that time she had met and married her second husband, Earl, a carpenter and stone mason. He was the uncle I remember—a gruff, grizzled, and likable man, a little Bogart machismo about him without Bogart's handsomeness. And he drank a little . . .

And a little more as time went on, so that Ole found herself broke again. She was not, I suppose, a good manager of money, and was at least partly to blame for her own troubles. Her health began to give out in her sixties and seventies, though it was never visible behind the disguise of Emeraude, rings, lavender dresses, and a fluff of elegantly coifed white hair. But when she was widowed for the second time, she cracked, overdosed on her pills for various ailments, and she found herself confused, almost comatose and broke. Involun-tarily, she moved back to the nursing home in her hometown, Minneota.

By this time I had moved back to Minneota, too, and saw Ole several times a week. As I approached my forties, I was a little old to go through the routine of crawling into her lap, but Ole was not past her part in the charade. Despite the rav-ages of bad luck, illness, and poverty, she remained a good-looking woman, her vanity intact, her Emeraude was still on sale at the drug store, and her bottle not yet empty.

The sunroom of a nursing home is not a cheerful place, de-spite the sun. Rather it is a sort of canyon floor, strewn with the wreckage of great falls from the cliff, the bodies not yet quite washed away by the river. Remnants of human beings sit strapped into their wheelchairs, leaking onto themselves, moaning in an undecoded language, half-asleep. Having known Ole in something like her prime, at fifty, I could see the ravages of her experience in her face, in her talk, in the slight disarray of her blouse; but in that room, even in her reduced grandeur, she was not a client but a countess come to visit the old, cheer them, and scatter the largesse of her elegance. At core, she was still Ole. She flirted. When a man walked into the room, twenty years dropped off her. Her eyes brightened, and I could almost hear her say: "Here we go again!"

One day I found her in a lively conversation with one of the other inmates. The other woman was kidding Ole about being broke, and in need of a man, preferably rich. "Why, Ole, old Steve is ninety-two, owns three farms, and one of the nurses said he could still get it up when she came into his room. He's the man for you, Ole."

Ole said, "I wouldn't touch old Steve with a ten-foot pole if his ass was plated in platinum." For better or worse, Ole married only for love. She was romantic to the end.

Another day, I brought a friend, an out-of-town girl, to meet Auntie Ole. Ole told her funny stories about the old Icelanders.

"What is an Icelander, Ole?" my friend asked.

Ole paused, but not for long. "An Icelander, by descent, is forty percent Norwegian, forty percent Irish, and twenty percent traveling salesman."

Her bawdy and vivacious wit never deserted her. But neither did her complaining. Those she had no interest in charming, she blamed. Every magnificent character has her own darkness, even if we choose for a while not to see it.

One day I came to visit only to find her gone. "Back to Sioux Falls," said the nurse, "into a nice apartment building for old folks. Everybody dresses up fit to kill there."

"She'll like being among the rich," I mumbled.

"You know," the nurse mused, "I could never figure out why a woman as fancy as your aunt came back here. She was always so gracious and kind, but you could tell she was used to money. She was classy. Was her husband a banker?"

I think I fell to the floor in a fit of involuntary laughter before I could reply. "Ole was so poor her whole life that she often had no money to eat, went days without food because she was too proud to use food stamps. She had," I emphasized, "neither a dime nor a pot to piss in for over seventy years."

"Well, you never know," sighed the nurse.

Indeed, you never do. Ole blossomed in her last few years, found a lively boyfriend, a good dancer, but he up and died of a heart attack, so she found another one—a retired South Dakota real-estate agent. The two of them were inseparable and probably illegal, but Ole was Ole, and nearing eighty is no time to moralize. They lived together, had little spats, made up, rolled their eyes at each other, and generally enjoyed life.

But even long lives end. John died, and Ole's will to go on seemed to leave her. Eighty was enough. I went to see her a few days before she died. I walked into her hospital room and found her still Ole. Her hair was lovely, though she apologized for it. "You should have warned me you were coming." She was wearing not a hospital robe but a silk dressing gown, and there was Emeraude in the air. Solicitous as always about male comfort, she insisted that her daughter Emmy Lou and I walk her down to the sunroom. "Damn fools in this place won't let you smoke in the room."

The three of us sat in the empty room full of brilliant sunlight, not talking much. Finally, Ole said, "There he is again!" I had been warned that she was having hallucinations—seeing people who weren't there.

"Who is it, Auntie Ole?"

"It's the little boy. He's there in the corner behind the curtains. He's following me; don't you see him?"

"Oh, Mother, there's no one there," said Emmy Lou.

"Well, if you say so. But he's there." Her angel of death was true to her character, a handsome boy. If a little girl had come, I think Ole would have refused the summons.

As I did for Sara, I wound up singing "I Walk in the Garden

Alone" for Ole. The chorus was weirdly appropriate: "He walks with me, and he talks with me / And he tells me I am his own." Jesus as a gentleman caller was the only theological image that made any sense to her.

After the funeral, drinking coffee with relatives, I proposed that the scheme for Ole's funeral had been all wrong. She ought to have been cremated, and her ashes taken up in an airplane somewhere over the American West to be dropped on a town full of lonely men. Many heads nodded in agreement.

A historian examining their bank statements and indebtedness would probably not find much difference between Sara Kline and Auntie Ole. Yet in actuality, a whole universe separated these two Icelandic women. The question of which poverty was more glad is not as easy to answer as you might imagine. One sank under the weight of her poverty, wearing its visible signs like Hester Prynne's scarlet A. The other used all her energy to stay visibly afloat and buoyant, even though sea monsters had fastened their tentacles around her legs, trying to pull her under.

The Garden of Love

After a scandal happens a thousand times, it loses its power to shock; it shrivels to normalcy, to the banality of the regular. This inexorable shriveling happens even in small, out of the way, conservative places like Minneota, or any of its thousand incarnations. Try this in 1995: She's seventeen and pregnant, he's married, she's going to have the baby anyway. Ho-hum. . . . Rain tomorrow? More coffee?

The same draining away of power inside events must occur in the lives of professional soldiers, executioners, surgeons. Another day, another mound of bloody bodies, another snapped neck, another amputation. The longer we live, the more of the peculiar, the monstrous, the scandalous we corral inside the circle of everyday experience. We tame it to ride it through the rest of our lives at a placid trot. We should re-member, though, that the mysteries of death and lust some-times summon up the power of rambunctious stallions to resist our best efforts to domesticate them.

Call her Hester; Hawthorne did, and it is as good a name as any. The time is the mid-1950s, and she is in high school. She lives in a neat and pretty house—white, of course—built just after the First World War. Inside are fine oak cabinets, oak floors, dormer windows, an etched glass door. A garden of irises, peony bushes, and a lilac hedge surround the house. The house is neat, clean, well maintained, with a basketball hoop for her brother nailed above the garage door. Father has a steady job—probably working for the government; Mother in her apron bakes fresh ginger cookies, whips together a salad with cream and canned fruit. There's the white-frame Lutheran church with a tall spire nearby, an old brick neo-Gothic high school a few blocks away, built at the turn of the century and showing its age. The wood stairs creak and sway under the weight of moving shoes when students clump from one class to another, wavery grooves worn deep into the wood. The big, drafty windows rattle in the stiff Minnesota wind. The town will build a new, more up-to-date school in just a few years, selling off the school grounds to a builder of 1950s ramblers. This is Hester's school, her neighborhood, her small but clean, serene world.

Minneota is a "nice" town; this is a "nice" school. Post-World-War II prosperity still thrives. Three or four implement dealers sell tractors and combines to local farmers. The land is fertile, prices for livestock and grain high enough to provide a good living. Local merchants offer a steady supply of groceries, overalls, bolts of cloth, wrenches, livestock feed, patent medicines, whatever you want or need. The farmers pay cash. Behind its hidden alley door, the municipal liquor store in the old brick City Hall sells whiskey to the thirsty and malcontented. Enriched by whiskey profits, the city has built fine curbs and gutters, sidewalks, paved streets, bought mercury-vapor street lamps and garish neon Christmas lights. "Downtown" Minneota, all four blocks of it, is full—no vacant lots, no crumbling eyesores. The wood-frame buildings with their false second stories rise hopefully into the air, concealing nothing behind them, the set for a movie that will never be shot. The only dark reminder of history is the handsome Art Deco Legion Post building with its dance floor upstairs, its basement bowling alley. The beginning of the economic and social end of a placid well-off little town like Minneota already rumbled under the music of its serene pleasure at being itself, but no one would notice for ten years yet.

Minneota was a half-and-half town—half bib overalls, half

crisply pressed white shirts, half Scandinavian Lutheran, half
Belgian and Irish Catholic, so the school was half-and-half too,
an exact microcosm. Half of the four-hundred-odd students
arrived on orange buses, hauled fresh from barn chores over
gravel roads to the brick school. Half strolled down the elm-
lined streets and arrived with cleaner shoes and more stylish
clothes. On Wednesday the school practiced a peculiar, now
probably illegal, ritual called "release time." For an hour,
classes stopped and the Catholic half marched a few blocks to
Saint Edward the Confessor, while the massed Lutherans
marched to Hope Lutheran, the granite fortress of the
Norwegians. What the Catholics learned was always a mystery
to me, but the Lutherans, among whom I was a spy for Marx
and Tom Paine, exhorted their young in the dangers of un-
reformed religion, the guns stored in the Roman church
basement, and the secret pledges signed by the Knights of
Columbus. Thus restored in confidence at their respective
good luck at having been born either Lutheran or Catholic,
the students returned up the creaky stairs to Calculus, Social
Problems, Pep Club, and other less spiritual endeavors. God
knows what a Methodist, or a Jew, or a Black Baptist would
have done in Minneota on a Wednesday afternoon in 1955. The
fifties were the last time in mainstream America when society
actually believed the old saw: A place for everybody and everybody in their place.

Hester, a Lutheran townie, sat through a hundred of these
Wednesdays—and Luther League and confirmation and choir
practice and Bible camp—and all the rest of the small town
religious rigmarole. What did she hear? Date no Catholics.
Don't let your glands carry you away. Save yourself. Be careful.
Live for Jesus. Above all—and here was the thunderous
mantra repeated over and over by church, school, family, your
gang of friends, the whole town, the United States of America,
the free world, who knew? maybe even all the whirling galaxies
of space—be neither too interesting nor too interested in

anything: art, your body, your intelligence, nature. Let the words passionate or curious never appear in a sentence attached to your name.

Imagine Hester seated in the pew, listening. She is sixteen or seventeen; raven-black hair falls over her shoulders, the only spot of darkness in a room of blond, red, pale brown heads. She has grown up early. There is nothing boyish or "little and cute" about her. Her breasts would have delighted the poet of the Song of Songs: "like two young roes that are twins, which feed among the lilies." She is simultaneously proud and unconscious of them. Her sweater, probably too tight for Minneota, fails to hide what ought never to be hidden. The sweater is red or black—a gypsy color—no pale Lutheran pink or baby blue. In the age of the stiff crinoline petticoats that made girls look like Little Bo Peep, she wears a slim wool skirt. The boy sitting next to her in the church pew feels the soft curve of her hip; he imagines her legs—not long, she is not a tall woman. He imagines—Oh, he imagines!—and how can he not? even as the shepherd of the Lutherans drones on about the dangers of Catholics and communists, warning against the unchecked lusts of the body. If he did not imagine at a moment like this, he would not be a human being at all, but a seedpod fresh from the hot new movie, *Invasion of the Body Snatchers,* playing at the Starlite Drive-In in Marshall.

And what does Hester imagine as the Lutheran droning drifts through the room? She is not listening; I know that. Behind her black eyes lives a formidable intelligence. With ease, she is the best student in her class, the idiot content of high school courses duck soup to her. She commits the most dangerous sin for a beautiful woman in a small town. She reads books, she thinks, she bides her time. Maybe she imagines her escape from Minneota—to San Francisco or New Orleans, or to an old eastern town like New York or Boston. Maybe she imagines Europe or Tahiti, somewhere with old cathedrals or warm turquoise water. Maybe she is writing her high school valedictory speech—a little irony, a few jabs, but mostly good-humored and gracious. Maybe she is thinking of a man she hasn't met yet—a witty, articulate, handsome man with a sense of adventure and humor, a daring risky man unafraid of the passionate life in a woman. She most certainly does not imagine the boy next to her in the pew who is so busy imagining her. She knows what he is doing—a beautiful and intelligent girl is never without her antennae. But Nature somehow made a little mistake with Hester. At seventeen she has grown twenty years past him in some way hard to describe. She still lives partly in the silly, dreamy world of teenage girls in the fifties, but she feels a core inside her for which perhaps no words exist, that has already flown far across the snowy, bleak plains to some place with light, brilliant sun, and an unconscious joy in the body. When D. H. Lawrence saw a girl like Hester on an English beach, he saw "that the glimmer of the presence of the gods was like lilies, and like water-lilies."

Every Wednesday after her hour with the Unknowable and Infinite, she walks back across Minneota to the school, maybe to cheerleading practice—for she is a regular girl, bouncy and bright-eyed, and the football fans love to watch her cartwheels, to watch her blue and gold sweater and swinging, pleated white skirt moving, warming the chilly late fall night. Or maybe she is heading to band practice where she sits balanced on the edge of her chair, holding her silver flute in midair, waiting to play the descant tune in the trio of "Stars and Stripes Forever." The band director, call him Art—as good a name as any—raps his baton and asks for the beginning of the trio one more time. Hester poises her flute again and counts, keeping her eye on Art Brightwald's beat, as all good musicians do.

Art, a rangy, tall, handsome man with a sideways grin and a thin rasp of a voice, is somewhere in his thirties, not quite old enough to have fathered his own band, but nearing it. His wavy, dark hair is slicked back from his high forehead and brilliantined until it reflects the fly-stained fluorescent light in the old band room. Art radiates a little of the wicked smoldering fifties style, the devil-may-care cockiness of a smooth-looking fellow who plays the tenor-sax tunes in the local dance band. But he plays on the sly, since the school board who pays his princely thirty-five-hundred-dollar salary for directing chorus, concert band, pep band, marching band, and for chaperoning bus rides and sock hops, has stipulated—among other things—no moonlighting during the school year. So Art keeps mum but packs his sax off to the Blue Moon, the Showboat, the Fiesta, Valhalla, and the Arkota three nights a week, resplendent in white dinner jacket and red bow tie, with an extra sheen of brilliantine to gloss his hair. Apart from the smoky glory of a little life on the road with the band, Art needs the money. He's got a gaggle of children at home—two, three, four, who knows?—babies numberless as stars, mouths to feed, feet to shoe, hands to mitten. The fifties were family time in America: no diaphragms, no pills, no easy abortions (nor any legal ones), rubbers for hoodlums only. A man proved his potency by the size of his brood, and besides it gave the old lady something to keep her busy. But the students knew about his secret life, and their parents (those whose religion didn't interfere with dancing and other carnal pleasures), danced to his mellow sax at the Blue Moon, and probably thought him a pretty regular fellow. There are no secrets in small towns, at least not for long.

A small-town teacher in the Midwest or elsewhere in the fifties had an easy time neither economically nor psychologically. School boards paid as penuriously as they could manage and they hired out of an easy market. Since you could always draft some live body, what difference did it make who you hired in this little place with mostly farmers? After a short flurry of "learning," they figured that children raised right would settle down to duplicate their parents' lives. Nobody here would think of going to Harvard for damn sure. . . .

Harvard? Where's that? Small towns got used to putting up with a succession of incompetent, neurotic duds: music teachers who couldn't carry a tune, English teachers who couldn't speak a parsable sentence or recognize one, history teachers whose idea of history consisted of film strips of World War II showing tanks in road gear and bombed-out cathedrals, capped off with true-and-false quizzes. Through blind luck, intelligent people sometimes arrived and stayed long enough to do some intellectual good. The best were driven out by the requirement that they coach something or other, baby-sit bus rides and school dances, and generally give up private lives as autonomous adults. When Minneota hired its teachers, they were instructed that should they choose to drink, they should never be seen entering either the front or back doors of the local municipal, the Power House, but should instead travel to Ghent five miles down the road or preferably further. If you smoked (still a possible pleasure in the fifties), under no circumstances should you be seen doing so on the streets of Minneota. Furthermore, female teachers will not be pregnant, and if so, promptly jobless. This sort of life at three-and-half-grand a year or so, 180 miles from a stoplight, didn't offer many attractions for genius. Art could play, he could read, he could lift a baton, he could hear a tuned chord, he looked good in white bucks at the head of the marching band half-time show. By Minneota standards, we had done all right.

But the shadow of the dance band hovered over Art. Like actors from the Middle Ages to the nineteenth century, or like heavy metal stars today, road band musicians were not quite respectable. Ballrooms still flourished in the fifties; ballroom dancing was a normal habit for normal people—whatever normal means. Minneotans fox-trotted, two-stepped, waltzed, polka-ed, and jitterbugged the night away once or twice a month. Teenagers smuggled contraband bottles of sweet-flavored vodka into ballrooms a few towns away in hopes of boozing their way into their first sexual adventures with some

Venus of the dance floor. The band, behind its brightly colored Art Deco bandstand, sweated and grinned, sometimes blowing what we thought at the time were some pretty hot licks. This was not the lugubrious music of Lenten services or the out-of-tune blatting of the marching band. This was the music of the body—the music of lust, of fun, aromatic with highballs, Lucky Strikes, "Evening in Paris" perfume, Bay Rum, bodies pressed close, damp silk blouses against limp white shirts with rolled up sleeves, hair-sprayed heads leaning against your shoulder, whispered negotiations for rides home and mysterious assignations.

Band practice is over. The tuba and the trombone boys shake out their spitty mouthpieces. The prim girl with the clarinet sees them, says "oh, ish!" and meticulously unscrews her reed from its mouthpiece. Hester folds her silver flute into its black oblong box. The room is filled with the noises of chairs screeching, giggles, idle chatter, plans for later, slamming lockers. Art reminds the pep band to show up early for the Friday night ball game. He gives Hester a beckoning nod, and she comes up to the podium. Her dark hair falls over one eye and she shakes her head to brush it away. "You okay with babysitting tonight? I'm playing the Showboat and the Mrs. goes to card club."

"I'll be there after supper, about seven o'clock. I'll walk over."

"I'll give you a ride home, okay?"

Not much of a conversation. Be patient. You've already figured out where it leads. The orange buses are loading to carry the farm-half home for evening chores. After that, maybe church tonight, maybe ball practice, maybe nothing. There's still not much TV in Minneota. The Townies disperse, many to the Dairy Lunch for Harvey's hamburgers, Evelyn's lemon pie, a cherry coke. The ball team suits up for practice in the basement locker room. The sound of a quivery tenor practicing "The Holy City" for a music contest drifts down the halls. The piano thumps triplets a little unsteadily, almost getting the harmony right. Another Wednesday afternoon in a Norman Rockwell painting.

If ever a place needed the sexual revolution of the sixties, it was the Midwest of the fifties. The fear and terror at the demands of the body, the conditioned embarrassment at its swellings, juices, impertinent demands, the forced yoking of natural glands with unnatural laws of religion and respectability made an almost sexually psychotic culture—CIVILIZATION AND ITS DISCONTENTS in Red Capital Letters. That fear and embarrassment persisted into adulthood, which in America is often only a gray-haired hypertensive adolescence.

A friend told a wonderful story about buying rubbers at the Minneota drugstore in the seventies. Long out of college and approaching thirty, he walked in sheepishly, hoping to find the male druggist working alone. No luck. Mrs. "Tankyou" was on duty, clerking back of the counter, duchess of the cash register and the hidden drawer everyone knew was there. Mrs. "Tankyou," a sweet white-haired lady in her sixties or seventies, earned her nickname, like so many Minneotans of her generation, from being raised in a first language owning no voiced "Th." My friend moved up and down the aisles, thinking hard, trying to inflate his courage by saying to himself: Here I am almost thirty, a grownup, buying a normal grownup product, socially responsible, recommended—even encouraged—by all the leaders of the Free World. What am I afraid of? This is damned foolishness! Meanwhile, he picked up a pack of Lifesavers, a tube of Colgate, a ballpoint pen. Finally, courage swelled. He approached Mrs. "Tankyou" demanding, though softly, should there be other customers:

"And a pack of Trojans, please."

She looked him bolt in the eye, grabbed under the counter for the rubbers and asked, (addressing him by name) "Will dere be anyting else?"

At that point, he recounted, he was, like Huck Finn, so far sunk in disgrace that he thought: The hell with it. I might as well go the whole hog. He imagined his voice saying, "Gimme a copy of Playboy, a tube of Kwell, and a box of Preparation H suppositories . . ."

Discretion triumphed as he silently handed her the cash. She rang up his condoms, handed him his bag and his change, smiled sweetly and cheerily, saying:

"Tank-you."

In 1955, at age twelve, I joined the orange bus riders, the new pink plump recruit from the farm. Before that, along with eight or nine neighbor children, I attended one of the last surviving rural schools in western Minnesota—District 90, Swede Prairie Township, Yellow Medicine County. It was a classic, a cliché in every way, a simple wood-frame building sitting on the corner of a section, two outhouses in back—Girls and Boys. Gravel township roads led off in four directions. My father's farm stood a mile away, others as far as two or three miles. A middle-aged Norwegian spinster with a six-month normal-school certificate presided, checking for dirt under our fingernails, praying in Norwegian, ringing her brass handbell to call us to order. For a library, we used a tall oak glass-doored bookcase stocked with Longfellow, Richard Henry Dana's *Two Years Before the Mast, Tom Sawyer,* Dickens, Poe, and Ernest Thompson Seton's animal books. The only extracurricular activities were blizzards and tornadoes. For the most part, children were left alone to their own dreaminess, so we all learned to read, or to think if we wanted to.

The triumph of the car doomed this most intelligent and effective of American educational institutions. Even the gravel roads became mostly passable and everyone owned a car. The buses arrived daily to carry the farm children to the BIG school where they would have intellectual advantages like football teams, indoor plumbing, central heat, administrators, pep club, and music lessons on a wind band instrument. There we farm hicks stood, huddled next to our mail boxes against the north wind howling over the treeless sections, waiting to step up onto a traveling room half the size and three times the population of our District 90 school. This was our baptism into urbanity, indeed into the real twentieth century.

The bus arrived in Minneota, at what seemed to me a vast, creaky old building, where we settled into a home room with thirty fellow students our same age. We moved from room to room carrying books for different classes. There we enjoyed watery Euclid, the bombing of Dresden, Silas Marner, the Communist menace, the principles of photosynthesis, day-dreaming, spitballs, secret notes, the wind banging the windows in their loose frames. Music had one room; sports had many. The library itself had a glass door, not just one for the bookcase. We jostled for space with high school students for whom puberty had already worked its fearsome changes— lowering voices, growing new hair, and swelling body parts, filling rooms with the mysterious eruptions of furry sexuality that at twelve or thirteen we had only begun to feel or imagine.

What I loved best in my educational Great Leap Forward was the chance for music. Without any genetic predisposition, I was born possessed by music and was luckily reasonably skilled at it. I started my career as a boy soprano soloist, warbling funeral hymns for dead Icelanders, meanwhile learning in school to finger a plastic recorder called a Tonette. I'd even begun to compose little tunes for it, ruling staffs on plain white paper, copying the notes in ink, then inscribing the title page: GRAND SYMPHONY FOR TONETTE, OPUS I, BY WILLIAM J. HOLM, 1954. I can't remember when reading a page of musical notation was not as easy as reading English, though I suppose someone taught me the notes in country school. With my baggy dress pants, my prematurely six-and-a-half-foot tall plump body and cowlicky orange hair, I was probably not destined to be a social success; but as long as music held out its beckoning fingers in my direction, I survived childhood in a state of moderate happiness.

My parents agreed to band lessons. I probably longed for a

violin or a cello and had already discovered the piano, but band provided a means to sit in a room with other humans trying to make agreeable noises. A clarinet would have been a wise choice, but it seemed to me at the time a girlish instrument, and God knows, I was nerd enough for multitudes as it was. I liked the shape, the sound, and the rakish reputation of the saxophone, so I began my career on the E-flat alto sax in 1955.

Because of the new school already half-built on the north end of town, any repairs, remodeling, or enlarging stopped on the old building, already well on its way to salvage. Band lessons happened wherever there was space enough to keep the awkward pre-musical squeaking and blatting from causing protest. My sax lessons took place in the boiler room, deep in the school bowels. The furnace, old, vast, full of clanks, wheezes, and sputters, was presided over by a janitor in greasy khaki work pants whose nickname was Tiny. At the time, I imagined that boiler as the engine of an old ship, a tramp steamer out of a Conrad novel clunking its way across the Indian Ocean. Though I'm afraid the Minneota Public School was never likely to sail across the tallgrass prairie, mental pictures of large bodies of water brought peculiar joy to people like me, trapped in the flat middle of a continent.

The boiler room possessed the additional charm of being what is called in the nineties a smoking zone. Tiny smoked. The furnace smoked. Adventurous high school boys copped a few drags on their way to study hall. And Art, the band director, smoked enthusiastically—Lucky Strikes. Music lessons were perfumed with clouds of Lucky smoke and decorated with tin cans filled with gravel and old butts. Even then I admired second-hand smoke, intending to graduate to first-hand as soon as opportunity knocked.

Mr. Brightwald, as we addressed him, lit up his first Lucky, pointed at the music stand and ordered us to play. And play I did. After the first instructions in fingering, embouchure, instrument draining and cleaning, and reed preparation, my lessons consisted mostly of playing the piece. If some notes misfired, or dynamics went cockeyed, Art told me to play it again. When it finally sounded right, he lit another Lucky and ordered, "next piece." I frequently found my own music at a local music store: a transcription of the "Flight of the Bumble Bee," "In a Persian Garden" arranged for solo, a grand march from Meyerbeer, a little chunk of Glazunov. Since practice was my joy and delight, I must have been little trouble for Mr. Brightwald. He could smoke in peace, half listening to me, half to the clanking furnace, while imagining more interesting moments in his life, either past, present, or yet to be.

Lesson over, I trotted back to the upper world, just in time for the end of the hour crush. Ring a bell anywhere in earshot and watch humans who have attended American public school begin herding together to shift location. Though resigned to the privacy of my nerd body and odd mind, what sensual life I hadn't sublimated or repressed noticed the immense sexiness, the glamour and mystery of the high school girls. I had been to enough movies to formulate mental pictures of the perfect woman who waited somewhere for me—who would by generous intuition spot the romantic male trapped in Alfalfa's body. She looked like Ava Gardner, a planet removed from the local, wholesome Scandinavian blondes and redheads, my cousins mostly. She had black hair, a throaty voice, a ripe womanly body—no anorexic models for me. She laughed; she found the world full of humor, bawdiness, and adventure. Her black eyes gleamed. She didn't exist.

But Hester came close. She was, as I remember, often laughing. She found the world funny. Her body moved differently from those of her chums, with an unashamed sensuality, nothing so sleazy or obvious as a Marilyn Monroe wiggle but instead a consciousness of her body as a lovely thing—fit not only for labor, duty, or weight bearing, but for joy. I suppose every boy in Minneota was at least half in love with her, infatuated, dazzled, speechless. She was the real thing—the Platonic Form of Woman, an ideal made flesh.

My first year in town-school I discovered a piano in the basement of the Icelandic Church across the street and spent my winter lunch hours reading through the four-part Bach Chorales in the black Lutheran hymnal, then trying the Beethoven and Mozart pieces I found in *Fifty-Nine Great Piano Solos.* I composed a "Grand Sonata for Solo Saxophone," but successfully sidestepped acquiring fame, glory, or an audience. With puberty well underway, I had acquired an incipient Heldentenor squawk for a voice. Like my schoolmates in Minneota, I was already dreaming and plotting my escape into the world of oceans and stoplights.

In spring, the clanking boiler mostly held its peace. I fetched my saxophone case from the school locker and trotted down the boiler-room stairs ready to go with Rimsky-Korsakov, lonesome for second-hand Luckys. But I encountered a strange silence and met no teacher. Tiny came out from behind the boiler wiping his hands on his pants.

"Haven't you heard, Billy? You got no lesson today. I guess nobody told you." He had an odd, sad look on his face.

"No lesson? Why?"

He waited a little, then said, "Well, you'll hear it anyway upstairs. I might as well tell you." A little pause as he hunted for the right tone, the right phrase. A man of natural courtliness, he understood that the tune of serious speech must be as consciously rehearsed as well-played music. "Art, Mr. Brightwald, he got Hester pregnant, and the two of them run away for Mexico or someplace a few nights ago. The police were hunting them down. I heard they caught them south of here, Texas maybe, or Oklahoma. The police are bringing him back to jail. It's just terrible—terrible for her folks, for everybody. So no lessons. You can put your sax away."

Probably I stood a while in stunned silence before turning back upstairs into the world of light. I understood none of it then and forty years later, I understand even less. This was my first scandal, at twelve, and I still judge subsequent scandals, private or public, by its high and rigorous standards. A few years later, I got blind drunk in public and found myself dumped unceremoniously in my father's front yard, puking and semi-comatose. Word got out. There was talk. But that was only tiny potatoes next to Art and Hester. When I tracked down a family skeleton, learning that my grandmother in Iceland had been the daughter of the hired girl and the farmer, it amounted only to an interesting detail, a mark more of pride than shame. One of my classmates and best friends turned out to be gay. So what? A schoolmate grew up alcoholic, dried out, then went into the basement to blow his head off with a twelve-gauge shotgun. I felt pity but no judgment in the face of this catastrophe. Then there were the public and political scandals of the seventies and eighties: Watergate, a lying President, the news that Jack Kennedy bedded Marilyn Monroe, that the manly Rock Hudson was gay, that J. Edgar Hoover had a secret life as a drag queen. Scandal is too small a word for Vietnam, a war that was a lie, a sham, a cynical con that took 50,000 lives out of my generation. But I judged even these events by their resemblance to the scandal of Hester and Art.

What is puzzling about the story of Art and Hester? It is ordinary as the rotation of the planets. An older man with a wandering eye and a boring job in the boondocks is fetched by the sensuous loveliness of a young girl—in the case of Hester, an extraordinary girl. She is bored and frustrated by the repressive life of her hometown, has a lively romantic imagination, and the burgeoning of a newly-awakened body that surprises even her by its loveliness. Maybe he makes a pass, half-drunk, after a ballroom job. She is embarrassed, diffident, holds him off, but thinks about it. He tries again. She says the hell with it, gives herself up to an hour or two of awkward lovemaking. She has a glimmer of what this means, but some new recklessness is born inside her. One thing leads to another. Or maybe, in her boredom, she flirts with Art. He knows better, hesitates, then says: the hell with it. She misses a period. She tells him. They quarrel. He knows he is in legal trouble. She is more than half-terrified. She knows she has struck through the mask of small-town respectability, but she refuses to believe that her own body and spirit have lied to her. Abortion is a world away, a coat hanger in a back room in Minneapolis. Her stomach already presses against her skirt. She will never be able to fool them, to carry it off until graduation. She demands they run away. Or maybe he does. One night, after faking a job at the Blue Moon, they meet on the edge of town. They have only small bags, a few things. He has taken what little money he can hide from his band jobs. Maybe the car is a '51 DeSoto, a lot of good miles left under the hood. They head south on gravel roads. She has a map. She imagines a place beyond the border, a foreign language, people even darker than themselves, sombreros, moonlight. The ditches are still half-full of snow, but violets have started to grow by the side of the road, too small to be seen in the headlights. Maybe she turns on the radio and they listen in the dark. Maybe the Platters are singing "The Great Pretender."

Is he no more than a seducer of young girls, the reprehensible cock-hound, the creep who chisels on his wife and a houseful of kids? It takes no genius to think that or to say it. Is she a sweet small-town flower, harshly plucked—or maybe a wild girl getting what's coming to her for not keeping her pants up? That shrinks Hester as a human, and the testimony is that she was large; she contained multitudes. Will any human ever know anything true about the interior life of Hester and Art's saga. Tolstoy tried to tell it in *Anna Karenina* at great length; Dreiser and Crane tried here in America. Soap opera will not do the job, though their story has the trappings of one.

What did Minneota think of its fine archetype of a scandal? What did it feel? What did it say? It felt righteous anger—

judgment—the lust for punishment—prurient interest in private details. Minneota clucked.

"Serves them right."

"They should send the son-of-a-bitch to jail and throw away the key." (So they did.)

"Who hired him?" (Minneota did.)

"She always did look like that kind of a girl."

Ad infinitum. Ad nauseum. There was pity for the innocent whose reputations were tarnished by connection. Some probably thought in the privacy of their souls that more had happened here than eye could see or soul could fathom, but not many said such charitable and diffident things in public. The Minneota jury had spoken. Art went to jail. Hester went to a home, probably in Minneapolis, to grow large with child far from the withering stares of her fellow citizens or her classmates. The boy with the rich imagination who sat next to her in church feeling the warmth and curve of her body, wondered. Probably he still wonders forty years later. I certainly do.

Every small town treasures its private code of taboos. Those taboos mark the limits beyond which neighbors must not trespass if they intend to remain neighbors; paying taxes amounts to only a fraction of what it means to live in a community. Taboos grow in the darkness under a sour mash of folk wisdom, fear, and religion. Had they never been useful in human history, they wouldn't exist. Natural selection ought to operate as ruthlessly with received ideas and habits as it does with thumbs, gizzards, or swim bladders; but in community life as in biology, some extraneous appendages, some psychic sixth fingers, don't atrophy and disappear quickly enough. They flop around awkwardly for generations, causing embarrassment, ungainliness, trouble.

Marriage has always been a rich hatching place for these taboos. In Minneota in the fifties, the young received two messages cut in mental granite: First, get married and settle down, sow your wild oats before you sign the license. After the kiddies come, your job is to act your part, do your duty—accept whatever boredom and failure live inside your marriage—stoically. In public, maintain a stainless-steel regularity. Relieve whatever misery you feel with jokes at the coffee table, hard work, a frenzy of trivial social activity, and a face of public respectability. We didn't need Tolstoy or Flaubert or Willa Cather to remind us of the discontents of those marriages or the consequences—particularly for women—for those who stepped outside the circle.

The second commandment went this way: If you get pregnant, then that's it. You've made your bed, now lie in it for fifty or sixty years. March down the aisle with your growing belly and in thirty years maybe you'll even like each other? But it doesn't make any difference. You did it; now take your medicine.

On one hand, these taboos seemed harder on women than on men. It was a woman's job to protect the gates of temptation; if she failed, the onus rested with her. Boys will be boys and so forth, but in a way, men faced equally dark consequences. They often suffered interior death—retreated into habit, passivity, a psychic automatic pilot, the rest of their lives mapped out from puberty to nursing home with manual labor to fill up the middle. Breakfast, lunch, supper; spring, summer, fall, winter—stretching onward toward infinity on the now completely apparent horizon. Some drank, some got religion, some made money. Few of them talked, except in jokes or prescripted chatter. Few acknowledged the presence of psychic disturbance. The arrival of TV with its multiple channels brought great relief. They could go straight from supper table to easy chair in front of the set, then into the blessed ether of snoring.

Hester and Art violated these taboos from every possible angle. Art had a wife, a houseful of small mouths, a job that was a community trust. He chucked them all for an under-age

girl. Hester possessed every accolade either the town or the genetic roulette wheel could award her—beauty, talent, intelligence, wit, charm, a promising future. And she chucked it all
for an already married, brilliantined lothario, a two-bit
Orpheus with a tenor sax. He couldn't even "make it right" by
marrying her and settling down to let the long passage of time
re-cement them into the life of the community. So let the town
pick up its stones; the lottery is cast.

A friend of mine, a lovely woman almost the contemporary
of Hester, found herself in Hester's predicament, pregnant at
seventeen. But the boy was local, single, anxious to "do the
right thing." They married, had a couple of perfectly normal
children, got normal jobs, lived in a normal house with normal
hamburger and normal TV shows. They "settled down." But
while her curiosity about the world grew and flowered, his
shriveled. She finished high school by correspondence, started
taking college classes on the sly, reading, thinking, having conversations on subjects other than hot dish, laundry, and grue-
some surgical procedures described in comprehensive detail.
She began to find pleasure in the world, wondering why there
was none in her marriage. He sank, probably into a diagnos-
able depression—but you didn't go to a doctor for that in a
small town. You bucked up to do your duty. He stopped talking. He drank—a lot and not gracefully. He lost jobs and
looked for no others. He sat like a stone. He watched eternal
TV. After about a quarter century of this, the woman asked
herself a sensible question. What am I doing in this marriage?
My duty. Why? Because both relatives and the town expect it
of me. Isn't this what a marriage is? Yes, often. Why don't I
leave? People would think badly of me for leaving him. What's
my choice? To die in this house, at a great age, miserable and
well thought of. She left. She misjudged the town and the culture a little. She is even envied now for her courage and happiness, for a lively and adventurous middle age. The fifties have,
thank God, died a natural death. The corpse isn't quite rotted

yet, and cynical contemporary politicians keep wanting to revive it with adrenaline shots of mildewed nostalgia straight to the heart. But pay them no attention. It's well enough dead. *Requiescat in pace.*

I liked one 1950s cultural institution, though; I even feel a smidgeon of nostalgia for the Saturday night outdoor band concert played from the screened gazebo in the Bum Park next to the railroad tracks, a one-time camping spot for Depression hobos. The concerts are safely dead now, the gazebo gone, railroad tracks disappeared along with the trains themselves, even the Saturday night of open stores finished.

The concerts were peculiar in a couple of ways. Older citizens of Minneota who still fancied playing their horns joined in with the high schoolers, much to our delight, but, even more germane, to the improvement of the music. These old codgers (so we called them—they were in their forties and fifties) could actually play!—with real skill, fire, and a too-long pent-up lonesomeness for music. Many, like Art, were danceband veterans. What a pleasure to watch Harry Smishek, who drove a fuel-oil truck, oompah on his tuba, cheeks puffed out as if he kept a pair of golf balls in the back of his mouth. Or to hear Leonard Allen, the courtly insurance man, cut loose on a trumpet lick like a honky Louis Armstrong. The hour of outdoor music always included old wind band standards: "The Carnival of Venice," "In a Persian Garden," a few peppy Sousa marches, and some jazzy arrangements of popular dance tunes. Parked cars surrounded the Bum Park on three sides. Elbows stuck out the open windows of '49 Fords, '53 Chevys, an Olds or two, maybe a sporty red Studebaker Hawk, a couple of Dodge pickups. No air conditioning in those days— either in car or house. At the end of each tune, whatever it's quality—the hell with the fluffed notes and missed entrances—car horns honked wildly for a full minute—a fine cacophonous, metallic chorus, courtesy of Detroit. After a polka or a Leonard Allen solo, the honking might last *two* minutes, setting off an answering chorus of howling dogs for a mile radius. It was a joyful noise—probably now induplicable. Car alarms and computer buzzers do not resemble it.

Only at those concerts on a summer night do I remember seeing Art and Hester in the same place. Those Saturdays were invariably hot and muggy—ninety degrees, only a small, damp breeze, the music scores so limp they could hardly stand upright on the music stands. Mosquitoes dive-bombed the screen, and a fair number made their way in, buzzing around the ear, humming in the wrong key, drawing a little blood during the *pianissimo* passages. Art was the only man dressed in necktie and white shirt, a requirement for the dignity of his job as director. By the third or fourth honking, the shirt sticks to his back, soaked, the rings of sweat curl down from his shoulders, his necktie limp, the shirt collar oozed open. But no dress code for summer band, so the high school girls are moistly dazzling in their shorts and cutoffs, their halter tops. How lovely the look of all those naked tan legs discreetly tapping a four-four beat in almost unison! Finally, "The Star Spangled Banner," the school song, "Go, Minneota," a *tutti fortissimo* of honks, and the now-soggy band disburses into the July night, the old codgers to the Powerhouse across the street for a cold beer, and the students to Carl's Cafe, the Dairy Lunch, driving around, or the Joy Theatre for the second show, maybe *Marty* or *On the Waterfront* but probably something worse, with cowboys and horses. Art hangs around to fold up the chairs, gather the music, tidy up the bandstand. Hester stays to help him. The town returns to its Saturday night sociability or goes home early. No one watches. Hester, resplendent in snug cut-off Levi's, a white silky blouse with the top buttons undone, leather sandals, is deeply tanned—even the slight visible curve of her breasts, her elegant ankles. No one worries about skin cancer in 1955.

Maybe Art invites her for a little ride in the country to cool off, maybe the deep-gully country a few miles south of town, the only forested, watered, sloping landscape on this horizontal prairie. Maybe first she says she should get home—a lot of stuff tomorrow, then says, maybe for a little while. Maybe they get in Art's DeSoto to drive slowly out of town. They roll down the car windows to feel the wind that's come up a little now after dark. Driving with one hand on the wheel, he reaches under the seat, brings out a pint of cheap Canadian whiskey. There's a couple of Cokes, he says. She pops the caps with a church key from the cubby hole and they drink a few inches. He pours carefully, filling the Coke bottles with whiskey. They turn first down a gravel road, then a rutty dirt path. They have driven up a few hundred feet over the town. The red elevator beacons and farmyard lights stretch out below them in a long ribbon. It is a clear starry night, the milky way vast and diaphanous, a three-quarters moon, the gully under them a blue-black emptiness. The bur oak and cottonwood leaves clack against each other in the wind now. The tallgrass swishes. Frogs ribet, crickets hum steadily, an owl hoots—maybe he's spotted something. Art turns the DeSoto off, and they get out, looking up, then down at the tiny lights flickering in this enormous blackness. They say nothing for a while, just sip their whiskey cokes, leaning against the warm car, feeling the breeze. He comes over to stand next to her, begins slowly to unbutton her silk blouse.

How can I go on? I have no idea what actually happened or if it is a fantasy in which I imagine myself an actor, though of course, I could never have been. Did they make love there, at the top of that gully, or was it a drunken, sordid fumbling in the back seat of a car? But who of us, in the midst of that imagining, could not say, with Hawthorne, that what they did, whatever sins the town thought they committed, had "a consecration of its own"?

A sexual scandal is like a religion in one way. It sets down a mystery before us, a paradox, an event or a metaphor about which our offering of opinions is beside the point. Reason deserts us; the mystery is—or it is not. We circle the scandal; we mutter, howl, sing. We cannot understand. It passes all understanding. What happened to Art or Hester in the forty-odd years since that morning of my epiphany in the boiler room is, curiously enough, of no consequence. Even if I knew, I wouldn't tell you. The event is complete. Your job is to reconstruct your own first scandal, your first glimmering of the power of taboo, of sexual life, of the procreant urge of the world. What workings did it begin inside you? In Hollywood movies these days, particularly social problem films, a paragraph of print frequently rolls over the last frame telling us how things stand ten years later or whenever, tying all the unresolved knots together, informing us how long a prison term, who married or divorced whom, whether justice was done. I want none of it. It's lies, all pure blatherskate. If you come close to getting a story right, or telling it straight, you still have no idea how it "comes out." That's the true idle fantasy, having nothing at all to do with the imagination.

I thought of Hester and Art again in high school when I discovered William Blake. How well Blake understood Minneota, though he died a half-century before any settler ever set foot there! "Sooner murder an infant in its cradle than nurse unacted desire." Well! The whole drift of American life in the fifties and long before was toward the suppression of desire for the public good. Desire, whether for sex, money, fame, a life completely lived out rather than regulated by expectation, represented a disruptive force to be kept in line by church, school, law, taboo. Making sure desire remained unacted was exactly what the town, in its function as moral and cultural policeman for the United States or Christianity, had in mind. Some part of us was supposed to be murdered in the cradle so that we could be proper neighbors and citizens.

By desire, Blake meant something more than getting laid, getting drunk, having a good time, raising a little hell. He described a world shrunk by "reason" and its blind guardians.

"Understanding," the world of Newton and the explainers of the universe, and "perception" were two different things. Hester cannot be understood but can be perceived. She cannot be diminished by explanation. Blake's *Songs of Innocence* and *Songs of Experience* "show the two contrary states of the human soul." Here's experience:

The Garden of Love

I went to the Garden of Love,
And saw what I never had seen:
A Chapel was built in the midst,
Where I used to play on the green.

And the gates of this Chapel were shut,
And 'Thou shalt not' writ over the door;
So I turn'd to the Garden of Love
That so many sweet flowers bore,

And I saw it was filled with graves,
And tomb-stones where flowers should be:
And priests in black gowns were walking their rounds,
And binding with briars my joys and desires.

Is this Hester and Art's song? In part. "Without contraries is no progression," and every event, scandal included, has inside itself two truths (or fifty), one the opposite and contrary of the next. To a country suddenly fallen in love with the bumper sticker, ONE WAY, Blake says there are two—at least. Two ways or more will never sell to a culture lonesome for judgment, eager to punish. I'm afraid "One Way" as a religious and political model leads to precisely the kind of cradle-murder Blake had in mind. We ourselves become the black-gowned priests binding with briars our own desires. We climb aboard the "marriage hearse," set our jaws, tighten our knuckles, and hang on.

In another little poem, Blake asks the question hidden under this essay.

The Question Answer'd

> What is it men in women do require?
> The lineaments of Gratified Desire.
> What is it women do in men require?
> The lineaments of Gratified Desire.

What do these lineaments look like to Blake in yet another poem?

[The Marriage Ring] The Fairy

> Abstinence sows sand all over
> The ruddy limbs & flaming hair,
> But Desire Gratified
> Plants fruits of life & beauty there.

Maybe what I saw as a boy in Hester—or indeed what the whole town saw, in the honest recesses of its private soul—was that longing for "gratified desire," the shadow of those lineaments. Her tragedy—and it is partly that—was that Art might not have been her desire gratified. Did he bring her ruddy limbs afire, or did the black-gowned priests do their work one more time?

Americans have always feared the physical world, both of nature and of our own bodies. We live as uncertainly inside our received ideas as we live on the tallgrass prairie. Neither topsoil nor sexual desire bring out our best intelligence or humanity. We attack nature with big machines; we throttle upwellings of desire with disapproval and judgment. We borrow these judgments from an imagined history that has now ceased to exist except in the dead cement around our opinions or in our vaporous respectability. Our niggling moral judgements are the psychic sixth fingers inside the consciousness, not yet evolved.

We magnify these overwhelmingly normal and human up-wellings of sexual desire into mighty scandals and cluck like chickens. Then in our national life, we eat small countries, honor large-scale greed, spoil our landscape, and elect felons, demagogues, and simple-minded salesmen to humor us with tales of our own virtue.

A lovely young girl on a summer night, caught by physical desire and frustrated by the desiccated mental and spiritual life around her, or a thirty-ish would-be Don Juan, tempted be-yond his powers to resist, and probably not much different from any man in his place or time hardly amount to a Tupperware cup of scandal. Rather wish the two of them joy in whatever consecration of their own that they discovered at the top of that gully, or wherever else they made love.

Art and Hester are gone and the memory of their story haunts those old enough to have lived through it. The young neither know nor care—they have their own scandals, their own stories. But writers can't let Hester go; two of her school-mates have spent years on long novels, trying not so much to make sense of that story, but to make it quiver with life as D. H. Lawrence wanted. And here I am telling the story, walk-ing around it, trying to understand it. None of us will ever get it right—but that's as it should, as it must be. You can't pour concrete around the feet of a mystery and drown it. It is buoy-ant. It rises. It looks us in the eye and asks us dark questions.

Maybe the novel and essay can't hold the truth of Hester's story. Since she exists now only in the imagination like a half-heard song of beauty, sensuality, the Form of Woman herself—maybe only a poem comes close. Carl Sandburg knew Hester by another name in some Illinois version of Minneota. This is the song he made about her and about Hester—and about desire.

> Everybody loved Chick Lorimer in our town
> > Far off.
> > Everybody loved her.
> So we all love a wild girl keeping a hold
> On a dream she wants.
> Nobody knows now where Chick Lorimer went.
> Nobody knows why she packed her trunk . . . a few
> > old things
> And is gone,
> > Gone with her little chin
> > Thrust ahead of her
> > And her soft hair blowing careless
> > From under a wide hat,
> Dancer, singer, and laughing passionate lover.
>
> Were there ten men or a hundred hunting Chick?
> Were there five men or fifty with aching hearts?
> > Everybody loved Chick Lorimer.
> > Nobody knows where she's gone.

Blind Is the Bookless Man

The Cure for Received Ideas

At about twelve, I publicly declared myself an agnostic and a socialist. Where does a young fellow "declare" in Minneota, Minnesota, in, say—1955? In a Lutheran Sunday School, or on an orange bus riding eight miles south to eighth grade at town-school, or to his cousins who liked to argue—and of course, to his parents, but this hardly shocks them. They don't even register mild surprise; this declaration seems, in fact, normal, even hopeful, a sign of independence and spirit. My mother cautioned me only by giving me a small list of relatives and old people who would not so much be shocked and offended, as prefer that I kept my opinions to myself where they belonged—at my current age or at any other to which I might subsequently live. That was all right with me; I had at least a primitive understanding of civility and its true function: keeping neighbors away from each other's throats, making sure you begin only necessary quarrels.

What perverse crankiness leads a twelve-year-old boy to make his small assault on the chief received ideas that covered the fifties like a lead quilt? Thinking back, I find several causes, some less flattering than others. I was a spoiled and self-willed only child, an early extrovert misplaced in the introvert culture of the Midwest, a "talker for victory" (as Boswell described Sam Johnson) in a place that honored silent stoicism as a high virtue. Keep your mouth shut so they can't tell for sure what a damn fool you are; open it, and they'll know fast. I was fearless in the presence of "they." I wanted, with a properly sharpened remark, to draw psychic blood, particularly from the pious, the patriotic, the obedient, the sentimental, the conventional. I kept an internal enemies list as long and distinguished as Richard Nixon's. It began with Nixon himself, proceeded with Joe McCarthy, J. Edgar Hoover, Bishop Sheen, Ezra Taft Benson, John Foster Dulles, Dale Carnegie, the Americanism Committee of the Legion, the Legion of Decency, and the Council of Lutheran Bishops. They were blissfully unaware that little Billy Holm had trumpeted his disdain for them and all their assembled notions of respectability from a farm on the summit of a very small hill in Swede Prairie Township. They continued running the public life of America as if nothing had happened.

The swampy nostalgia of nineties politicos conceals the truth that there was plenty to loathe in fifties America. My first memories of radio were the voices of Roy Cohn, Joe McCarthy, and the Vice President ferreting out un-American activities, exposing atheistic communism in the Army, the State Department, the movies, maybe even Minneota. Why not in the chicken house where red eggs probably lay hidden under the warm butts of disloyal hens?

Whether by reaction or immersion, our parents usually baptize us into their own religious and political convictions. My father was a Floyd Olson-Franklin Roosevelt Democrat who thought Republicans the enemy of anyone who did any real work in the world, having failed to swindle or inherit enough to loaf and trumpet conservative opinions. The only reason I could ever imagine for veering toward Republicanism might have been to spite my father, but I had no interest in doing that. He was not a spiteful man. To be large-hearted and generous was, like him, to be a Democrat. To be shrivel-hearted, suspicious, smug, and greedy meant to more clearly resemble Nixon, the Vice President, and his cohorts whom my father cursed grandly every time he heard their voices on the radio, or saw their names in the newspaper.

My parents dropped me off at the Icelandic Lutheran Church on Sunday because that's where children were supposed to be. Although they attended only two or three times a year, I was a regular. I was a budding musician, after all. They exhibited no particular interest in Lutheran dogma (such as it is), thinking that, at its worst, it hatched the seeds of intolerance, narrow-mindedness, superstition, and the mistrust of common sense. But at its best, it gave you good stories, a history, magnificent old language, first-rate songs and a chance to practice singing them in four proper parts, occasional sound moral advice, and a place to gather with friends, relatives, neighbors, and fellow Icelanders, all having a weekly try at being high-minded. They allowed for the possibility of spiritual life existing inside the church but didn't insist that the church was its only home. Church was a habit, a neighborly duty, a way to raise children decently—who then could make up their own minds how much religion they wanted. Because of that immense sanity on their part, I remained and remain a loyal if moderate Lutheran, even during my twelve-year-old agnostic flurry. The agnostics didn't sing Bach chorales or repeat the rolling cadences of that grand old prose; there were no organs to finger in the Agnostic Temple. The only sin for which I've never forgiven Lutherans is the attempted willful destruction of their tradition of ancient language and choral singing. Each revised hymnal grows steadily stupider in its efforts to be fashionable and to remodel the prose and voice leading of its betters.

That loud-mouth twelve-year-old still lives in a now-middle-aged body, its once pink dimpled cheeks shrouded in white whiskers. Part of him never recanted his declaration—the theses still nailed to the church door and the town hall. But after a premature passion to "shock the bourgeois," the real roots of his declaration come from what moves him still as a grown man: the glad poison of books, the unsettling habit of reading as many pages as can be turned in a single lifetime, and the perilous sloughs where reading might lead—to contrary thinking and to profound mistrust of any public truth presented as an incontrovertible fact. Everything is controvertible in this universe if you keep mulling it over, and if nobody has controverted it so far, then it is your duty to do so now before it does serious harm to human beings, even to civilization itself. There is always one more idea. That's the best thing the experience of books teaches us.

Though far removed from colleges, libraries, and bookstores, Minneota was a luckier birthplace than it might seem for a passionate lover of books. Marx was not entirely wrong when he attacked "the idiocy of rural life," and promised to invigorate the mental lives of farmers by industrializing and moving them closer to the mental means of production. But the Icelanders who settled in Minneota kept their Old Country habits of bookishness and contrariness in argument. Reading, owning overstuffed shelves of books, spending money on mail-order books, and decorating your conversation with quotations seemed to them normal habits for working-class people. School degrees or social position had nothing to do with intelligence. The rich and self-important might be more likely stupid or badly read than the neighborhood farmers, carpenters, store clerks, and domestic help. That's probably the immigrant Icelander's best advice for us: Don't whine about your poverty and brainless labor. You can read, can't you? Get thee to a library and foment rebellion—in both inner and outer worlds.

The Icelanders were not alone in this peculiar habit. My mother was a great friend and admirer of the doctor in Minneota, a French Jew escaped from Hitler's maelstrom. He had a house full of books in several languages, even poetry, and somehow interested her in reading novels and histories about the ghettos of Europe. The immense respect for learning among poor Jews impressed her mightily, and for a while she was convinced either that the Icelanders were not Scandinavians at all, but a lost tribe of Jews wandered too far north, or that the Jews were discontented Icelanders who had taken it into their heads to travel. I've always thought that as accurate and sensible a racial genetic theory of human character as any other, and a good deal funnier and sweeter. I think she even hoped I'd find a Jewish wife to bring the family IQ up a point or two.

These habits, willful contrariness and bibliomania, survived among old people in Minneota, the first generation of not-yet-Americanized immigrants, still bilingual, in some cases tri-. My generation is only lingual, and after us, who knows?—the silence. I found this touchstone story in the memoirs of the greatest Icelandic immigrant poet, Stephan G. Stephansson. He came first to Minnesota and North Dakota in 1875, finally settling on a lonesome farm in the brush country next to the Rockies in Markerville, Alberta. He lived not so much in a particular country as in his head, leaving a major corpus of untranslatable poems in Icelandic, written between bouts of hard farm-work. He tells in an autobiographical sketch of his longing to attend school while still in Iceland, of being too poor, of seeing his friends riding south to begin classes at a district school. Finally he says, "What I felt was pain, not envy, and I began to sob. I hid myself in a hollow among the grass tufts." Ashamed, he told his mother the cause of his weeping. Years later she said to him that, "at the moment she had found poverty harder to bear than at any other time." So Stephansson stayed home and devoured books. Here's a story of the uses to which he sometimes put them:

I have noticed one thing which I cannot quite explain. It has happened that I have said something in jest, in order to shock people, which I have later had to defend as if it were my sincere opinion. In doing so it has become my opinion. There was a certain woman working as household help in Mjóadalur when I was there. She was very argumentative and used me as bait often, though she had nothing against me. Sometimes I tried to avoid the confrontation. Once several of us from the farm were riding together to church. I was silent, absorbed in the beauty of the valley on that midsummer day. She began to praise and panegyrize the Bible, turning to me. I was half angered by her interruption of my pleasure, and the Bible was far from my thoughts. She kept harping on this until I had to say something, namely: "The Bible is no more praiseworthy than other 'bibles' like the *Edda,* for example." I had in reality no opinion about this and had never heard or read anything to substantiate such a view. It was spoken in malicious jest. At this, however, she began to argue in earnest and I had to defend my exaggerations. I knew both books well, and for every proof she provided from the Bible for her position, I found an equally convincing one from the *Edda,* until she was beginning to find her defence of the Bible difficult. This discussion lasted all the long way to church. I believe now that I unintentionally formulated a better argument than I expected to do. Such has sometimes been my experience.

That story shows a healthy instinct that Americans ought to imitate more often. Sometimes by vigorous and contrary argument we come a horsehair closer to understanding. Assent does not lead in the general direction of wisdom. Truth is an organism, not a lightning flash in the brain that comes clean once and for all.

Stephan G. Stephanssons by many names still lived in Minneota in the fifties and between their book hordes and their proud crankiness, they nudged the plump, young agnostic-socialist to make his public declaration, fortifying his spirit for whatever disapproval or argument might follow. They also taught him that though you make every argument with all the mental and verbal energy you can summon, you oughtn't to be too anxious to win, even ought to imagine yourself making the opposite argument with equal spirit. You're at least as likely—

maybe even more so—to learn something from your failures as from your triumphs. Who knows what new book might bring you up short? I'll give two portraits of old Icelanders who helped ruin me as a boy. They owned by no means the only libraries in Minneota, but I loved these two in particular, so I try to bring them back to life for you as homage, as just thanks for gifts too princely to be repaid.

Stena

My parents seldom left their only child to play in the street when they traveled from the farm to Minneota for some errand. Part of any town adventure included visits to old Icelanders. There I learned something about the separate worlds of men and women. My father's social calls usually began with a card game in the Round-Up after which he and whatever friend or old relative showed up would adjourn either to the back room of the liquor store or off to their houses in town. A child, on those occasions, invariably turned into a pest, so my father did his best to see that I spent more wholesome time in the company of women. Whenever my mother visited Stena Dalmann, that policy was all right with me.

Stena lived in my favorite flat in Minneota, a misnomer since it was not a flat at all but a height, part of the second story of what in the fifties was the town newspaper office and print shop, a wood-frame building once half-occupied by her father's grocery store. Old Gudmundur Dalmann, born in 1856 on an Icelandic farm buried by volcanic ash and fresh lava in 1875, emigrated to Minneota in 1879. He started work as a manual laborer on the new railroad, soon got a job clerking in a general store, and finally, in 1889, went into the grocery business for himself. Meanwhile he established a reputation as an essayist and journalist in Icelandic newspapers like *Heimskringla,* writing commentaries on religion, politics, and the various quarrels inside the Icelandic immigrant community. A book of immigrant genealogy describes him as a *"rauðheitur* Democrat."* The adjective translates as "red hot" but I have a feeling from the context and withering tone of the Icelandic that dark connotations lurk underneath. Old Dalmann was a prairie radical—a populist.

His number was legion among Scandinavian immigrants. Fired by disgust at the hide-bound conservatism, rigid class-structure, and "screw the poor" callousness of Scandinavian government bureaucracies, the new immigrants already arrived as *rauðheitur* radicals, preaching the cooperative movement, regulation of banks and credit, and stern taxation for the new generation of robber barons, land-rich plutocrats and speculators. The populists particularly disliked the railroads, Dalmann's first employer. They thought them real-estate swindlers fleecing the local farmers who had to ship their grain and meat to market. The radical populism of Minnesota, fueled by the rebellious energy of these immigrant Scandinavians, remained vigorous through the triumphant Farmer-Labor movement of the thirties, but began to peter out before I came to consciousness after World War II. These immigrants came from a tradition in some odd way similar to that of William Bradford and the Puritans who arrived in Massachusetts in the seventeenth century, determined to practice a form of communal ownership of property. The Puritans were our first precursors of socialism. Both groups suffered quick defeat in the presence of vast properties and easy profits available for the taking in the New World. Americans have never been able to long resist the "mania of owning things." We sink fast to greed after we arrive on this continent, like children who come to a toy shop with a rich uncle's credit card. We want it all for ourselves, and are not about to let the silliness of principle slow us down in our lust for property. Old Dalmann became a grocer selling slabs of dried fish, rye meal, cured meat, sour-milk curds, and coffee to the new immigrants, and to anybody else with ready cash. He had a family to feed and he fed them, whatever his political or economic convictions. Then he argued, read more books, and argued again—while counting change and making home deliveries. It's a small version of the story of America.

Elmer Benson, Minnesota's last Farmer-Labor and probably the only true socialist governor, was interviewed on television just before he died in the late seventies. He had been soundly drummed out of office in 1938 by the young Republican Harold Stassen. Elmer, who inherited the governorship when Floyd Olson died in office in 1936, shared Floyd's convictions, but not his charm. He returned home to Appleton, Minnesota, a small farm town, to become for the next forty years the most prosperous banker in the district. The interviewer asked him if there wasn't some cognitive dissonance in the fact that a committed radical populist—still, in fact, an unashamed socialist, a scourge of the corrupt power of banks—should become a banker and a rich one at that. No, said Elmer, nothing curious at all about it. He offered his political and economic ideas as plainly and squarely as he could, laying all the cards of his convictions on the public table. The electorate, his fellow citizens, just as plainly rejected those convictions, so he found himself in his forties washed up for political life and unemployed. He had a family to feed and having studied banking so thoroughly, understood perfectly well how to be a banker, still a legal profession despite his best political efforts. He implied that he would have preferred that the last forty years had gone differently in the national life, but in a democracy, the citizens speak, and that is that. Dalmann would probably have said the same. The *rauðheitur* populist grocer died of a heart attack at seventy-six, falling to the sawdust-covered floor from his rocking chair next to the stove in Dalmann's Grocery while reading the newspaper. This was 1932, just after the triumph of Roosevelt and Floyd Olson. I suspect that a cracker barrel sat on the other side of the stove.

Old Dalmann was long dead and his grocery store closed

before I arrived in 1943. Three of his four children moved away from Minneota. That left only Stena, the unmarried daughter who did her proper duty by staying home to tend her aged parents and run the store. Born in 1890, by her mid-fifties she had retired from the grocery business. She sold the big family house to move downtown into her flat above the *Mascot* office. A small, squarely-built woman, not handsome, her face mixed iron determination not to be deprived of her own say in matters with impish ironic humor. When she said severe things, she simultaneously lifted one eyebrow and wrinkled the corner of her mouth ever so slightly as if to say: "What I am telling you is unfortunately true, but you have my permission to laugh." As a small boy, I loved her utter refusal to patronize children. Having had none herself, she was unused to children and treated them in the only way she knew how to treat human beings—as equals. She said adult things and expected you to rise to the occasion and behave like a civilized rational creature with a functioning brain. Stena spoke not a syllable of baby talk, no cooing or baa-ing or ain't-that-cuting. She spoke English, unless she spoke Icelandic, in which case what she was saying was neither any of your business nor ever would be. Only old affairs happened in that language; children lived exclusively in English.

Her apartment was a magic place. After forty years, I still dream of it; sometimes I think I've imagined the whole place—that it never existed, this Minneota pleasure dome of Kubla Khan, but then I meet others who were inside and remember it exactly as I do, but whose memory can be trusted better than mine.

You entered from the street by a broad wooden door next to the *Mascot* office behind whose windows you heard the clanking of iron presses, metal printing plates being noisily piled in a corner. The wide but dingy and unpainted stairs creaked and squeaked as you ascended. At the top, there were two small apartments to the left, both homes to elderly

Icelandic bachelors, and Stena's door straight ahead, decorated with a brass knocker. When you knocked, she answered, "Come in." Visitors piled wraps on an antique coat tree.

The oddly built flat had been for most of its history a photographer's studio and had never, thank God, been remodeled into normalcy. You entered a long, narrow shotgun-shaped parlor with three shotguns running off from it, two to right and one to back. I never saw the inside of the first subsidiary shotgun, Stena's bedroom; the second, a little sitting room, had a huge pocket door at the back. The parlor, formerly the photographer's front office, led to these two side rooms, dressing and primping stations for customers before their formal sitting. The kitchen, running straight back from the parlor, must have been the darkroom; so windowless and cramped that only small Stena could penetrate its recesses for cookies and coffee cups. Those skinny rooms felt like a train car, presumably parked high in the air.

But what treasures lived there! I remember the whole place flooded with greenish light—green patterned wool rugs on which sat Victorian love seats, chairs of leather and plush, carved wood tables with marble tops, the walls lined with glass-doored oak bookcases and cabinets full of a century's bric-a-brac: ivory, amber, bronze, porcelain. The already thin rooms shrank to anorexic narrowness with that generous collection of thingamabobs, whatchamacallits, and doo-dads, with a few thousand books to boot. On the walls hung portraits of dead Icelanders in heavy gilt frames. Even as a child, my outsized body knew enough to sidle delicately through that labyrinth of stuff. Break nothing—knock nothing over, were Stena's two house rules for children, and presumably for adults too, should they show up drunk or wobbly, inclined to wreak havoc on her good order.

But while Stena and Jona coffeed and gossiped in the parlor, I ambled past the bookshelves finding choice items to look at. Stena liked to see children read; aside from intellectual benefits, it kept them quiet, but eventually house rule number three came into play: Put it back where you found it. I would accumulate a handful of old books, then make my way past the heavy oak-slab of pocket door to my true destination—the dining room.

Claustrophobia ended here. The room seemed vast, flooded with light from an enormous skylight fifteen feet above the floor and majestic ten-foot-high windows on two walls. The air above your head always floated with gossamer dust particles that orbited in calm majesty through the light coming in from all directions. This must have been the old studio where the dead Icelanders stood for long minutes, one hand resting on an ornate pillar, mouths closed tight, eyes straight ahead in a transfixed stare while a voice from under a black shroud called out, "Hold it now, just a little longer." This room was full of ghosts, transcendental negatives circling toward the faraway ceiling in a disembodied waltz. The cameras, pastoral backdrops, pillars, stools, decorative armchairs, and light stands were replaced by a tall Victorian sideboard, a buffet with mirror, and a huge oak clawfoot table with eight leather-seated chairs, all resting on an almost threadbare Oriental rug. On the walls hung more dead Icelanders in even grander gilt frames, more bookshelves beneath them.

Though that princely room was a goad to the imagination, I never saw anyone use it. Stena served coffee to visitors or took her private meals in the little kitchen and parlor. The dining room was always slightly cold, only half-heated in winter, if at all. Snow blown with blizzard vigor penetrated the skylight now and then, leaving little drifts on the tablecloth. The room belonged to its ghosts or to children who loved it. It was a museum to a life I could only fantasize.

If you were young and limber, the space under the table made yet another room. I remember lying stretched out on the rug, reading, resting the spine of my book on the carved oak clawfoot. It was a little hiding place for me to ruminate on whatever curiosity I plucked from behind the glass doors.

And such books I found there! What damage they worked on my status as patriotic American, devout Lutheran, contented farm boy! No television ever presumed to the awful unsettling power of those crumbly yellow signatures. How can I remember them forty-odd years later? I use the best mnemonic device of all: I own them, and they sit on shelves in easy distance from this old kitchen table where I write. Goethe's *Faust, The Stones of Venice, Fanchon the Cricket* by George Sand (to my amazement, judging by the evidence of the frontispiece, a woman), Herbert Spencer's *First Principles,* Emanuel Swedenborg's *Heaven and Hell and the World of Spirits and Things Heard and Seen,* the complete Milton with an inlaid leather cover and etchings on heavy paper of Satan talking back to God, mysterious books in Icelandic whose contents I could then only imagine. What was a grocer who had never set foot inside a school doing with these books? Reading them—mostly in his second language, acquired only after his twenty-third birthday. They are signed, marked, dated, well-thumbed, but immaculately kept. Someone loved those books. Someone still does.

Here are three of the great poisons that did me damage, still living close at hand—in my consciousness and in my house. All three are plain black books, like Bibles.

Old Dalmann had bound three small books together in leather and boards (probably at the *Mascot,* also a bindery in those days): a pamphlet by Kristofer Janson, the controversial Norwegian Unitarian who argued for Jeffersonian reason and tolerance inside Christianity rather than fire-breathing fundamentalist piety; and two books by Tom Paine, another radical immigrant, *The Rights of Man* and *The Age of Reason,* Paine's passionate defense of deism and free thinking grafted to his savage attack on brutality and superstition in the Bible. All three appeared in 1889 reprints; Dalmann must have ordered them from a mail-order book dealer and had them bound in the same year his last daughter Stena was born. There I am, still a Sunday school student who sings "Living for Jesus the Life That is True" once a week, lying under Stena's table examining this title page:

THE

AGE OF REASON:

BEING

An Investigation

OF

TRUE AND FABULOUS THEOLOGY.

BY THOMAS PAINE;

MOVER OF THE "DECLARATION OF INDEPENDENCE," SECRETARY OF FOREIGN AF
FAIRS UNDER THE FIRST AMERICAN CONGRESS, MEMBER OF THE NATIONAL
CONVENTION OF FRANCE, AND AUTHOR OF "COMMON SENSE,"
"THE CRISIS," "RIGHTS OF MAN," ETC., ETC.

CHICAGO, NEW YORK, SAN FRANCISCO

BELFORD, CLARKE & CO.

1889.

And finding on the first page of text this creed:

> I believe in one God, and no more; and I hope for happiness beyond this life.
>
> I believe in the equality of man; and I believe that religious duties consist in doing justice, loving mercy, and endeavoring to make our fellow creatures happy.
>
> But, lest it should be supposed that I believe many other things in addition to those, I shall, in the progress of this work, declare the things I do not believe, and my reasons for not believing them.
>
> I do not believe in the creed professed by the Jewish church, by the Roman church, by the Greek church, by the Turkish church, by the Protestant church, nor by any church that I know of. My own mind is my own church.
>
> All national institutions of churches, whether Jewish, Christian, or Turkish, appear to me no other than human inventions, set up to terrify and enslave mankind, and monopolize power and profit.
>
> I do not mean by this declaration to condemn those who believe otherwise; they have the same right to their belief as I have to mine. But it is necessary to the happiness of man, that he be mentally faithful to himself. Infidelity does not consist in believing, or in disbelieving; it consists in professing to believe what he does not believe.

I probably quoted to myself, slightly out of context, Martin Luther's famous sentence that prefaces his explanation for each article of the Apostles' Creed: "This is most certainly true." I did a little research in school afterwards and discovered that Paine was one of our great patriots and a mover behind Jefferson's prose and ideas in "The Declaration of Independence." After publishing *The Age of Reason* as an old man, Paine was beaten and turned out of his house and away from his town by his fellow citizens to punish him for his blasphemy. I had, even then, a little glimmer of how dangerous it actually is for an American to behave like an American. We've never

believed a word we've said from the Bill of Rights onward.
What conceivable right do we have to feel smug about the
fatwa imposed on Salman Rushdie by fanatical foreigners? We
don't do badly with *fatwas* ourselves.

The second black book was the *Complete Lectures of Colonel
Robert W. Ingersoll,* an Illinois politician and orator famous on
the nineteenth-century lecture circuit for his free-thinking spell-
binders. A philosophical descendent of Tom Paine, his only
shortcoming for Dalmann, the *rauðheitur* and for me, was his
unfortunate membership in the Republican Party. He supported a sound business climate and the gold standard and even
gave the nominating speech for James G. Blaine at the
Republican convention of 1876. But he was a brave lambaster of
narrow-minded Christianity; he would not have much liked the
school-prayer movement. Here he is in "Mistakes of Moses."

> I want to free the schools of our country. I want it so that
> when a professor in a college finds some fact inconsistent
> with Moses, he will not hide the fact. I wish to see an eter-
> nal divorce and separation between church and schools.
> The common school is the bread of life; but there should be
> nothing taught except what somebody knows; and any-
> thing else should not be maintained by a system of general
> taxation. I want its professors so that they will tell every-
> thing they find; that they will be free to investigate in every
> direction, and will not be trammeled by the superstitions of
> our day. What has religion to do with facts? Nothing. Is
> there any such thing as Methodist mathematics, Presby-
> terian botany, Catholic astronomy or Baptist biology?
> What has any form of superstition or religion to do with a
> fact or with any science? Nothing but to hinder, delay or
> embarrass. I want, then, to free the schools; and I want to
> free the politicians, so that a man will not have to pretend
> he is a Methodist, or his wife a Baptist, or his grandmother
> a Catholic; so that he can go through a campaign, and

when he gets through will find none of the dust of
hypocrisy on his knees.

This was the fiery public oratory Whitman loved so much that
he used it as one of the roots of his long rolling line. That's a
true American voice, turned up on high, but it doesn't always
preach sanity and tolerance. Father Coughlin and Gerald L.K.
Smith also sang their harangues to this tune. The grandilo-
quent music inside it—the voice of the lecture circuit, the
Chautauqua, the public oration—ought to be sweet to one
American ear, but we had best keep the other carefully tuned
for content. Dalmann bought his copy of Ingersoll's *Lectures*
on March 6, 1885, six years after he arrived from Vopnafjörður
for the first time. It cost seventy-two cents. The binding has
dried and cracked from age and hard reading.

The *Communist Manifesto* sat glowering on the shelf, of
course, and I read it, even while Joe McCarthy's voice belched
out of the radio, proclaiming lists of commies it held in its
claw. But the economics book Dalmann clearly loved best was
Progress and Poverty by Henry George from California.
Though George wrote better prose than might be expected
from an economist, I had a hard time keeping my mind on his
arguments. I fathomed the general idea—of a single tax imposed on private gain on any public resources, and his lovely
notion that Americans owned their country and its riches in
common. If you want to mine our communal iron or gold, pay
us for it with a little tax: 100 percent on profits. After all, we
own the Vermillion Iron Range and the northern forest in
common, not J.P. Morgan or Jim Hill. George confirmed
what I already suspected: that entrepreneurial-laissez-faire-
monopoly-free-market capitalism was not only morally vile,
but provided an excuse for large-scale theft. How I loved
proposing those notions in social studies class in high school!
Dalmann owned a 1907 edition of Henry George; I imagine he

wore his first copy out. George was a popular man among the *rauðheitur* from the rural Midwest.

A few years ago, I saw an old home-movie of my father and mother not long after their marriage standing in front of Dalmann's Grocery with Stena in 1935 or '36. The images rolled by on a jerky, antique 8-mm projector, giving me for one weird moment the sense that these people were still alive—Bill and Jona Holm young and handsome in their twenties, Stena in her forties, hair still colored. They're all dressed up in their Sunday clothes, admiring the old heavy-footed workhorse and his waiting dray-wagon labeled "Dalmann's Deliveries, Phone 33." I imagine that horse arriving at my door a few blocks away laden with bags of hard fish, coffee, Hershey's chocolate, Arm & Hammer baking soda, Lucky Strikes, Monarch canned peas, Schilling's cardamom, Morton's salt, a bag of prunes for making *Vinarterta*. It's a blustery November day in the mid-thirties, steam rising from the horse's nostrils, curved hoof-prints making a trail in the snow from street to street. The horse wears a fine hat in the old movie, though that may not have been its everyday couture.

I think I try in my mind's eye to lasso into consciousness the decade before my birth—the look, feel, smell of it, the colors of hair I knew only as white, their crooked backs suddenly unbent and erect, the dead I knew telling stories again, burned and demolished buildings like the Round-Up Tavern and Dalmann's Grocery risen up on their foundations to line Main Street once more. I want to hear the conversations that led to marriages and quarrels, to my own conception and birth. I wait, invisible, watching books with now-dead names on the fly leaf arrive by train, soon to have their virgin bindings cracked under kerosene light that falls over a leather rocker. I watch lips moving and mumbling as ideas and stories make their way into some brain—like Stena's or her father's—now lost to me and to you. Can that consciousness be brought back? Should it?

In 1954 I got a red autograph book for my eleventh birthday, August 25. School started soon after, so I began gathering the autographs of schoolmates, and of any unsuspecting visitors to the farm. What an insufferable little prig I must have been! I hauled the autograph book to town too, and pestered all my mother's and father's friends to sign it. Stena, neither at a loss for wit nor inclined to humor pesky children, wrote this:

> Sept 4
>
> Dear Billie : —
>
> Blindur er bóklaus
> madur. (you know, Mr.
> Shakespeare)
>
> Stena

She refused to translate for me. She knew an arrogant little twerp when she saw one—though she loved him in spite of it. "You know everything; translate it yourself." So I did, probably with a borrowed Icelandic dictionary. It means, "Blind is the bookless man," an old Icelandic proverb. It's still true—and one of the important things you need to know on earth.

Stena died in 1957 when I was fourteen. She left me the pick of her father's books. I try still to be a good steward, to bring back to life the quality of mind and spirit that read and loved them. There's another grocery store now under the ghost of her apartment, Finnegan's, not Dalmann's. Her dining room table must sit just above the meat cooler, an open copy of Ingersoll or of Poe's stories floating in the ether over the pork chops and chicken wings. Sometimes buying meat, I cock my head up in thanks in case any forty-year-old molecules still drift around looking for home.

Einar

The Dalmanns loved truth; Einar Hallgrimsson loved beauty. You could find whatever books, ideas, and views of the universe didn't live above the *Mascot* office by walking down the unpainted stairs, traveling across the street to the Big Store and taking a left into the alley past Eric Heggeseth's blacksmith shop, Clair Frakes's cabinet-making shop, to Einar's compact little house, a bookshelf with its own concrete foundation and shingled roof. Stena could have looked out the back window of her flat and waved to Einar, hardly 150 yards away as a crow might fly in a proper landing. Einar could have sat in his green leather reading chair, peered over the tops of his trifocals and blown a kiss to Stena. I doubt the dead will contradict me when I tell you that neither ever did.

Einar, like Stena, never married. He was born Einar Oddur Jónsson in Vopnafjörður in 1891 and emigrated with his parents in 1903, first to Canada. Old Jon and Sigridur came south to Minneota with Einar's sisters just when America embarked on its adventure in the trenches of World War I, but Einar didn't follow his family here until 1926. He was a skilled carpenter and cabinet maker who prided himself on never needing a level. "My eye is a perfectly reliable level," he said in his slightly lisping, still thickly Icelandic voice—the *s*'s hissed and *r*'s trilled, and the *v*'s and *w*'s standing in for each other. Oddly enough, he was right about his eye; Einar's cabinet doors glided elegantly shut with seamless joints and properly right angles. He liked to be given a goal, but not your directions on how to achieve it, your opinions about the proper materials to use or your frenzied demands that the job be hurried. When you hired Einar to build, you got Einar, not a faceless flunky to obey orders. You consulted Einar; you didn't buy him. He couldn't be hired for mere money; though if you didn't pay him for years, he was unlikely to put up much of a fuss. He simply removed himself permanently from the possibility of your asking him any more questions, or making use of his level eye and impeccable hand. There was no conscious arrogance in this; Einar simply knew his own value. A man of great intelligence and curiosity, he honored language well used, whether Icelandic or English, and prided himself on the unexpectedly proper word in the proper place, the right tone with just a

YOUR VOTE AND SUPPORT RESPECTFULLY
SOLICITED BY
E. O. HALLGRIMSON
Candidate for
COUNTY COMMISSIONER
SECOND DISTRICT — LYON COUNTY

GENERAL ELECTION NOVEMBER 7, 1950

(Prepared and Circulated by E. O. Hallgrimson, Minneota, Minn.)

Proof of Einar Hallgrimsson's run for county commissioner in 1950, pasted into the author's autograph book.

touch of sharp irony to keep you thinking after he walked away. But a large part of him was given over to shyness, diffidence—even humility. He would have called himself a simple man—without education, vast income, connection to the "important world" outside Minnesota. He would, of course, have been partly right insofar as we are all "simple" viewed from one angle. Thoreau, for instance, was simple; so was William Blake. But Einar's imperious independence came from being Einar, and that had better be enough since that's all one was ever likely to be in this world.

I have puzzled over the apparent unwillingness of these old Icelanders either to marry or reproduce. They were neither ugly, stupid, without verbal or physical charm, nor (most of them) trapped in a gay closet. Besides, as experience demonstrates, the ugly, stupid, graceless, and gay marry every day in vast numbers and reproduce mightily—sometimes hatching lovely and intelligent children who might not marry. I thought about it a long time but can't even propose an explanation. It's merely an intractable fact, a mystery like so many others.

Einar and Stena were almost the same age, spoke the same two languages sharply and precisely, and between their two sets of bookshelves owned a comprehensive library. So why didn't they at least live in sin and read to each other? The idea certainly never occurred to either one of them. On the other hand, I got to make use of the best of both of them by sticking my determined nose into their libraries.

By the time I was old enough to remember him, Einar was almost sixty. He had made enough money to satisfy most of his desires: fresh supplies of books, shelves to store them, a tavern close at hand, a place to play cards and argue with his friends, a bar for more serious whiskey and arguing, and most of all, time to read whenever he pleased. He still worked now and again, particularly if begged and flattered, but regularly took a few months of travel in winter, always to a big city: Denver, Chicago, Seattle, Winnipeg, Minneapolis and Saint Paul. He arrived home laden with fresh cases of books, probably gathered by walking from one used bookstore to another, combing shelves until he accumulated what he thought was another year's worth of pleasure. Back in Minneota he unloaded his stash, sat down in his green leather reading chair, poured a Sunnybrook and water, lit a cigar, put on his trifocals, and opened to the frontispiece.

He built his house exactly to his taste and needs. He bought the back end of a lot that faced an alley behind the Big Store as the site for his four-room wood-frame cottage. The house sat over a basement workshop and garage filled with Einar's saws, planes, clamps, hammers, vises—but no level. He filled the built-in shelves on every wall of the house completely with books—even in the bathroom. There you sat on the throne facing a few hundred spines, plus piles of old *National Geographics* within easy arm's reach. Carlyle, anyone? An Anatole France to pass the time? Vilhjálmur Stefansson's essays on life with the Copper Eskimos?

Einar loved poetry best. He acquired fine nineteenth-century "household" editions bound in half calf of all the major poets of Europe and America from antiquity to about 1900: Goethe, Longfellow, Pope, Gray, Dante, Poe, Whitman, Homer, Wordsworth, Tennyson, Browning, Scott, Emerson, Whittier, Heine, François Villon, Schiller, Shakespeare—all! And Mrs. Hemens and Hannah More for gender equity. He read Icelandic as well or better than English so all the Icelanders stood there too, usually in full leather: the *Eddas,* Halldór Laxness, Snorri Sturluson, Hallgrimur Petersson's *Passion Hymns,* Jonas Hallgrimsson, Stephan G. Stephansson, K. N. Julius—and all the prose sagas from the Middle Ages. Einar was catholic in his picks; he ignored the modern academy's distinctions between "poetry" and "verse." Between Milton and Dante sat Paul Laurence Dunbar's black dialect poems, Eugene Field's Hoosier verse, "Casey at the Bat," "The Highwaymen," and Einar's particular favorite, Robert Service, the Canadian sourdough poet. He loved them all—their noise when read aloud, their high sentiments, their ingenuity of image and form, even their elegant look on the half-white page where the margins are wide, leaving you space to think and imagine.

My father and Einar were pals. Frequent partners at whist or rummy in the Round-Up, they often finished their card games by getting a pint at the Power House, the local liquor store just through the back alley, then strolling a half-block to Einar's kitchen for "Just von little nip of viskey." I loved tagging along on those afternoons though I'm not so sure my father was always pleased to be shackled with the tending of his over-sized son. At least at Einar's I could be easily pacified— kept permanently quiet, my prepubescent nose safely out of adult business, buried in a book. Einar installed me in his green chair, ordered me to read, then disappeared into the kitchen with Big Bill and the pint of Sunnybrook. Sometimes they talked English, sometimes Icelandic, most often a mixture of the two incomprehensible to me. I paid no attention to what they said. I was lost in Einar's library, light years away from Minneota and the farm.

I didn't merely read. I walked up and down past the shelves fingering the books, petting the leather, stroking the marbled flyleaves, carefully lifting the sheer India paper away from the engraved frontispiece, feeling the heft and weight and balance of some complete works in my hand, smelling the ink and leather and sometimes mildew, flipping the pages so the gold edges moved like a kaleidoscope. In these days of CD-ROM and books on disc, we forget the physical charm of books, their weight, texture, color, odor. We love them with our hands, noses, and eye for design as much as with our minds. A book is a kind of skin—a genuine epidermis—over the words, ideas, and songs inside. We love books sensually, not abstractly, the same way we love a woman, or a tree, or dinner. We cannot love an idea without a body or we sink; the humanity drains out of us and we become capable of anything.

Surely, this ghastly brutal century should begin to teach us to mistrust the love of abstractions that so easily turn to excuses for cruelty.

I first saw *Leaves of Grass* in Einar's house, a well-thumbed copy. I loved the mysterious title (no "Collected Poems" for Whitman!), the look of the long-breathed lines on the pages, the grandly be-whiskered face and sly sideways look of Walt—not Walter—like Bill, not William. Longfellow was not Hank, nor Lowell, Jim, nor Holmes, Ollie. Walt was my man; I knew it almost without reading him. As I later discovered, he liked being held whether you read him or not. I opened the book:

> I have said that the soul is not more than the body,
> And I have said that the body is not more than the soul,
> And nothing, not God, is greater to one than one's
>   self is,
> And whoever walks a furlong without sympathy
>   walks to his own funeral dressed in his shroud,
> And I or you pocketless of a dime may purchase the
>   pick of the earth,
> And to glance with an eye or show a bean in its pod
>   confounds the learning of all times,
> And there is no trade or employment but the young
>   man following it may become a hero,
> And there is no object so soft but it makes a hub for
>   the wheel'd universe,
> And I say to any man or woman, Let your soul stand
>   cool and composed before a million universes.
>
> And I say to mankind, Be not curious about God,
> For I who am curious about each am not curious
>   about God,
> (No array of terms can say how much I am at peace
>   about God and about death.)

In Einar's green chair, turning the pages at random, I reached "The Songs of Parting," to find these lines:

Camerado, this is no book,
Who touches this touches a man,
(Is it night? are we here together alone?)
It is I you hold and who holds you,
I spring from the pages into your arms—decease
　　calls me forth.
O how your fingers drowse me,
Your breath falls around me like dew, your pulse
　　lulls the tympans of my ears,
I feel immerged from head to foot,
Delicious, enough.

Now *that* was what reading meant, what lived inside books. Einar and Stena and fifty others and maybe-dead Walt showed me the possibility of a life—what a real vocation felt like as you held it in your hand while your heart overflowed with the exquisite joy of being simply alive in this world, a body and soul that can't tell each other apart.

My internal clock stopped while I sat in the green chair so I never had any notion of how long it took Einar and Big Bill to finish their business and their nip. When they did, Einar came in to fetch me out of his green chair. "So you found a little something to read," he said. He was a large man, maybe six feet and heavily built. He wore thick glasses (to protect his level eye, presumably) and dentures that seemed a little over-sized for the mouth they inhabited. His hair was gray and bristly, and his hands looked like they could, without benefit of a hammer, shove nails into a two-by-four with a slight push. Yet there was an odd delicacy about him when he moved, a kind of primness, as if he were afraid that with an expansive gesture, he would break something valuable. He dressed most often in workmen's khaki, but since he had been ceremonial mayor of Minneota for years, he owned a couple of good suits and silk ties. "He cleaned up nicely," as my mother said of working men who occasionally duded themselves up like Republicans. His voice was a little whistly (probably because of his unwieldy dentures) and his English bore no resemblance to ordinary American speech. He had arrived in Canada at age twelve, lived mostly among Icelanders there, and came to Minneota when he was thirty-five. I thought his brogue elegantly musical with its hisses, buzzes, trills, rising and falling inflections. Stoic flatness hadn't taken up residence in Einar's throat—yet. Usually, I suppose, he was a little tight after his afternoon Sunnybrook. I loved the manly smell of whiskey, cigar smoke, snuff, peppermints, Bay Rum, a little sweat in the flannel shirt. I often used the whiskey to my advantage by encouraging Einar to read a poem or two for me, and whether weakened by Sunnybrook, vanity, or pity, he often obliged. I rose from the green leather chair cushion; Einar settled in to begin scouring the shelf or leafing. Since I liked hearing him read Icelandic, he often read or recited fifteen or twenty lines of something to warm up, to sharpen the consonants and get the vowels flowing, then a passage from Shakespeare, or a stanza of Poe's "Raven" building to the grand finale—what I *really* waited for—a Robert Service tale in Einar's inimitable odd voice, maybe "The Shooting of Dan McGrew."

> A bunch of the boys were whooping it up in the
>   Malamute Saloon;
> The kid that handles the music-box was hitting a
>   jag-time tune;
> Back of the bar, in a solo game, sat Dangerous
>   Dan McGrew,
> And watching his luck was his light-o'-love, the lady
>   that's known as Lou.

I have no interest in your opinion of the literary quality of that poem. It is a masterpiece and that is that.

Einar contributed to my twelve-year-old agnosticism too. As with so many of the Icelanders, both in the Old Country and here, Christianity did not quite "take." The notion of the atonement—that a God died to pay for your sins before you ever thought of committing them—seemed to diminish the independence of human beings too much. The old Icelanders wanted to own up to their own mistakes or shortcomings; they wanted to take their own consequences. It seemed a little presumptuous of God to shoulder your responsibilities without even asking in person. I'm not sure that "sin" in any kind of accurate theological definition meant very much to them. Quite clearly, they came out of a shame culture. It's probably still impossible to make an Icelander feel guilty; to shame him is easy. Just repeat these mantras: "We brought you up better than that . . . ," "I thought you were more intelligent . . . ," "You've let us down badly. . . ." Still works like a charm. Try it.

Theosophy and spiritualism interested old Icelanders more than dogma or piety. God might not exist, but ghosts certainly did. To judge by sagas and folklore, the Icelandic dead were livelier and more mischievous than most Los Angeles street gangs. Swedenborg, a regular on immigrant bookshelves, even in otherwise conventional Lutheran houses, frequently kept company with Annie Besant and Madame Blavatsky. I'm not entirely certain that these long-dead Icelandic immigrants wouldn't have embraced channeling with at least half-credulity.

Einar went to church at least once a season, and even, I think, wrote checks to keep his name on the books. I often heard him tell my father in his fine hiss of a voice "Christianity is primarily superstition." Superstition had five clear syllables in Einar's brogue: "su-per-sti-*se*-on." He valued Sera Guttormur (Reverend Guttormsson), the intelligent, kindly, and soft-spoken old minister, and during the sometimes interminable sermons, Einar leaned forward onto the next pew with an elbow crooked under his chin, listening closely, trying to follow—and afterwards to defeat—the logic of Guttormur's propositions from the pulpit. The more pious and devoted members of the congregation frequently snored in their pews, heads lolling on leaning necks as elucidated dogma drifted past their off-duty ears. I sat twenty feet above it all at my post in the choir loft looking down at this small comic drama, wondering which parishioner old Guttormur preferred, the sleeping believer or the alert free-thinker taking the sermon seriously enough to exercise his mental muscles on it. Or which company God might prefer during the more tedious stretches of eternity. Einar, no doubt, was better company. If God had any sense, he would notice that.

The grand moment arrived during the creed, the Apostles' on a regular Sunday, the Nicene on state occasions like communion, and the Athanasian for handy reference. In Lutheran churches, the congregation rises to its feet out of chivalrous respect for dogma, no doubt, and intones the words in unison. For non-Lutherans, I'll give the old version—the right version.

THE APOSTLES' CREED

I BELIEVE in God the Father Almighty, Maker of heaven and earth. And in Jesus Christ, His only Son, our Lord; Who was conceived by the Holy Ghost, Born of the Virgin Mary; Suffered under Pontius Pilate, Was crucified, dead, and buried; He descended into hell; the third day He rose again from the dead; He ascended into heaven, And sitteth on the right hand of God the Father Almighty; From thence He shall come to judge the quick and the dead.

I believe in the Holy Ghost; The holy Christian Church, The Communion of Saints; The Forgiveness of sins; The Resurrection of the body; And the Life everlasting. Amen.

Each clause is prefaced by: "I believe," not "I think," or "most of the time it seems to me," or "sometimes." I believe. Hard words. Heavy stones. Congregations, of course, mumble them automatically like the alphabet or a childhood tongue-twister, a form of theological "chin music," (as my friend the poet, John Rezmerski would call it). The Apostles' Creed is a habit, not a statement. Einar, in this regard, was not a habitual man. Whiskey was a habit, or cigars, but that had to do with liver and lungs; a creed had to do with mind and to say it Sunday after Sunday, you had to stop thinking. Einar refused to do that for man, state, or God, so he rose to his feet as a gesture of politeness and solidarity with his peers whom he had no wish to insult and remained resolutely silent during the recitation of "I believe . . ." What Einar believed on any given Sunday was a matter to be taken up between Einar and God. "It vas none of anyvon else's damned business." That eloquent silence gave me heart at twelve. It gives me heart at fifty-two, and will go on giving me heart until heart stops.

A few years ago, I heard another story about Einar's life. I think it's even true. Einar, behind his ironic exterior and his reputation for quick wit and brooking no opposition, was a romantic soul. He had fallen in love with an Icelandic widow who worked in the Big Store just across the alley from his house. He was too shy to speak to her, he instead wrote her passionate romantic letters, many in verse, all in Icelandic. She had decided not to remarry and had no wish to embarrass Einar, so she simply collected the letters in a box, never answering them. These two must have passed each other every day in the street, saying a hello and ain't the weather grand and never a word of the secret they shared but would not bring to speech. Einar walked past the Big Store to drop his letter at the post office, then walked back to his house again; she walked home from the Big Store to find another letter, written at a table not fifty yards from where she worked. She read the letters and saved them, and after they were both long dead, her children found them, and I heard about it. I do not want to see the letters or read them, but I might hold them in my hand for a while if they were ever present in a room where I sat—probably in a green leather chair.

When Einar died, just short of seventy and a year or two after Stena, his sisters invited me to have my pick of his library. "Einar wanted you to have the poetry," they said. "He often told us how much you loved it." They also gave me a pair of large etchings in gilt frames that hung back of his green chair of an elk or caribou in an Arctic landscape. They willed me the green chair too. I still own it. It is not for sale. You cannot have enough money even to make an offer. When I find some mad child in love with books, he or maybe she shall have them all— chair, etchings, books, Einar's ghost.

Eight-Millimeter Ghosts

One morning over coffee years ago, I praised a thirties movie I had just seen to an old friend. I remarked on the liveliness of the faces, the actors' physical grace, the presence of a woman of amazing loveliness who ended her career playing crazed hags in seventies slasher films. "Think of it," he said, in a low, melancholy voice. "All those people are dead now, while we sit here having coffee, talking about watching them move, flirt, say things to each other. . . . You are watching premature corpse-shadows." His voice trailed off; he looked up through fingers of steam rising from his cup to sigh—a long mournful sigh. It had been such a sweet, inconsequential morning—a little idle chat before breakfast in a crowded diner. Two tall almost middle-aged men sat, in broody silence, examining the ceiling tiles with some care, ready to weep.

The moment was, on the other hand, also comic. Both these fellows had been to college where they were taught to fear the slippery slopes of sentimentality, nostalgia, laving yourself in a hot bath full of the obvious. Of course these actors were dead! This was the late seventies, almost a half-century after the movie's premiere. A contemporary of these actor-corpses would shortly be elected president of the United States, but neither of us had the foresight to know that then. Had we been prescient, we both might have begun actually weeping and howling, followed by gnashing of teeth and rending of garments. Instead we just finished the eggs-over-easy, Italian sausage, and soggy whole-wheat toast with occasional sad mumbles between bites.

An old lady lived in the tiny house next to my mother in Minneota. She came from as deep in the rural countryside as possible in the age of drivable roads. When I knew her in the sixties, she must have been well over eighty. She grew up with kerosene lamps, horses, cisterns, hand pumps, cob stoves, chamber pots, and walking plows. Her farm was poor and far from town; her life must have been an endless round of too much hard, mind-numbing work, too many children, too little money. It was a life with no room left for books, newspapers, trips anywhere except to neighbors for coffee, or town once a month for groceries and supplies. While she slogged through that long life, the automobile, radio, airplane, electricity, telephone, indoor plumbing, nuclear weapons, moving pictures, space satellites, ICBMs, lasers, computers, and television all arrived. By the time her children moved her to her little house in Minneota to live out her last years in relative comfort and convenience, these contraptions had come to seem normal to her neighbors. But they were not normal to her! A light switch, a flush-toilet, or a disembodied voice on the telephone that even sounded like someone you might know seemed to her a world of wonders—of science fiction come home to roost. She was a nice old lady, and I often visited with her. She was a kind of walking future-shock with gray hair wound up in a bun. But television almost unhinged her.

Her children bought her a small color TV with an aerial that could pick up channels from the Twin Cities—Minneapolis and Saint Paul, to her only names on a map. She liked soap operas more than anything and watched them all with a kind of fundamental religious intensity. Since she had lived most of her life in an almost pre-literate world, her memory for the details of who was screwing whom or dying of what or embezzling or conniving, or whatever it is that happens on soap operas, was exact, precise, and literal. She followed not amorphous waves of feeling but the sinuous lines of event. She gathered not impressions but facts. She was not—to use the modern construction—"into" nuance. She became a geriatric one-woman *Soap Opera Digest*. Neighbors with busier lives stopped by to chat, catching up on whatever developments they'd missed. Her summaries of half-hour shows took almost exactly half an hour. She neglected most of the commercials since they were concerned with persuasion, not narrative—her only passion. Besides, she neither wanted nor needed to buy anything. Her children brought groceries and paid the rent and utility bills, and the TV set, so far as I know, never went on the blink. What conceivable use could you have to spend money or go any place? Even outside this context, that is probably not a bad question for the twentieth century to ask itself now and then.

I depend on my mother's truthfulness for the evidence of Grandma's unhinging. I was not a witness. Whenever Jona baked, she made up a little plate of cookies or bars or cake to deliver next door for Grandma's afternoon sweet snack. One summer day, Jona heard someone speaking in the tiny sitting room. It was Grandma's voice—worried, excited, a voice tense with warning. Jona peeked in through the screen door to see if something was wrong. There sat Grandma in a straight-back wooden chair leaning forward, a few feet from "As The World Turns," or whatever she was watching, shaking her finger at the flickering screen. "Laura, you should have seen that Alex was a bad guy—why, he drinks and cheats on Sandra. He'll tomcat on you too. You should know better, girl! You ought to be ashamed of yourself, behaving like that!" And on and on. Jona stifled her giggle, discreetly left the plate of chocolate-peanut-butter-crunch bars on Grandma's kitchen table and slipped back through the yard. "She thinks the TV is alive. She talks right back to it," Jona told me the next time she called with the digest of Minneota news. "Why shouldn't she?" I answered with a sigh. "It is." That's what we've got to be afraid of—all those artificial people imitating nature with electricity and fooling us.

The chat about old movies over breakfast and the image of the old lady lecturing her television set came back to me many years later when the Holms, probably for the first time in history, decided to have a family reunion.

A cousin I hadn't seen since the mid-1950s arrived unannounced at one of my bookstore readings in Minneapolis in 1991. She strode boldly up to the podium afterwards demanding to know if I recognized her. I blinked a few times, speechless, finally mumbling, "You are the ghost of Auntie Sophie . . ." It was indeed cousin Frances, grown into her own mother, a blond, hearty middle-aged woman. Her sister, Eileen, just behind her, took after her dark Irish father. We adjourned to a nearby bar for a drink and a little old-Minneota talk, telling funny stories about our parents and childhoods, catching up on the news. "So you're a grandmother now . . ." I had last seen the two of them when I was twelve, they sixteen or seventeen.

As we called down the roll of cousins, who was where or up to what, an idea came to the two sisters. Why not have a reunion? Why not indeed? Auntie Sophie, like most Icelanders of her generation, a pack rat, filled every closet in her large house with memorabilia, photos, old letters, junk too good to throw away. She preserved her own history, of course, as we all do. Hoarding relics implies confidence that history moves from generation to generation in an orderly, coherent way. Even if we don't believe that, we probably ought to behave as if we do. It's an existential leap in the direction of sanity. The treasure in Sophie's closets was a metal canister of 8-mm films, presumably undisturbed since 1945 or '46. Eileen had opened it once, identified it, and promptly shut it tight again. Little air, dust, or light had penetrated that canister since around V-J Day. Next to the films, still in its original box, sat the old projector to show them. Sophie's husband John had a good job throughout the Depression while the rest of her relatives—and most of America—scrounged to survive. He bought a movie camera in the mid-thirties and used color film after 1939, the year of "Gone with the Wind." Wouldn't it be fun, she said, for everybody to get together and watch those films? Yes, indeed. That canister turned out to be the family equivalent of the tomb of Tutenkamen.

My great-grandfather brought four sons from Iceland to America in 1882. Their son, Sveinn, and his wife Emma Holm had five children between 1896 and 1906, two sons at either end, Bjorn and Bill, and three daughters in the middle, Sophie (1898), Dora (1900), and Olympia (1904). Sveinn died in 1909, not yet fifty, from pneumonia caught in an April blizzard. His widow, Emma, raised the five children alone. They all married, among them producing five sons and five daughters. When Dora, the last of them, died in 1988, that generation disappeared, causing a strange uneasiness in their children—now middle-aged and bereft of parents, uncles, and aunts. In 1992, the ten cousins ranged in age from sixty-eight to forty-nine. I was both the junior at forty-nine and the only one still living in or connected to Minneota in any way other than memory or nostalgic imagination.

The next summer, after phone calls, seeking out airline specials, changed plans, and the usual difficulties of assembling any random handful of middle-aged Americans, the gathering was set: it included a tour of Minneota and the old farm, a stop at the nursing home to survey the survivors of one's childhood, then on to South Dakota where cousin Roger had bought for a song the country villa of a crooked speculator in some sort of agribusiness scam. He left behind a behemoth rambler with six or seven bathrooms, a handful of living rooms, and a kitchen big enough for medium-sized state dinners, as well as beds, couches, and flush-toilets for a whole army of Icelanders. The house sat three miles off the major highway, ten miles from the nearest town, just east of the

world-famous Corn Palace in Mitchell. The treeless prairies of
South Dakota rolled off toward the edge of the horizon on all
sides, making a fine metaphor—reunion forces converging not
far from the bull's eye of the continent, equidistant between
oceans, earth and sky, birth and death.

What are reunions of relatives like in America? For years, I
hated even the idea of going to one, but we age into them.
After a while, we become grateful for the connection to others
by blood, shared memory, chance, or whatever brings us together. When the generation of adults who were your age
when you were a child dies, followed by the next generation,
and then when your own generation starts to disappear here
and there, it occurs to you that you will probably die yourself.
I mean "occur" not in the obvious way; even a sixteen-year-old
when asked will tell you that yes, indeed, he is going to die.
Don't we all? I mean the interior consciousness of generational
roll-over. This moment in most lives gives birth to the longing
for connectedness. Partly this longing acknowledges that we
cannot escape being tangled into the tissue of history—the
long thread of conscious life on the planet. Reunions awaken
our curiosity to see how others age, what the world has done
to them—or for them—in a half-century. We want to compare
gray hair, scars, fat, close calls. Even if we loathe our biologic
parents, we discover that they exact a kind of ironic final revenge. Cellular determinism takes over in middle age when we
grow into their bodies, wrinkles, ailments, hair, faces, voices.
Sometimes without awareness or recognition, we put on the
overcoat of their opinions and prejudices. We should be a little
careful about that since something can actually be done to
avoid it, unlike hypertension or a rising hair-line.

Eight of the ten cousins arrive for the reunion; two have
fishing plans that can't be changed. The next generation shows
up, too, even a few from the generation after that, a nice as-
sortment of teenagers and children, braces and diapers to lend
charm and thicken the plot. Two out of the ten are childless

and divorced (the same two), not a bad record for stability and continuity as things go these days in America. Everyone still has a job, though a few retirements loom imminent, again a lucky crew. No deaths or major diseases among them yet—one happily sober twelve-stepper, a few allergies, a lot of high blood-pressure, a cataract or two, the usual lower-back pain. Pretty good for a bunch in their fifties and sixties. They have become—or married: trucker, carpenter, machinery salesman, bookkeeper, agronomist, mechanic, engineer, beauty operator, even one lawyer, and worse yet one school teacher and book-scribbler. A half-dozen still smoke, some have quit, some never started. Everybody likes a drink or three or four except the twelve-stepper, and he enjoys bartending; not a vegetarian for fifty miles. A few vote Republican out of bad habit, but mostly we're old Roosevelt Democrats, a fair shake for the working man and the farmer. Two were raised Catholic—Auntie Sophie married an Irishman—but the rest remain half-baked Lutherans who don't much think about it. They may write a check and go to church a few times a year, or they might not. Conventional piety does not weigh heavy among them. Jesus comes up in conversation only as an occasional expletive—followed by Christ Almighty!

First we get a drink, then reminisce and exchange photos. There's a table full of albums, loose pictures, and memorabilia that everyone brought from the bottom of their closet or back drawer. We tell affectionate stories of our parents' quirks—of Auntie Ole's sharp witticisms and flirting, of Auntie Dora's kindness and calm, her brown bread and *lifrarpylsa* and *Vinarterta,* of Big Bill's heroic cussing and generous nature, of Auntie Sophie's endless repository of useful advice—the oldest sister who wanted to bring everyone up to snuff. There are stories of Grandma Emma whose sweetness touched everyone who knew her, of Auntie Dora's midnight ride on the train from Garretson, South Dakota, to Minneota when Emma was dying in 1943, the month before I was born; of Uncle Bjorn's

World War I medallion, of the carefully censored postcards and letters from the French front to his mother and sister Sophie, how once having seen Paree, you couldn't keep him happily down on the farm after 1919; of Bjorn nearing his death at almost eighty, sitting down on a church step in Sioux Falls before his grandniece's wedding and telling me "You know, I didn't think either you or Johnny would grow up to be worth a shit." Bjorn, like my father, had one son in middle age. "But now I think you'll both be all right, pretty good men." For maybe the first or second (and maybe the last) time in my life, I felt blessed. I was in my thirties then; it may have to last me.

Stories, stories, stories, one anecdote rolling off another, the next surging in before the last one rises to the punch line.

"Remember the time? . . ."

"You weren't there, but . . ."

"She always said . . ." More drinks, more crackers and cheese, more laughter, more bullshit of a high order (as my father would have described it). Time to eat. Just shut up till after dinner. Freshen that drink?

We eat half a neighborhood pig, barbecued by a local farmer, probably in an old fuel-oil tank with a cut vent and a half-horse motor attached. Brown buns, potato salad, baked beans with chunks of more pork, sweet cole slaw—all made by a lady in the next town.

"Doesn't she do a nice job? She did the co-op dinner last year."

At the end, *Vinarterta,* brownies, pie, a big church-basement percolator full of thin coffee.

"Don't get grease on that picture of Grandma!"

"Get the hell out of my potato salad—there's more in the kitchen . . ."

"This pork is damn juicy."

"Pretty good sauce they use."

"Wasn't as good as Ma's . . ."

"No more whiskey; you got milk?"

"Save room for *Vinarterta?*"

"Always room for that . . . "

Coffee, a little smoking, some cardamom flavored crumbs on the table, the old citizenship papers, the homestead deed, wedding certificates—all these pieces of paper, yellow and brittle, folded and filed for too many years, passed around, admired, commented on and anecdotelized over. Then we moved downstairs to a big room full of couches and easy chairs where cousin Walt has already got the 1939 projector set up and humming while cousin Doris puts the films in order. A few false starts before the mechanism actually works. "You'd be a little rusty, too, if they hadn't plugged you in since 1947." Finally, lights out. A silence. The projector whirrs; images flicker jerkily onto the screen. The room fills with that odd, chemical acidy smell of old movie film, the smell of the projection booth in the Joy Theatre in 1949. When D. H. Lawrence, as a grown man, heard a piano play music from his childhood, his mind's eye saw a child sitting under it "in the boom of the tingling strings," . . . [betraying] "me back till the heart of me weeps." That smell might have worked for him, too.

We lived an extraordinary hour together, breathing that acrid film smell, sitting in semi-darkness, surrounded by middle-aged cousins stuffed with pork and cake, half-tight with whiskey and sentiment, watching each other watch their past lives, their own faces and bodies fifty or sixty years earlier, hair magically regrown, its original color fact rather than memory. Dead parents, dead pets, dead tractors, dead cars, are brought back to life as if by magic; dead people are moving again, smoking, grabbing, laughing, waving, posing, kissing, mugging, a tiny momentary illusion of life raised like Lazarus from the long sleep of time. It was a kind of seance without mumbo-jumbo—the levitating going on inside where it belongs.

Whatever arranging, chronological or otherwise, that had

been done to the films was a mystery to me and to the others. Chaos and chance provided the arrangement; we were continually surprised by whomever happened to appear on that screen looking at us. There's Ma! Isn't that J. B. and Lecta? Is that Ab's place or your dad's? Who owned that F-20? Is that George? We established time by context: Moved there in '41; had to be after that. Alice Ann wasn't born yet, so it was before '39. The films veered from 1939-color to black-and-white and back again to color. 1939 was a dividing line—for those movies, as for so much else in the world.

Here's a little review and summary of what we saw in those old films, with this small caveat: If you watched them, you would be bored beyond imagining. You would long for windy Victorian novels or insurance manuals to bring you back to life. On the other hand, I watched them with the same passionate attention usually reserved for say, *King Lear*. But the other humans in the room made an even better show. Maybe that's true of the response to all works of art, even of our response to nature. Watch not so much the work unfolding as humans in its presence in the process of being affected. No work of art, not even a deeply private lyric poem, can lay any claim to real existence until a human apprehends it. Yeats thought art ought to aspire to exist in a "Byzantium" beyond human imperfection. Walt Whitman thought otherwise and it explains a little about his craving for a vast audience. His passion was not so much to be famous, as to be invisible. He wanted to glide silently into rooms where a human sat with *Leaves of Grass,* to watch them finger the pages, watch their eyes and their hands (and Walt being Walt, probably their private parts), and, after a while, sidle over to plant a wet, invisible kiss on their cheek. Your job as a reader is to superimpose your own remembered faces on the ones we watched, while you join us in your mind's eye in that room in South Dakota. That is true interactive art.

The earliest films were from about 1935, the latest from

1945. They created a small picture of that decade in American life when so much changed with such headlong speed. What did those films show? They showed wind blowing for ten straight years: farm groves swaying, leaves gyrating, a garden full of peonies, roses, irises, almost bent over, hair always in motion, women brushing permanented curls out of their eyes, wheat vibrating in a field as if it grew in a van Gogh painting. I hadn't thought of it till that August night, but until pictures began moving through a projector at the turn of the century, there was no way to make wind visible. For all those thousands of years before, human beings had to take the existence of wind on faith—or experience if they happened to go outdoors on the tallgrass prairie. Wind, aged a half-century, didn't look much the worse for wear.

Old machines—automobiles, steel-wheeled Farm-All tractors, swathers, binders, and rakes—were more beautiful than new machines, their design and shape more elegant. They fit human beings better than our new cars—too small—or our tractors—too big and brutal. Cousin Roger is at the wheel of a handsome cream-colored coupe, about 1940. He was ten or eleven, dreaming of becoming the grown-up owning and driving that car! Did the whole country fight the war so that Roger could own that cream coupe? Maybe. My father's F-20 just fits him, the iron tractor almost an appendage of his body. In one grand sequence he mounts his tractor to swath grain, cigarette clenched in teeth like Roosevelt, a big grin, a tweed cap. The swather blade moves with smooth precision through the wheat. (Pronounce that word: swat-ter—no *th*-sound in it. If you don't remember that, you will be thought a stranger.)

You can easily tell the difference between city men and farmers in the thirties and for a long time afterwards. Uncle John comes from Milwaukee to visit his in-laws in his notion of country clothes: a gabardine suit with vest, crisp white shirt with collar pin and dark tie in tight windsor knot, braces holding up knife-pressed pleated trousers, two-tone wing-tip shoes (and presumably garters under the pants), a straw bowler or felt fedora depending on season, occasion, and time of day. Uncle John's idea of informality, when it must have been over ninety, was to loosen his tie slightly, remove his jacket, unbutton his vest, and neatly fold up the sleeves—twice—on his white shirt. A city man born and bred, he was a college graduate, worked for a "company," drove a fine Oldsmobile, elegant and strange, parked in the driveways of his in-laws' windblown farms. Sophie, his wife, escaped Minneota to get an education at the University of Minnesota. With a degree in Home Economics, she knew a dessert spoon from a teaspoon when she saw one. In pictures, she is six-feet tall, heavy, blond, smiling, ready to feed you at a proper table, exactly as she was in life. I remember John as a gracious, modest, soft-spoken man with fine manners. As my mother said with heavy emphasis: a *real* gentleman. But you would not mistake him for a farmer. My father and Sophie's brothers-in-law wore overalls or heavy work pants, tweed or engineer caps. My father's neck, even when he was under forty, shows a clear red line above which the sun and wind baked and leathered him. Sometimes their wives bamboozled these farmers into suits and ties that almost fit, but their bodies do not look at home in gabardine. Not only clothes, of course, showed that gulf. Farm men move differently, with a kind of cocky ease and bravado through wet barnyards, dry stubble fields, stony pastures, their boots already joyfully dirty. John, in the old film, moves diffidently as if a giant cow pie lurked just in front of his foot. The rural men's hands are rough meat hooks; a heavy ring adorns John's clean white fingers.

Even in the Depression, American families vacationed, taking photos as grimly comic as any from your own family trips. John and Sophie probably picked up Minneota relatives in their dependable car, motoring off to view scenic vistas for family fun. The earliest is a late thirties trip in black-and-white to the West Bend Grotto in Iowa, a pre-Disneyland concoction of broken glass and crushed stones set decoratively in poured concrete, imitation medieval turrets interspersed with statues celebrating patriotic and religious motifs. Imagine the pleasure of seeing yourself gambol through these wonders almost sixty years before, watching the stern looks of now dead parents warning you to behave. In the forties, the vacationers traveled in color to the Needles in the Black Hills and to the Petrified Forest in Lemmon, South Dakota, where once real trees turned to stone. Tonight at age sixty-two, you climb them again while your mother beams at you with affection and a little worry.

Animals and children, standard clichés in home movies, are not surprisingly present in great profusion: kittens, puppies, horses, cows, pigs are squeezed, petted, cooed over, scratched, held up by small hands to confront the camera with terrified, confused eyes. Here's cousin Roger with a piglet not long out of the sow, cousin Emmy Lou with a wriggling cat held firmly by the tail. Presumably that piglet turned into pork chops and the cat disappeared under a truck tire fifty-five years ago. Some long-lost pets inspired heartfelt outbursts of grief and pleasure from their owners. On seeing himself pet his beloved boxer for the first time since 1938, cousin Wally exclaimed: "Buster Bullshit Benson, the best damned dog I ever had!" Buster Bullshit Benson . . . gone—but now miraculously cocking his ears and running off camera into the vacuum of history.

As the projector whirred, voices called out of the darkness to identify scenes and characters: There's Rachel—she died in 1948. That's Lecta with colored hair; she was white by 1940. Is that Stena next to Jona? Look how cute; that's in Milwaukee. Those are dad's relatives.

More drinks arrived from time to time while the sentiments deepened. There's Ab—died in '46, such a young man. Mother always missed him. Look at Virgil—so handsome! I meant to go visit him before he died last year.

Laughter and near-weeping mix. We are betrayed like

Lawrence under his piano, by the insidious mastery of those images, people brought to life again for a while, moving and laughing as if they meant to step off the screen back into the room, years after their respective deaths, join us for a drink and give us big wet kisses and jovial handshakes, telling us how good we look, even after all these years.

My mother and father appear often in pictures of the old farmstead where I lived until I left Minneota, the barn, granary, grove, Swede Prairie Township, stretching away in all directions, bleakly lovely on those summer days well over a half century ago. It's odd to see pictures of your parents before your own birth, before your nagging presence altered their lives forever. My mother was a beautiful woman in the thirties with brilliant red hair, a willowy body, flashing green eyes full of humor and flirtation. My father sported a kind of rakish physical gaiety in those pictures that I seldom saw in him. I think it would have returned in the presence of his son if he had lived long enough, but he didn't. I missed that when I saw it in him before my arrival. Whenever the two of them show up together on camera for some group shot, he smiles wickedly and grabs her hind end. She looks at him sideways, seeming to scold him or be embarrassed, but she doesn't and she isn't. However their lives happened afterwards, they had that grand moment of lust, affection, joy in the body and in the world. I felt it in the way my father leapt onto the tractor grinning, then came over to fondle my mother. For a few moments in that dark room, I felt guilty at being born, at damaging that joy. But I didn't. We take too much credit for our effect on the world, whining about our misery and guilt, what others have done or not done to us. The world runs its normal course like the river of Heraclitus—new water passing by on its way to the sea. Still water is dead water. We are all here where we are to thicken the plot, as the Zen monks say.

As the night deepened, those old home movies transformed us into philosophers. Kermit saw his wife, Emmy Lou, at her wedding shower forty-seven years earlier clowning around with her girlfriends, shaking her red hair, grinning. In a voice close to weeping, sunk in longing, he called out, "Oh, Jesus, look how pretty she was—oh God she was pretty—oh, Jesus." She was sitting next to him, but Kermit, like all of us, lived for a while in a world gone backwards, the dead come to life, age defeated by youth, lightning sucked back into the clouds to bide its time.

I thought, as the baby of the cousins, that by virtue of lucky chronology I might avoid seeing myself. No such luck. Uncle John nailed me in 1945 during some sort of family get-together at the farm of my father's cousins. A row of mothers and children appear on camera, then a plump carrot-topped two-year-old looking deeply unhappy at being photographed, even exhibited. His mother looks embarrassed by his recalcitrance and disappears off-screen. His girl cousins grab him, hold him by his red head, and point him at the camera. He wants to escape. They don't let go of the head. Forty-seven years after that scene, I wanted to scold them, to shout out, "Damn it! Leave me alone!" Cousin Walt, still manning the projector, says: "That's Jane Ferguson and there's Dean." I silently absolved them of their sins.

The last film flapped out of the projector. Somebody hollered, "That's it?" Walt said, "Yup," and the shuffling procession to bathroom or to the kitchen for another whiskey begins. The seance ended; the table slowly sank down to its right place on the floor. If anyone had thought of Homer at that moment, he might have said he felt like Odysseus coming back from his side trip to the underworld, happy to have been there to meet the dead, to hear what they had to say; but happy too, to be back in the world of light, alive, ready for more adventure.

We had been fooled, of course, more victims of the "magic of moving pictures," like boys who daydreamed of taking home Ingrid Bergman or Ava Gardner, or of saddling up John Wayne's horse to ride off and save the town. We were all, for the duration of that flickering, old Grandma next door delivering moral lectures to the characters on "As The World Turns," imagining for the same flicker that they would buck up and improve by next Monday. All art depends on illusion for at least part of its power, but the technology of moving pictures (much less the inventions that have arrived since) ups the ante a little. Moving images imitate nature almost uncannily. Nature moves too; a painting or still photograph doesn't, except in the mind's eye. A novel can begin an interior moving in you, characters walking back and forth through your frontal lobe, but even Grandma wouldn't be fooled in the same way by Tolstoy or Melville or Balzac. The novel is not smaller than life or nature but larger. Nature can't read. Lawrence demanded that the novel be the "Great Book of Life," that it quiver when touched, be sentient as a plant, animal, or human. He asked of the novel what we imagine we want from electric flickering. His own great books go on quivering far longer than the movies made out of them. *Women in Love* on the big screen is partly alive, but we don't talk to it. On the other hand, when we read *Women in Love* alone in a silent room, we all become Grandma chattering with Lawrence himself—and with Ursula, Gudrun, Gerald, and Rupert. Film images shrivel reality by giving you the temporary pleasure of seeing the world imitated so exactly that for their duration, your wishes take over from your senses, much less from your reason.

Think of that reunion of cousins in a South Dakota basement, watching those over-fifty-year-old moving pictures of themselves as children, of people they loved now dead, of great occasions in their own lives, slipped irretrievably away in time. The dead cannot be brought to life; you will not be a child again; that grand afternoon is gone forever. You can't pluck an image off a screen to sleep with it and expect it to keep you warm. Its feet are permanently cold—colder than you will be able to stand.

It was lovely to watch those fifty-year-old home movies

with a room full of warm, breathing humans, to hear and join the high-spirited patter—the conversation with those images flickering on the screen—to lave in humor, nostalgia, even a kind of useful sentimentality that humans need a little of once in a while—but not a lot of or often. It was fun to see the electrically-moving faces of the long-dead you loved, but more fun to have a nightcap with warm, sentient bodies or to kiss cousin Doris goodnight or to shake cousin Wally's calloused hand. The true pleasure of those home movies was that they cemented a connection between a stray batch of humans gathered almost by chance—or historical accident—under the same roof. That connection said to them and to you: The planet is not so lonely as you thought. "Only connect!" was E.M. Forster's passionate cry. Without connection is no community; without community, no civilization. Without connection is no love, no order, no real freedom to be alive as we ought, while we are still lucky enough to be sentient ourselves.

One cousin copied those old movies onto videotape, so we could each own a personal cassette, play it five times a day if we wanted to, ten on lonesome days, or talk to it endlessly in a dark room. I haven't played it for a couple of years—and then only at another family reunion. I wasn't sure I could find the videotape when I started writing this essay. I knew that a responsible author should watch that film to take mental notes before describing it for whatever end he had in mind, so I sat down in front of the VCR at midnight, notebook in one hand, pencil in the other. As the images rolled by in silence, I scribbled "wind . . . cream coupe . . . boxer . . . two-tone shoes . . . swathing . . . Roger with pig . . . shower . . . grotto . . . more wind . . ." But when the pictures of my mother and father in 1935 or '36 arrived, I took no notes. I suppose those pictures will always cause a swell of grief. But I don't intend to play that tape often—and never except as a kind of cement to the fellow feeling in a room with live humans, preferably having a drink and a good time. As we age, our parents' deaths remind us of our own. It is us we grieve for. That is a connection we some-times don't want to acknowledge. The world offers us no choice. If we're smart, we make our necessities into our joys. Technology won't be much help to us in that process.

We are not suspicious enough of our own gadgets. We think moving pictures have slight consequence in the life of human consciousness. Watch them and use them, of course, but be a little careful, a little alert if you get signs that they are using or watching you. Remember, as a higher mammal, it's your biological duty to be the boss—of your electronic toys, of flickering images in a dark room. The next time you go to a movie theater or sit at home with others watching TV, wait for your eyes to adjust to the dark, and then watch not the screen, but the faces around you. Does that look like higher intelligence? Or better yet, be alert for the tiny moment when the images stop and the house lights first come on. What do you see? Faces drained of consciousness, seed pods, raw material, empty vessels. Your face, too, if you could see it in the mirror. Like furtive Walt, glide invisibly into a room where a human sits reading a novel—or maybe this essay. Look at the face. Is it different from a face hypnotized by an electronic image? Kiss it!

I think that's what my old friend in the coffee shop wanted to drop like an ironic stone onto my breathless praise of old movies. Remember: those people are dead now; they are only corpse-shadows. True connection exists somewhere else, both internalized in memory and history, and still alive in rooms full of sweating, breathing fellow-humans. Have some more coffee.

The Art of Brown Bread
and Vinarterta

"Fat! Fat! Fat! Fat! I am the personal.
Your world is you. I am my world.

You ten-foot poet among inchlings. Fat!"

Wallace Stevens sang my song in "Bantams in Pine-Woods"—
the song of the fat boy, blubber-belly, lard-ass, tub-of-guts,
piled-high-and-deep. He's just big for his age. He's so tall, he
carries it well. He'll trim down when he gets older. No, he
won't. At fifty-two, he's still portly, broad, big-boned-so-you-
don't-notice-it-so-much, large-framed, distinguished, etc. *Fat!
Fat! Fat! Fat!* as jowly Wallace chanted, before our ten-foot
poet among inchlings was born. In 1995, he is the owner of a
middle-aged spread with history; it began spreading in 1945.
Old "built for comfort not for speed." As his beard whitens,
strangers stop him in the street and ask, "Do you work department stores at Christmas?" Or begin chanting at him, "Ho,
Ho, Ho and a bowl full of jelly." Jolly old Saint William with
his marsupial paunch full of the gifts of a lifetime of cream and
butter, and the fat on roasts, and whiskey and chocolate—the
sweet gifts a benevolent god gives us to take and eat, rewards
for braving a life in this vale of skinny tears. In a world where,
as Dorothy Parker said, "you can never be too rich or too thin,"
he is neither, nor will he be. While newspapers and magazines
and junk catalogs fill with ads for Nordic Track and Nutri-
System, he sits quietly with a book and a sandwich, watching,
reading, as H.L. Menken, another portly fellow did, the

obituaries of his friends who exercised and dieted. Whatever is
is right, so sing it! *Fat! Fat! Fat! Fat!*

On the Holm farm, labor divided precisely, a great gulf
fixed. My mother cooked and my father ate. My mother
washed the dishes and reset them. My father napped, his substantial middle bearing the similarly napping gray cat,
Bootsocker, up and down, up and down. My mother did not
enter the tool shop or the barn. She neither would nor could
locate a socket wrench or a pliers. She was a stranger to cow
manure and intended to remain in that state. My father knew a
frying pan existed, but neither its location nor function interested him. Thus the amiable division of their labors.

I was of my father's party, an eater, though I was also of my
mother's party in being incapable of tracking down the pliers. I
lived in the best and the worst of both worlds simultaneously.
A fat, pampered, bookish boy, I got what cant psychology calls
"mixed messages." On the one hand, my plump, pink enormous body got the blame for my laziness, sloth even, sunk in a
book and unmoved by the pleasures of farm work or monkey-
ing with machinery. On the other, the prune whip, creamed
pheasant, lemon pie, bottles of hot fudge sauce, loaves of
brown bread spread with a quarter inch of butter and straw-
berry jam were gifts of love, gratitude even, for a child who
had the courtesy to arrive and exist and show some signs of
mental function. So I ate—and read, and then had a snack.

Only desperation roused my father to cook. My mother's
youngest sister moved east to marry an Irishman who wanted
numberless olive-shoots at his table. During her sister's rapid-
fire pregnancies, my mother would board the Great Northern,
going east for a month to be useful while the two Bill Holms,
Big and Little, found themselves suddenly bereft of roasts,
gravies, and proper pies. Compassionate neighbors helped
with invitations, but a niggling sense of honor always compelled my father to locate the black iron skillet and practice his

recipe. I use the singular carefully. He had one and one only. I'll give it to you.

He threw a pound of ground meat, most often hamburger, but if we were lucky, pork, into the black skillet. After a successful search for the pilot on the gas burner, he even managed to light it. He knew the principles of machines though this one didn't interest him. While the meat fried, he hacked up an onion (sometimes even skinning it . . .), then added it to the bubbling mass. The onion congealed and softened in the hot meat-grease while he attacked the last stage of his recipe. After a search through three or four drawers, he would discover the can opener, then apply it to a big can of Campbell's pork and beans. He dumped the can into the skillet, stirred once and, if fancy moved him, passed the salt and pepper shakers over the now-brownish mass. It swapped around together for a minute, Huckleberry Finn fashion, exchanging flavors and textures. Then he hauled out two plates, a bottle of ketchup, a piece of whatever bread retained its original color and texture, a beer for Big, and a milk for Little. Bon appetit! The recipe was unvarying and eternal. If what was in the frying pan looked a little short for two more helpings, he simply recharged the recipe with fresh infusions of the three ingredients. Why lose the honorable history of the seasonings and blended flavors by cleaning the skillet between batches? The pan sat on the stove in black crusty majesty until my mother came home after three or four weeks, and either washed it or threw away the ghosts of Big Bill's all-purpose hot dish, trusting that Gislason's Hardware would sell her a fresh model. What a joy for me when life resumed its regularity, Jona at the stove and Big Bill back in his domain of cows and combines.

Minnesota and its neighboring states share the dubious honor of being America's chief source of bad-food jokes. In Europe that honor goes to the English. A friend once told the story of his invitation to dinner at the house of a professor in

Devon. He arrived, shook the rain off his coat, complimented the host on a fine garden, drank a small sherry, and was summoned to table: an off-white soup with floating mushrooms, a boiled fish with white sauce, boiled potatoes, a limp, boiled cauliflower with a sort of floury crown, these on a white plate with a crisp white linen table cloth and napkins, and a flagon of white Bordeaux to wash it down. He looked down at the juices mingling on his plate and asked for the pepper. It was white. Though he owned perfectly good dentures, dinner in a thatched cottage in Devon did not require them.

Nor would Minnesota food. The jokes, while funny, are mostly true, and I will resist them. Yes, Jell-O, bars, and a goop called "hot dish" are omnipresent. Yes, it can all be gummed or slurped. Yes, it is unseasoned; one bulb of garlic or one jalepeño pepper lasts a long time in a normal Minnesota kitchen. Yes, a beef commercial is, locally, two slices of white bread, a slab of overcooked pot roast, a scoop of boxed potatoes, a ladle of floury brown gravy over all. Yes, the locals eat this stuff with ketchup. Me, too. Yes, I can take you to lunch this very day in a hundred cafes in easy driving range and we can find these concoctions—and probably fried Spam too—and we can pay our $3.25 and sample it all, washed down with astonishingly thin and colorless coffee, topped off with a piece of not-too-bad pie, probably garnished with a little dollop of Cool Whip; we can get change for our fiver and a toothpick to ream out the gummy patches and stroll out into the ever-present gale-force winds with our choice of snow pellets or soggy humidity, and we can tell withering jokes about gourmet eating in the Midwest. We shall not, however. You are on your own for lunch today.

This is not an essay about the comedy of food, or even the history of my own fat and how it shaped or smothered my life. I mean to think about what food means in the life of a town, a community, a family, a state, a civilization—pick your own boundaries.

We eat, all of us, from necessity and desire. We must eat. We want to eat. We even long to eat. Cravings, whether from stomach or imagination, propel us sometimes to New Orleans or Hong Kong, sometimes to refrigerators in the middle of the night. I read stories of young girls who fear and resist food as a way of loathing their own physical bodies, starving themselves to death in houses stocked with millions of beckoning calories. This is a madness unimaginable to me whose interior food-chimes ring with the precise regularity of a Swiss clock. Offered my last meal on the way to the gallows, I would order two, just in case. If what we eat makes no difference to us, then either we are premature saints, or are already psychologically and spiritually sunk. To live without true desire is not to live at all, whatever the Buddhists may argue.

Virtuous eating infects Americans at the moment. We eat what no sane person could desire in order to reach some amorphous and ethereal "higher good," whether eternal health or political correctness. Desire will neither sink nor elevate us, whatever fashionable illusions we entertain. It is simply desire and makes only the inexorable argument that we are, after all, human. That's it, that's all there is. To long for a crêpe, or a square of old bean curd, or a herring, or a dried Madeline, merely qualifies us as card-carrying higher mammals. The Taoists concocted potions, elixirs, pastes, dishes to ensure longevity, even eternity. These ancient Taoists are all now dead, and their progeny will join them as time goes by. Wait and see. From one angle, at least, we are only the sum total of our meals—a mound of hot dish, vindaloo, pot-au-feu, Wuchang carp, menudo—gone back to earth for thrifty recycling.

How is desire nourished in us and what does the history of our desires tell you about us? Think of lutefisk, not as a joke, but as a desire, a fish with history, a metaphor with tentacles stretched around the life of a community or culture.

Just before Christmas in 1994, the *Minneota Mascot,* the local weekly, ran a story that, as the old line goes, got me thinking.

The front page headline read "Please Pass the Butter; Charlie Wants to Put Away Some Lutefisk." Imagine translating that headline in an English-as-a-Second-Language class in Botswana or Grozny or Malibu! When you have penetrated what that headline actually means, you have slithered inside another corner of your culture and language well past the obvious.

Here is some cultural information to start with. Lutefisk means literally: lye-fish, cod (or some other stock fish) hung in the open air, dried until it resembles an off-white board, then brined in a lye solution. By this time it will keep, probably for centuries. It's cheap, or was before it became a nostalgic fashion in the Midwest, and will keep you alive if the potatoes freeze, the cow dies, and the landlord or the tax collector comes with a warrant. If you clean and soak it meticulously— lye after all is poison—it won't kill you, but it's hard for those born with no cultural connection to imagine being pleased by it. When you boil it, the house fills with a faint smell of lye and fish grown older than nature meant it to. When done, it jiggles slightly in its bowl like softened white rubber. This is Christmas food, appearing in its plastic bags on the fish counter only in November, gone back into its lye bath for another year by February. Small-town Scandinavian churches host lutefisk feeds before Christmas, usually offering meatballs on the side for the sensible. Die-hard Norwegians eat it on Christmas Eve as a family celebration before going off to bellow Christmas carols and open gifts. The Saint Swen's Youth Handbell Choir, playing "It Came Upon a Midnight Clear" in three keys and two-and-half rhythms, is probably the right music to help you digest lutefisk.

Is lutefisk food at all? Marginally—it *can* be eaten, but that is not the point. The fifty percent of nineteenth-century Norway that emigrated and whose descendants now populate the central Midwest eat it, whether consciously or not, to honor their ancestors, the poverty, grief, and uprooting in their own history. Lutefisk means bitter Passover herbs for jackleg Lutherans. It is human, even decent or noble to make a road back into your grandfather's life by lifting the same fork of jiggling odorous fish to your mouth—you in your middle-classness, he in his awful poverty. It is a sort of historical Eucharist when we take and eat the stuff. We change the ancient language of ceremony at our peril. We cannot make what has already happened fashionable, "now," or more to our taste and current opinion. Liturgy is liturgy for good reasons; the Chinese knew what they were doing when they chiseled their ancient philosophy and history onto ten-foot black marble stones standing on an old turtle's back, wreathed at the top by a guardian dragon. These words mean something in human history, the dragon and the turtle say. Touch them at your peril. The smell of lutefisk, a kind of olfactory dragon, wafts the same message through the wintry air.

Back to our headline. Charlie, the lutefisk eater, is an old schoolmate of mine. We were two of the three tallest fellows of the class of 1961, but Charlie is still reasonably gangly, while I had no gangle to start with and never acquired one. He is the head bus-mechanic and director of the school bus garage, a man handy with wrenches and fan belts, and a useful citizen by any definition. And his descent is Norwegian . . .

Madison, Minnesota, thirty-odd miles north of Minneota, claims to be the lutefisk capital of America, proclaiming that fact with a gigantic fiberglass fish in the park along the highway that runs through town. Before Christmas, the town hosts a Norse Festival, one of whose touchstone events is a lutefisk-eating contest. Minneota had never fielded a contestant. Somebody suggested Charlie, prevailed on his good nature, his appetite, and his local patriotism, so off he went to prove himself the Achilles of Lutefisk.

Here's the event described in the words of the local editor:

> The four contestants were seated at a long table, with salt shakers and glasses of water at hand. To eat this much

lutefisk, however, butter was not used. This contest is for the true Scandinavian lutefisk lover!

Three judges were in attendance, with one's job to weigh each batch of lutefisk. Exactly one pound of the white fish was placed on each plate, and then served to the contestants. The whistle blew, and the contestants began to eat.

Said Charlie, "The pound of lutefisk covered the plate, piled in the middle. But it was nice and flaky, and really tasted good." He also mentioned that the fish had to be served at exactly the right temperature, as he soon found out. If the fish was too hot, it would burn the throat as the men ate it so quickly.

The contestants were given five minutes to eat the first batch—and all four did. The curtains on the stage opened, and the gathered people gave them a round of applause. Then the curtains closed, the variety show went on, and the contestants were served another pound of lutefisk.

Again, all the contestants finished their lutefisk in the allotted time. A five-minute break, and the group was ready to go again. The contestants began to eat, and this time everything went a little slower. . . .

Said Charlie, "This is when I failed. I had one little square left of that third pound. I just couldn't eat any more." The other three finished their plate full, and took another five-minute break.

The next contestant stopped on the fourth pound, and two remained. Said Charlie, "They started the fifth pound, but it was slow. One faltered and quit. The Champion from previous years finished that fifth pound, and was declared Champion again.

While the competition took place, video cameras also whirled. One of the tapes is destined for a television talk show, as they are always looking for something unusual. So who knows, we may see this on television one day.

Four grown men behind closed curtains battle mounds of lutefisk on a public stage, applauded between jousts for surviving. They act for the audience and do the town's work—indeed the work of a whole small section of a civilization. They eat history over and over again, pounds of it; they manifest heroic desire in the presence of their neighbors.

We cook and eat not only for ourselves, but as an act of community, of love and necessity. That is true even when we dine alone. The Chinese set a place for the ancestors at their New Year's table, after preparing their favorite dishes. They leave the dead to dine in privacy, a simple enough courtesy toward those who hatched you whether they be dead or alive. After finishing dinner, the ghosts presumably return to the astral spheres, smacking their invisible lips, while the family gathers to finish leftovers and toast their presence. How generous the dead are at table, leaving you the best morsels of the richest dishes!

M. F. K. Fisher, America's greatest poet of food, often tells the old story of Lucullus, the Roman host and famous gourmet, dining alone. One night the staff relaxed a bit; even the sauce for the carp "lacked that tang for which the chef was justly famed." The wine was "a shade too cold." Lucullus summoned the major-domo to complain. The servant explained, "We thought that there was no need to prepare a fine banquet for my lord alone—."

"It is precisely when I am alone," the great gourmet answered, icily, "that you require to pay special attention to the dinner. At such times, you must remember, Lucullus dines with Lucullus."

We respect ourselves and thus our neighbors by paying close attention to our desires. The Puritan streak in America denies this; visible pleasure insults moral earnestness and correct living. Balderdash. That Puritanism is one of the black stones at the heart of our discontent. It is abstract, bloodless, truly dead, unlike the Chinese ancestors. Though we are better off done with it, we show no public signs of letting it die a natural death.

M. F. K. Fisher goes on to tell the story of a modern Lucullus, an old man in the Victor Hugo Restaurant in Paris:

He was dressed carefully in rather old-fashioned dinner clothes, with his feet in tiny twinkling pumps, like a doll's.

He ate little, and drank a half-bottle of wine with his meat. For dessert he went through a never-varying formula with the intensity and detachment of a high priest.

An avocado was brought to him, cradled in a napkin. He felt of it delicately, smelled it, usually nodded yes. It was cut in two with a silver knife. Then he himself detached the stone-skin from each half, placed one part of the fruit gently on a large plate before him, and sent the other back to the kitchen.

Powdered sugar was brought, and the old man pressed it into the hollow of the fruit. He spent some time over this, making it firm and even.

Next the *sommelier* appeared with a bear-shaped bottle of clear Russian *kümmel*. He poured a generous liqueur-glass of it, waited for the old man's sniff of approval, and went away.

Drop by drop the *kümmel* disappeared into the moon of white sugar, very slowly, very patiently. Very delicately it was stirred and pressed down and stirred again.

Finally the old man ate a small spoonful of the smooth green fruit-flesh, then another. Sometimes he stopped, sometimes he finished it. Then he drank a mouthful of coffee and left.

When I finished reading this story, I was, like Fisher herself, half tempted to go and buy an avocado and a bottle of *kümmel,* but I resisted. The dish itself is not quite the point. She says that "Very clear in my memory is the expression in the old man's face. He was happy. . . ." Happy as Lutefisk Charlie's face is happy in the *Mascot* photo above the news story. It is not just lutefisk or *kümmel*-soaked avocados that make us happy. They are the instruments of our unashamed desire.

When is your own face happy like this? That is the question, the point.

As much of a town's history lies buried in its cookbooks as in its tax records, or even its roll call of war dead. I own two of the three cookbooks published by the "Young Ladies Union" of Saint Paul's Icelandic Lutheran Church. The 1905 edition has disappeared from the planet so far as I can tell, like Shakespeare's thirty-eighth play, Beethoven's tenth symphony, Venus de Milo's arms. That first cookbook may have been in Icelandic, though I doubt it. The Icelanders had been here twenty-five years, sent children off to war and college, anglicized their citizenship names, published a town newspaper in sterling Victorian prose, and in general—Americanized. They would never quite get to California, but they would never go home either. There was no more for them to eat in northeast Iceland than there had been when they left. Like so many American immigrant groups, they left the old country not so much for freedom as for dinner. They preferred a more regular arrival of food on the table than was ever possible in Vopnafjörður.

The second edition in 1913 is distinctive mostly for its complete lack of distinction. Aside from the names of some of the young ladies who contributed recipes: Gudmundson, Askdal, Gislason, Bardal, Jokull, etc., it is almost indistinguishable from a church cookbook that might have been published in Ohio, Wisconsin, Vermont, Oregon, Kansas. The south might contribute a few new wrinkles, but no where else. It's peculiarity lies not in "Icelandic" or in "Lutheran" but in "1913." "Take a lump of butter the size of an egg," "Fry in hot lard . . . ," "Take some meat," "Add a pint or so of sweet cream to thicken . . . ," "A pinch of mace, or lemon rind if liked. . . ." The Y.L.U. Cookbook assumes that you have always on hand: "good stock," "sweet drippings," "a jar of butter," "a veal knuckle." The few Icelandic recipes are mixed into the sections with proper gringo recipes. *Vinarterta,* a prune layer-cake, lives with the other cakes harmoniously. *Kleinur* (an Icelandic donut) is in "Breads and Pastries" and *rullupylsa* (a pickled sausage borrowed from the Danes) in "Meats." The old ethnics longed not for "identity" or "self-esteem" but to slip discreetly and harmoniously into the mainstream of pre-First-World-War American life. There was no "butter the size of an egg" to add to the sauce with wild abandon in the kitchen at Haukstaðir—a farm within walking distance of the Polar circle.

I'll give you a couple of gems to remind you what turn-of-the-century cooking was like. Here's a recipe whose name I fancy from Mrs. S.G. Peterson of the Ivanhoe colony of Icelanders.

Veal Wiggle

Three c. veal, 1 pt. cream, 1 can peas (drained), 2 tbs. flour, a lump of butter, pepper and salt to taste. Take cold boiled or roasted veal and chop fine. Put the cream, veal and peas in a stew pan and heat. When it boils, add the butter and flour which have been rubbed together. Season with salt and pepper.

Imagine a veal wiggle presented to a San Francisco-food yuppie!

Here's the soup my mother made whenever anyone was ill. She called it *Saetsúpa* (sweet soup). Mrs. Th. S. Eastman (probably something like Thorlákur Sigfusson Austmann in its original incarnation) translates the title into "Scandinavian Soup."

One large cup sago, 1 lb. raisins, 1 lb. currants, 1 lb. good prunes, 1 tbs. vinegar, pinch of salt and several cinnamon sticks, add sugar to taste and water to make like thick sauce. Cook several hours. Just before serving take out cinnamon and add 1 pt. good red wine. Keep thin with water.

When my mother was diagnosed with melanoma in her sixties, she came back to her house and made a batch of this soup. My cousin who lived upstairs smelled the soup and realized immediately that she had received a sentence of death. The soup didn't work its magic, but then neither did a couple of hundred thousand dollars worth of neo-scientific fol-de-rol. The soup had at least the virtue of being cheap and pleasant to the tongue. Presumably Jona enjoyed it. Try it yourself—you don't need melanoma as an excuse.

The third and last pure edition of the Young Ladies Union Cookbook appeared in 1926; no legal glasses of red wine in the sweet soup now, no infusions of brandy in the *Vinarterta*. Now the book is in a practical ring binder; a few veal knuckles and butter lumps still appear, but the tablespoon, the measuring cup, and the packaged mix have advanced. There's still not a single oven temperature—your oven was either on or off. A few of the ads even list phone numbers: Dalmann's Grocery announces that "We deliver your purchases, and our phone is 33. Call us. We are here to serve you." You seldom see sentences like that in the Thrift Club Warehouse Market.

What had not changed were the names of the Y.L.U. members. When I was a boy in the forties and fifties, the Y.L.U. still met and functioned. Originally, it was intended only as a stepping stone to Ladies' Aid, the church club for august and properly married women. But few of the Y.L.U. ever married nor did their numbers increase. A few died, a few moved, but most of them simply aged. I suppose the average age of the Y.L.U. as I first remember them was sixty or more. By now, as the century gets ready to turn again, only a few members are left. One is ninety-eight. Even the Ladies' Aid, once the repository of congregational vigor, has an average age well over seventy. So do the unmeltable ethnics dissolve into the stream of American life. They age, they go, and there is something else. All that's left? Maybe only a stack of old cookbooks, a few choice recipes.

I like the modesty of Mrs. J. G. Isfeld's title for bread. She understood, by instinct I suppose, that single vision does no more good in making bread than in making politics, religion, or the life of a community.

One Good Way of Making Bread

Pour 1 pt. potato water into a jar and add to it while hot ⅓ c. sugar. When lukewarm add yeast (1 cake makes 4 or 5 loaves). Mix well, cover and let stand in warm place over night. In morning add 1½ qts. water or scalded and cooled milk, salt and shortening and flour to make a sponge. Set to rise. When light (in 1½ to 2 hours) add more flour and knead to rather a stiff dough. Let rise again and knead down. When light make into loaves and let rise about an hour. Bake 1 hour. The room should be free from draughts and the temperature warm and even. This recipe was a great help to me many years ago. I hope it will interest some young housekeeper.

This essay has so far hidden its true subject with anecdote, speculation, and digression, but I will now, like a poor poker player, show you my hole card and hope for the best. You are reading a long preface to recipes for *Vinarterta* and brown bread. What is *Vinarterta*, you sensibly ask? It is, I suppose, an immigrant Icelander's version of lutefisk—or *jiaozi,* or *vindaloo,* or *perogi,* or *latke,* or whatever ties you into your imagination of your own history in a place. Here's Mrs. Pete Jokull's version in the 1926 cookbook. I know this recipe has been lovingly made a thousand times; the cookbook falls open to the page after seventy years and written in the margin in the squiggly hand of my mother's old friend Pauline Bardal is the gloss: "Bake at 350 degrees, 10 to 15 min." Pauline, unlike Mrs. Jokull, lived into the age of the modern oven with its optimistic temperature gauge and automatic timer.

Vinarterta

1 c. shortening, 2 c. sugar, 4 eggs, ½ c. sour cream, 1 ts. each soda, B.P., cardamom, vanilla, 6 c. flour. Cream butter and sugar, beat in eggs one at a time, add cream and dry ingredients. Roll and bake in layers. Filling: Stew 2 lbs. prunes until stones can be removed, return to juice, boiling until prunes can be mashed. Add ½ c. sugar. Juice of ½ lemon or any fruit juice or nutmeg may be added. Thicken with cornstarch if too thin. This makes 2 cakes, 5 layers each.

Say *Vinarterta* in a room full of the descendants of North American Icelandic immigrants and quarrels begin. In Canada, *Vinarterta* is in six or seven layers, flavored with almonds, frosted with butter cream—wrong! One lady (with a Norwegian half in her family) used apricots instead of prunes between layers—wrong! Some leave out cardamom—oh-so-spicy, you know—wrong! A fearless and large-hearted Icelander in Minneapolis spikes her prunes with bourbon or brandy. This is daring and unconventional—the bobbed hair or pierced ears of *Vinarterta*-dom—but it might possibly be right.

Now, mention *Vinarterta* in a room full of real Icelanders from the genuine Old Country, and they'd give you a quizzical look? *"Vinarterta? Hvað er það? Ekki Íslenska!" Vinarterta?* What is that? It's not Icelandic. They've heard of it, but not in any form recognizable to North American descendants. In Iceland, it's a cheap bakery item—not for company. The word itself merely means Vienna cake—something in layers on the Austrian model probably arrived in nineteenth-century Iceland via the Danish colonial landlords who owned eggs, butter, cream, fruit, and brandy in quantities sufficient to pile them in layers. Prunes and a simple cookie dough flavored with cardamom hardly seem to them worth the trouble of sentimental preservation. Yet I am as attached to the last crumb of an old *Vinarterta* as Proust ever was to his stale madeline, and my number is legion in my own generation, in Minneota, and (I almost add) among sensible people of discriminating taste anywhere on the planet. Perhaps that is an exaggeration; perhaps not. A proper *Vinarterta* makes me happy, like Fisher's old man in the Victor Hugo cafe, and that is a truth that passeth all argument and understanding.

The history of *Vinarterta* probably bears bad news to the new multicultural and ethnically alert. Once the great sea change to America takes place without your permission or conscious compliance—and it seems to begin to happen almost instantly as soon as the first ancestor breathes New World air or takes a stroll through New World grass—you have become that confused and partly unsatisfactory species of human: the American. You aren't hyphen-anything; you're a sort of grand mess. You have inherited irony and the necessity to use your imagination, whether you think you need it or not. All your neighbors, no matter how odd or unsatisfying they may look to you, are in your boat—with an oar in their black, brown, yellow, pink, or tan hands. Row quizzically, my brethren, toward we know not where: the great pow-wow of history with some hot jazz playing while the Declaration of Independence and the IRS audit form flash in neon lights and an old lady with her hair in a bun stands at the back of a church basement folding table full of *Vinarterta* beckoning you to take and eat with her arthritic flour-dusted hands and her rheumy maternal eye. The prunes will do you more good than bran fiber, organic wheat germ, or macrobiotic miso, and the cardamom will bring excitement and danger to your life. The butter won't hurt you either, whatever any damn fool says.

The last edition of the Minneota Icelandic Church Cookbook appeared in 1965. The nostalgic ghost of the actual Y.L.U. cookbook lives in it, but by now the Y.L.U. is well over seventy, the Icelandic synod has died away, and the church itself is only Saint Paul's, "formerly Icelandic Lutheran." The preface announces its function "to perpetuate the traditional foods of this cultural group . . . but will add newer western delicacies that can happen only in an American cooking pot." All that's left of immigrant life are *Vinarterta, kleinur,* and thin pancakes. The western delicacies include: Ice-Box Muffins, Can't-Fail Caramels, Chicken Chow Mein (with two cans of Campbell's soup, celery and mushroom), Low-Calorie Vegetable Soup, Tuna One-Dish Meal, and Lazy-Day Hot Dish (with optional onion, and salt only, no pepper). Oven temperatures are precisely noted, and there are no more butter lumps scooped out of a tub. Now it's margarine by the pre-measured stick. Telephone numbers are four digits now, a hundred percent Great Leap Forward. "Call Bob Alleckson at 6491 for home delivery of Oak Grove dairy products." "Nordquist and Bourgeois, funerals and fine furniture, dial 4241." Progress has marched inexorably onward, a grim, steely cast to its mouth and an ice-cold eye. It has just eaten Chop Suey made with two cans of soup, finished off with a couple of Coconut Macaroon Cup Cakes, wiped crumbs from its thin lips, and decreed the end of the New World Icelanders. This will be the last of "those" books from "those" people, thank-you very much. And so it was, sang Civilization as she put another mile or two on her odometer.

What are my credentials to give you recipes? I eat and show visible evidence of that fact. Sometime in my thirties, I even began life as a cook and have come, after twenty years of practice to possess reasonable, if limited, skill at it, enough to talk sauces, larding needles, and *mirepoix,* to join in arguments about the relative merits of flour and cornstarch, fresh grated nutmeg or tinned, and the quality of wine in the stew. What has lead the only son of my principled father to travel so far into the domain of women? As is so often true of change and reformation in a man's life, not ideology, but necessity. I ran out of cooks before I had exhausted the desire to eat.

As a young man, I went plumply from the custody of mother to wife, both skilled cooks and devoted attenders on the daily needs of husbands and sons. Then in my thirties, within a year or two, one died and one left, and I found myself standing in a kitchen, alone and hungry. Lightning did not exactly strike me on the road to Damascus, but a certain mental turning occurred. I could read, I could taste and smell; with some practice I might even be able to chop, boil, stir, add and correct seasoning. A love of music and desperate privacy had driven me to a passionate life with the piano; why shouldn't the love of eating be able to work as well with a stove? I opened *The Joy of Cooking* and Julia Childs' *Mastering the Art of French Cooking*, patted my fat tenderly, and have never looked back.

My mental picture of a table began with my life on the farm, and aside from refinements and additions, it has probably not changed much in its Platonic form since my childhood. On a throne at the center stands something majestic with a bone: a roast of pig or cow or sheep or a whole bird, chicken, duck, or goose, or in hunting season, a pheasant or a haunch of deer. Paying tribute in their steaming bowls that encircle the bone, sit potatoes in some incarnation, a vegetable or two, softened then thickened with cream, a bowl of gravy, a bowl of whipped cream with whatever fruit could be plucked fresh from the can that day, a neat stack of brown bread, soaker of juices, a bowl of butter, and tributary bowls of pickles and condiments, watermelon rinds, blood-red vinegary beets, small cucumbers, horseradish. The queen, a lemon pie, is dressing in her chambers and will make an appearance after a while to sweeten and charm the retainers.

I make only one profound change in this metaphor. My father worked his way toward the roast with a whiskey or two (no change there!) and sometimes washed dinner down with a beer; but wine was only for the old, the sick, the cowardly, and the sentimental. I populate the table with a bottle of good red wine, standing unashamed next to the bony throne of roast. By such small gestures does civilization advance. Paint a good picture in your mind's eye to begin, then refine and improve the details. That's a not a bad philosophy of cooking—or of writing, composing, inventing, legislating, worshipping, or loving either.

If you operate out of the solid base of this metaphor, vegetarianism will come to seem not merely a failure of taste and imagination, but even a kind of moral aberration. What sort of higher mammal with presumption to intellectual functions are you that you imagine life without bones? You have them, then chew them; they will nourish you. G. B. Shaw and I would have had interesting chats on this question over boiled eggs and brown bread finished off with a slab of the Queen's pie. He had as vigorous a mental picture of a table as any Scandinavian farmer. I would have drawn a mental line in the sand at lunch with his fellow vegetarian, Hitler. That mind had no mental pictures at all, but rather a black shroud covering the true imagination. A favorite cousin of my father's refused all vegetables except a dab of potato. "Corn," he said, "is, strictly speaking, indigestible by human beings. That's why I prefer to run it through the pig first. Pass the pork roast and a little more gravy, please." He died in his late eighties still owning a good appetite.

The status of cooking as an art, or at least a craft requiring skill, imagination, and intelligence, has risen immensely since my childhood. If you said "cook" to an American in the forties or fifties, the face of Betty Crocker materialized in the mental eye—old Betty with her freshly beauty-shopped hair, her benign, even vacant smile, and her crisp white nursely collar. That face knew the seven basic food groups, and where to find the canned soup for a shortcut sauce; that face gave multiple choice exams in seventh grade Home Ec. and ordered you to spit out your gum and sit up straight. That face wanted cheerful conversation at table, something that might please the Vice President and his absently smiling wife and daughters while making one-of-the-gang jokes about cottage cheese and ketchup and sweet boiled dressing for the canned pineapple salad. That was the voice of The American Way.

But some benevolent worm turned in American public life,

and television, for once, probably had something good to do with it. Say "cook" now, and the large gawky intelligent face and hooty voice of Julia Childs clicks in, fresh from a joyous whack at a *Coquilles St. Jacques ala Provencale* or a *Coq-au-Vin* or a *Charlotte Aux Pommes.* That face is handing you a glass of a perfectly drinkable côte-du-rhone, inviting you to a table of finely crafted dishes—a sensual delight on the order of a Mozart serenade. That is the voice of true civilization, of irony, of high-spirited talk with literature and political sarcasm and bawdy wit and flirting and adventurous traveling inside it. How different from the voice of mere respectability, of bourgeois stodginess, of wholesome food for busy families. How uncomfortable, thank God, the Vice President would have felt at that table. Fine cigars—probably smuggled from Havana— were about to be smoked after that dinner and cognac drunk in big thin snifters.

Cooking now reached out a firm hand and welcomed men into the club, even here in the United States. France and China, the two great old repositories of gastronomic wisdom, always understood cooking as a manly art. But here the news made its sea change with Julia and with the ambrosial essays of M. F. K. Fisher. What a fine paradox! Women, one more time, making gifts to men. Fisher, a woman of class and style, would put Betty Crocker in the back closet where she belonged, once and for all. Clubs always do better when they get larger—more inclusive, less full of judgment, dogma, cant. Religions and political movements and fashionable end-of-the-century ideologies might learn something here. If you want an art to be practiced intelligently, drain the opinions out of your crankcase, cultivate humor, and invite everyone. The only two requirements are a sense of joy and of irony. Nothing else needed, though a little genius is nice.

Intelligent women who cooked, of course, always knew this—silently, wisely, with the magnificent alertness of a sleeping tiger. They put their Betty Crocker on the shelf should

J. Edgar Hoover or a Hauge Synod minister arrive for coffee, ignored her, and went about their business, calmly adding a pinch of this or a jigger of that, feeling the butter under their hands, letting their eye follow lovingly the marbling labyrinth of fat that circled lazily through proper meat. Every town, maybe every family, had and has its touchstone cooks—artists with flour, yeast, apples, shoulders, loins, breasts. You know them too. Think for a minute. Take a private Rorshach. What mental picture, or smell or face or pair of hands, comes to your interior eye when I say: bread . . . ginger cookies . . . a chicken frying in a black skillet . . . a meringue rising toward heaven . . . vegetable soup on a blustery day. I'll try to conjure one of those cooks that I knew and loved and give you a recipe or two to try, but while I'm at it, do a little of your own conjuring. If you've got about a half-century of mileage on you, those cooks are probably women—pre-Julia America. But if you are a son maybe they are women anyway. A table may be a man's first and best experience of affection, civilization, and its un-expected complications that both bedevil and instruct us.

My Auntie Clarice could never have been mistaken for something other than what she was: a Scandinavian, a farmer's wife, a mother, a small-town Lutheran, a quilter, a cook. She had the look of someone for whom the apron, the knitting needle, and the spatula were not adornments or accidents of fate but a part of the body itself grown into the skin like some miraculously speedy operation of natural selection.

But to the everyday eye, she was just a tall blond woman al-ready grown heavy—not fat, but majestic—in middle age when I first knew her. She was Auntie, not by blood, but by marriage to my mother's older brother Adalbjorn Josephson, called always Abo by his neighbors and relatives. Not only was she not Icelandic, and therefore in a mixed-marriage, she was herself a product of race-mixing: Her father was Norwegian and her mother Swedish. By such ominous increments does the mongrelization of America proceed, the racial sins of the

fathers visited unto the children, and one thing invariably leading to another. Keep this up and God knows what relatives
Americans might accumulate. It is a slippery slope. Clarice
once told me the story of the quarrel leading up to her wedding to Uncle Abo in 1929. Abo announced (in Icelandic) to
his immigrant father Herman Vigfus that he was going to
marry a Christianson girl from Minneota. His father eyed him
sarcastically and inquired, *"Getur þu ekki gifts Islending?"*
(Couldn't you find an Icelander to marry?). But Clarice's humane charms, and probably her brown bread, soon worked
their magic on her father-in-law and he died thinking Abo had
married upward. My mother and father stood up at Clarice
and Abo's wedding, and the old photo of the four of them is
one of my treasures—the pale blond Dorothy-Parker-thin-
Clarice in her flapper dress, the brilliantined Abo looking like
an Icelandic Rudolph Valentino or a Chicago mobster gone
straight, my rumpled rakish father in a rare necktie, and Jona,
my mother at nineteen, her red hair Clara Bow-ed and a mysterious privacy in her eyes. The four remained lifelong neighbors and friends. Clarice and Abo's children arrived mostly in
the middle of the Depression, and Clarice had just finished
winding up motherhood in the early forties when my mother
entered the business.

My early memories of Auntie Clarice are always connected
to a kitchen. She is reaching into a stove, setting bowls on the
table, buttering bread, turning chicken in a black pan, mixing
coffee grounds with a beaten egg, dribbling frosting over
something. She was responsible, of course, for the whole
house; but I was a child, a farm-work-avoider, an avid eater.
Kitchens in old Minnesota farm houses were often the only
truly warm room in winter. They smelled lovely—at least
Clarice's did. They were the middle earth between the ma-
nured overalls and five-buckle boots of the porch, and the
starched and disinfected parlor with its crocheted slip covers,
heads of dead relatives, and green lampshades.

Clarice was not a farm girl, but a Townie. Her father Carl, the Norwegian, worked as a lineman for Great Northern, repairing track and bridges. Jim Hill's kind-hearted benevolence and public spirit didn't extend to his employees, so Carl's salary fell a good deal short of princely. Clarice's mother, Anna, the Swede, came to America with her father who worked in the mines in Colorado until that likewise princely salary moved him to find farmland around Minneota. Anna bore Carl ten children, seven sons and three daughters, and while he repaired bridges in western South Dakota or wherever, she raised and tended them. Clarice was baptized early into work—cooking, weeding, canning, wood chopping, lamp cleaning, laundering by hand. Like so many women of her generation, it never occurred to her to complain of poverty, hard and brainless work, too many mouths, too few rooms, too little butter, too much weather. That was life and you lived it and, as the Icelanders said, *"Það er nefnilega það"*—That is namely that."

Clarice was raised stoic more than Lutheran, and in that resembled most of her neighbors. In middle age, she had a bout of what used to be called "nerves," and disappeared for a while into the "sanitarium." Making believe that depression was tuberculosis was a local euphemism, not quite a lie since in small towns everyone knows everything. Just dress a fact up in its Sunday suit, scrub its face and hands, and instruct it to behave itself in public. Clarice emerged from her depression, and that was, indeed, that. Abo retired from farming though he continued active in the hog-selling and margarine-smuggling business. They moved to town into the house vacated by the death of Abo's oldest brother, August, and Clarice reorganized a new kitchen to her satisfaction, turned on the oven, and kneaded a large batch of brown bread.

When my father died in 1966, Clarice cooked and consoled her old classmate, Jona. When Jona died in 1975, she cooked again and consoled Jona's only son with brown bread, caramel rolls, lefse, *Vinarterta,* dinner on Sunday. She seemed worried that her orphaned nephew might starve. When Abo lay dying in 1981, the Lutheran minister came to pray and visit them. Abo's dying had been a long ordeal, and Clarice never left his side—not for years. She had probably kept him alive much past his celestial appointment with brown bread, vegetable soup, and endless patience. The minister, meaning to express kind feelings, thus giving her an easy opening to unload her grief and frustration, asked if she didn't find her long sick-bed duty difficult. Insofar as Clarice was capable of iciness, she fixed him with a chilly look, and said, "Of course not," in a tone one uses for obtuse children who failed to notice the obvious, and that was that. I hardly remember a funeral without Clarice in her apron, cutting sandwiches, lifting brownies from a pan, slicing cake, doing her business in the church kitchen with her "circle," then afterwards appearing at the house of the bereaved with bread, pastries, and roast chicken. One of her sons who moved away has thought about the irony of this protocol for years. First you die, then everyone eats. When news of death arrived, Clarice turned on the stove and swung into action. What did it mean? Death be damned, somebody is still alive and hungry; "life goes on" sings the oldest cliché of all. It is a good tune. We shouldn't weary of it easily. Clarice certainly didn't.

Sherwood Anderson noticed the connections between death and feeding in his great short story "Death in the Woods." One harsh winter day, a poor old woman dragging old bones and meat scraps begged from a butcher to feed her men and animals, takes a shortcut through the woods, gets tired, rests under a tree, goes to sleep and freezes to death. Her dogs drag the body into a clearing, take the bag of scraps and bones, strip her of her clothes, and leave her naked but untouched in the snow while they circle the body in a strange sort of ancient mammalian ceremony of praise, gratitude, something older, who knows? Anderson's narrator has thought about this story, this scene, all his adult life, trying to get it to come right in his head and reveal itself. He thinks:

> Well, things had to be fed. Men had to be fed, and the horses . . . and the poor thin cow. . . .
> The whole thing, the story of the old woman's death, was to me as I grew older like music heard from far off. The notes had to be picked up slowly one at a time. Something had to be understood.
> The woman who died was one destined to feed animal life. . . . when my brother told the story that night when we got home and my mother and sister sat listening, I did not think he got the point. He was too young and so was I. A thing so complete has its own beauty.

What, indeed, is the point? What is the beauty or completeness in this? The faint suggestion these days that the notion of feeding as a vocation and "woman" might appear in the same sentence will summon Euripides' furies to do what furies do. And yet . . . Clarice, as a human, contained the usual multitudes. She had been a good student and proud enough of her high school work to have saved her A+ essay on *Hamlet* for well over sixty years. In a juster, newer world, she would have trotted off to college on scholarship and gotten a real education; but given poverty, the Depression, her immigrant culture, and Abo, she contented herself with wide reading and making sure her children went off to Lutheran colleges. She read my books devotedly and was one of my most intelligent and exacting critics. She disapproved of two things in language: exaggeration and profanity. She was proud of her eccentric nephew but kept notes. After I'd written a book of Chinese adventures in which I quoted my own angry, grandly cussing voice for humorous effect, she confessed to one of her children that she had kept meticulous count. Little Billy had used the G.D.–word sixty-seven times, the SH–word twenty-one times, and even the F–word once. He needn't have done that, she said. He's smart enough to think of the right way to say things. I was, in fact, honored and delighted by Auntie Clarice's criticism, but I would never have had manners bad enough to have confessed it to her. She had more of the Hauge Synod in her than the Icelanders did, and there was nothing to be done—that was namely that. Besides, on reading of my lonesomeness for *Vinarterta,* she brought me one, apologizing that it wasn't one of her best, and it if it was no good, I could just throw it. It was ambrosial—and she knew damn well it was!

I imagine that Clarice's own mother, Anna, didn't so much teach her to cook as allow her to absorb the act of cooking by osmosis, since her function in the house was to be in the presence of food as it was kneaded, chopped, brined, stuffed, lifted into and out of heat and cold. Cookbooks (or domestic science books) are an ancient literary genre, but from *Mrs. Beeton's Household Hints* to the latest California pasta contraption that gives you exhaustive instructions on making glorified macaroni and cheese—noodles reborn with virtue, jargon, and pretense—they are a last resort, not a proper education. If you have not absorbed what you ought to know without language, self-consciousness, compulsion, or credentials, then you will have to resort to a book to remedy the hangover of a misspent or deprived youth. Real cooks practice their art with offhand skill and gaiety before it ever occurs to them that they are doing something less natural than breathing or moving limbs or speaking in complete sentences. If you have to ask—or be taught—you'll probably never get the point, as Duke Ellington said of jazz. By the time Fritz Kreisler or Arthur Rubenstein owned their first long pants, the question—when did you start playing and how did you master music so elegantly?—would have made no sense to them. In the dark of my mother's womb? Before my first tooth forged down from gum to the bright air? Would you like to hear a minuet of Padre Martini? Or a Chopin etude? Please pass the watermelon pickles and the crust on the end of that loaf. As a grown man, I *can* cook: I *can* even play the Chopin Etude after a fashion. But I am not a cook, nor am I a pianist. I know something about table and piano. Clarice, on the other hand, was most certainly a cook, although she never used the actual verb or noun in normal speech. She did not cook supper; she fixed it. The eternal form of supper already lived in her head; she merely tinkered with details as she went about fashioning its body and bringing it to table to take and eat.

Having lived through that process—a kind of unconscious apprenticeship in the Guild of Cooks (or as her own mother might have said: of woman, of human being), she passed it on to her own daughter. I doubt she thought that was what she was doing. She thought she was being a mother, or to broaden the circle again, being normal. We seem these days to have lost track of the fact that "normality" is not a political statement nor is it ordained by God in some secret text owned only by your most fanatical right-wing neighbors. It is the accumulation over thousands of years—maybe millions—of what one generation has taught another about survival on a planet full of sometimes harsh surprises. The boundaries of "normal" are larger than any of us imagine; our job before death is not to use the word as a blunt instrument to cudgel our neighbors into a shape more like what we imagine our own, but to stand in awe and wonder at its presence and use our powers of reason to try to understand it so that we can praise with more intelligence. "Normal" is brown bread; it is not talk radio.

My cousin Marilyn describes the scene in the farm kitchen over fifty years ago. While Clarice went through the steps of the yeasting, rising, punching and kneading of dough, she brought a chair into the kitchen and set a small pan—a sort of Suzuki-method bread dish on the counter, tiny Marilyn's trainer pan. With Marilyn next to her standing on the chair to reach the bread board, Clarice pulled off a corner of dough sized for a child's hands and mother and daughter kneaded together: Not so hard, keep a regular rhythm, roll the dough away from you, your hands need a little more flour, more flour on the board, just a drop or two of water, this is what it should feel like now, punch it down, see how it rises, now shape the loaf, put it in the pan this way, give it room, be careful not to drop it, this is how hot the oven should be, take it out now, doesn't it look nice? Doesn't it smell good? There's the butter. Let's have some before the men come in from chores.

Were the Renaissance painters who mastered the art of those endless pietas and adorations normal? Or the children who conquered the notes to sing and play Bach's cantatas every Sunday morning in Leipzig? Or the nameless carpenters who did the elegant oak cabinet work in fine old houses in Minneota and learned to feel the grain and shine and joining of wood? Is that normality? Maybe things are supposed to go on and on in this way if the world works right, turning on its axis properly.

When Marilyn finished telling the saga of her apprenticeship in bread, she said, "I've still got the little pan upstairs, do you want to see it?" I didn't have to, but it comforted me to know it was there. What genius in Clarice's method! It kept a child happy, quiet, and useful. It taught a skill that, like a foreign language, is best mastered before self-consciousness destroys the hour of splendor in the grass; and finally, it gave birth to proper bread—an incontrovertible good in this vale of tears and tasteless "boughten" wonder product.

Clarice's son, Charles, was one of the men out in the barn, riding the baler, or cutting pigs while the mysterious bread bubbled and rose in the darkness, the secret realm of mother and sister. He moved off the farm to Chicago, but the sensible longing for his mother's bread haunted him. One Saturday afternoon, he literally took matters into his own hands and started bread dough. Among other things, he discovered that a strong intelligence, several advanced degrees, a career as a book editor, reasonable skill as a keyboard player and singer, and gastronomical longing will not teach your hands the proper feel of the dough, nor will it teach you what is not in a simple prose recipe. No piece of paper can ever teach the one crucial, necessary skill in cooking, as in music or language—improvisation, spontaneity, knowing how to "make do," to invent something else that will work, to remain open to the infinite currents of the universe (Emerson's transcendental eye), to trust intuition, to practice forgetfulness and strict attention together, or as Clarice might have put it more simply and truly: "You just know—then you do it."

Charles was reduced to the telephone, an unsatisfactory substitute for a fragrant kitchen, floury hands, a voice. But in desperation, we make do. He called his mother many times asking: How is it supposed to feel now? When do you punch it down? What happens if it rises too fast? When is it ready to go? What do I need to know that's not in the recipe? Clarice did her best by long distance, and after a few false starts and botched tries, her son managed bread that was a reasonable facsimile of his mother's. AT&T was happy, and for a little while the quality of bread in south Chicago rose, making it a more fragrant and delicious place.

Learning the language of bread is a little like learning Chinese—indeed any foreign language. It is one thing to read about the four tones of Mandarin or the nine of Cantonese in a do-it-yourselfer book, but it is quite another thing to make those noises accurately if you have never heard a human being utter them. I doubt anyone ever learned to speak intelligible Chinese without hearing it, preferably from a native speaker who unconsciously made the tones. If you wanted rice, you said "fan." If you didn't say it properly, no one would give you rice. That is the true foundation of learning. Small children carted off to China on their parents' teaching expeditions learned flawless accentless Chinese in a few months, without having any idea what a tone was. They learned to read packages without having the foggiest notion of radicals or stroke numbers. Meanwhile, their parents drudged gloomily along on: *Ni hao, Ni chr fan ma?*, the distinction between *tz, dz,* and *ts,* and the rising and bending tones. Little children, like small Marilyn in the farm kitchen, were rewarded by nature and happy circumstance with their own internal bread dish, their own mother's hands inside their still unselfconscious consciousness. Past a certain and very early point, humans never master a foreign language without an accent or without mammoth labor. Our ear atrophies young. Do the nerve ganglia in your hands that can feel bread under the fingers age as quickly? With what labor we try to quicken them in middle age!

After this long exhalation of language and speculation, you shall have your recipe for brown bread. Do you think it will be simple? It is Pandora's box—a conundrum, an inpenetrable paradox, a quandary, a spiritual exercise, a Zen koan. Take this recipe or recipes far enough into the sphere of unreason and you shall have murder, war, fire, and apocalypse. Start anywhere and this might happen. Humans, only peripherally conscious most of the time, should remind themselves to practice reverence for the few things they've partly mastered, to cultivate modesty, humor, curiosity in the presence of bread as in the presence of politics or religion. Eschew certainty, experiment fearlessly, expect little, be grateful for everything. There. Now, you are ready for brown bread, and after that *Vinarterta*—your reward.

Here is Clarice's Ur-recipe, typed on a now-brittle yellow index card and filed in her recipe box soon after her marriage in 1929.

Brown Bread

6 cups water
2 cakes yeast
2 cups graham flour

1 cup sugar
1 cup lard
1 cup molasses
2 tablespoons salt
White flour

Dissolve yeast in one cup lukewarm water. Add to the other
ingredients and enough white flour to make a stiff dough.
Let rise about two hours and knead down to let rise another hour when it is ready to make into loaves.

Much is left unsaid here. It represents a kind of private
shorthand, useful to those who already know what they are
doing. There is a kind of terse, gnomic poetry in this recipe as
in the language of so many old recipes, whether for bread or
spiritual enlightenment. Only the gist—never the steps or the
variations or the possibilities. "Go ye therefore and do unto
your neighbor as you would have him do unto you." Now
there's an ethical recipe with loopholes and room for
argument . . .

In 1979, after that recipe had aged for fifty years, Clarice
found herself interviewed for a local oral-history book. She
confessed that she had revised her recipe, substituted rye for
graham flour, oil for lard, added whole wheat to the white
flour, and introduced oatmeal and cold milk. She told the interviewer in typical Clarice phlegmatic fashion, "I've tied it in
with the Icelandic and it's worked out all right. . . . If you
wanted to change it to Swedish *limpa,* just add orange rind,
anise, or caraway." Get a clear mental picture of bread, then
you can monkey with details until the Second Coming.
Recipes are organic and alive as bread itself. Their function is
not closure, but germination.

Clarice gives the interviewer one valuable cautionary sentence, "It's best to put it in the middle of the table so if it spills
over—if you put plastic over it you can oil the top—and then a
cloth over that—then it won't dry out." Bread grows. It is alive

and moving! If you don't watch it, it will take over! Notice the fractured syntax of Clarice's sentence. She was an intelligent woman who spoke clearly and correctly in brief parsable sentences. Those halting phrases are the record of a mind at thought, trying to bring to consciousness an automatic action, asking itself: Now what in the hell do I, in fact, do?

When her son made his phone calls for bread lore from Chicago to Minneota, he pried a few trade secrets out of his mother. She confessed that her recipes were as much a matter of touch, chance, and timing as of measurement. "Sometimes I throw in a handful of Cream of Wheat. . . . You have to feel the butter to know how to use it. Sometimes it's different. . . . Always let the bread rise before you add salt, because it hurts the rise. The yeast doesn't like salt." To make bread you must be a chemist, a biologist, a diplomat, a massage therapist, a psychologist, a poet. And cooks disingenuously claim their art is less than painting, music, philosophy, literature! What would a mere novelist do in the face of angry yeast or peculiar butter?

My mother lived only a few houses away from Clarice and Abo and when I came home on holiday, we often joined them for Christmas Eve supper. Abo was by this time ill and sensibly not pleased with that state. He was cranky and frustrated, more interested in pork-belly futures than in taking his pills or being carved at by surgeons. Clarice always made lutefisk because Abo liked it, so I endured it silently; but once I had a curious small epiphany as I watched her come out of the kitchen with dish after dish: meatballs, scalloped corn, gravy, fresh brown bread, last summer's rhubarb sauce, pies, *Vinarterta,* lefsa with brown sugar and butter. The food existed to soothe and calm Abo, to keep alive the possibility of praise and pleasure in his life, as long as it could be managed. Abo was in the process of being fooled into thinking he was enjoying himself. The fooling worked so well that he did. "Now that's brown bread!" "Pretty good lutefisk this year. . . ." "Don't you eat it,

Billy?" I picked politely at a corner of the jiggling fish, asked for another meatball and sopped up the gravy with a slice of brown bread, waiting patiently to begin on the *Vinarterta*.

Clarice went on cooking even after Abo's death when she had nobody left to fool. She cooked for her children, their children, her brothers, her neighbors, the church bake sale, the quilter's club, her plump nephew. Years later, when her own death was imminent, she went on cooking, though by this time her pleasure in eating must have disappeared. Walt Whitman, old and sick in Camden, went on writing small poems until the day he died, knowing perfectly well he had finished his real genius work years before. But if a man was a poet, he wrote poetry, even after the tenth stroke. Poetry was not a duty, not a drudge job, but a way to be alive in the world. You no more set your pencil down than stop breathing. When Clarice went to the hospital for the last time, her daughter came home and found a half-finished pan of something on the stove. It took a few days for her to summon courage to throw it away.

The aristocracy of cooks passes its mantle from generation to generation without ceremony. When one dies, another is born. The town now agrees that Jeanette Konold is the new local empress of the stove. She is my source of brown bread. Her Icelandic brown bread is perfect; her *Vinarterta* almost, though not quite, matchless. Here's a fact for the multicultural squad. Jeanette is neither an Icelander nor a Scandinavian, nor a Lutheran; she is a patriotic Belgian. It's white jazz, Irish silence, the disorderly Japanese, the Chinese spendthrift, and the Swedish sense of natural rhythm. Genius is genius as any damn fool knows, and its appearance is a matter of luck, not genetic engineering. And bread is bread if you know how to make it.

I asked Jeanette if she could remember learning how to cook. Her answer was what I think Clarice's would have been had anybody asked her. "No." She paused and thought a bit, "I cooked with my mother when I was little, and learned more in 4-H, but I always just cooked. Every time I put my hands on something, it tasted all right." When Mozart fingered a harpsichord for the first time, his father heard genius. Music already existed in his hands; whatever he touched sounded all right. I asked Jeanette if she ever had failures in the kitchen. She said that she once quit cooking for a while, maybe a few months, and when she came back to it, the feel of bread dough under her hands was strange, a little awkward. "If you don't keep it up, you lose your touch." Mozart practiced continually too — even though he complained. Great gifts are often great weights, as much burden as joy. I asked Jeanette the secret of brown bread, why it was Icelandic rather than Belgian or Ukranian or Absaroka. "I use Runa Anderson's recipe from the Y.L.U. cookbook, and she was an Icelander." How simple truth is — sometimes. Runa lived with her daughter Sibby who had a beauty shop in one wing of their house. While the globe dryers whirred over curled heads with *Redbooks* in their laps, the smell of bread and cookies mingled with the whiff of permanent wave solution. Runa was one of the touchstone cooks of the generation before Clarice. Notice that Clarice's recipe is a variation of Runa's. Brown bread is a little like Anton Diabelli's waltz that he sent out to half the composers in Europe in 1820. They all contributed a variation a piece. Schubert is there, the child Liszt, Czerny, Hummel, and finally, greedy Beethoven who baked thirty-three different loaves of Diabelli, trying to get to the bottom of the mystery of music — the mystery of bread in another incarnation.

Runa's Brown Bread

2½ cups milk (scalded and cooled)
2 cups luke warm water
1 cup sugar

3 teaspoons salt
¾ cup melted lard
¾ cup molasses
2 cakes yeast (dissolved in a little lukewarm water and
   3 teaspoons sugar)

Make sponge and beat well. Mix 5½ cups white flour,
1½ cups dark flour into sponge by hand. Let rise twice and
push down each time. Let rise again and make into about
4 loaves. You can add more liquid for this amount
of yeast and make 5 or 6 loaves. Bake 1 hour at 350 degrees.

MRS. RUNA ANDERSON

Were there any secrets in this recipe? Any shibboleths to
keep the true bread from any but initiates? Jeanette had three
cautions. Grocery-store yeast won't do. Get live yeast from
bakers and tend it yourself. Oil or shortening will not do.
Bread wants lard and since the decline and fall of the old lard-
hog, make friends with a farmer or butcher and render your
own. Finally, real graham flour has almost disappeared from
the market. Whole wheat, whatever the current cant, will not
do. It is not not smooth enough. Find a source for the real
thing, whatever trouble it may cost you.

Now, you are almost ready to make bread, but not quite.
We have to go one layer deeper into history to find the *enigma,*
the unannounced absent tune at the bottom of Elgar's variations. The 1913 Y.L.U. Cookbook prints Mrs. Gunnar B.
Bjornson's recipe for brown bread. She was wife and mother
to the most distinguished family of Icelanders in Minneota—
her husband was the newspaper editor and master of English
prose; her children were politicians, journalists, composers.
She was a Canadian Icelander from the large Winnipeg colony,
born Ingibjörg Áugustína Hördal. After marrying Gunnar, she
came to Minneota, a young wife unconnected to the local immigrant community. On her first shopping expedition to the

Big Store, Minneota's Icelandic emporium and supermarket combined, 1900-style, the "girls" who worked there asked her name.

"Ingibjörg," she answered.

"What an ugly name," they all said. "Do you have another?"

"Áugustína," she answered. (All this in Icelandic.)

"Then we shall call you Augustine," the "girls" agreed. "It's a pretty name."

To her dying day, seventy-odd years later, she was Ingibjörg north of the border and Augustine south. But brown bread is brown bread by whatever name we call it. Here's her newly minted English prose from 1913, the best written of the recipes you have had so far.

Brown Bread

At noon, when potatoes are cooked for dinner, drain off the water, using it to scald a cup of flour. When this is cool, add 1 cake yeast, which has been dissolved in ¼ c. warm water. Mix well and let stand in a warm place till evening. Then add 2 qts. warm water and stir in enough flour to make a stiff batter. Cover and set in a warm place over night. In the morning add ¾ c. molasses, ¾ c. brown sugar, 2 tbs. salt, ½ c. lard, 1 qt. graham flour. If not stiff enough to knead, add white flour. Knead well. Let rise and knead again. Make into loaves and set in a warm place till light. Bake 1 hour or 1¼ hours.

Mrs. G. B. Bjornson

Beyond this point we cannot go, if we wish to remain on the North American continent. The roots of this recipe will go back a thousand years if you follow them — or longer. Nothing has happened easily, singly, or suddenly on this planet so far.

After bread, *Vinarterta*. I already a gave a sound recipe

many thousands of words ago, and if you paused in reading to make it and succeeded, then there are crumbs scattered on the margin of this page, little blotches of prune filling disguised as exclamation marks. Your fingers are sticky as they turn these pages. Don't wash them, lick them. But if you hold *Vinarterta* in your hands now, you know all these things. Auntie Clarice used Mrs. Jokull with one caveat noted in her recipe card; after shortening, she lists the real ingredients (lard or butter). I have a feeling lard is right, but butter is satisfactory.

The other school of *Vinarterta* in Minneota uses this recipe

Vinarterta

    1 cup butter
    1 cup sugar
    2 eggs
    4 tablespoons sweet milk (part cream)
    4 cups flour
    3 level teaspoons baking powder
    1 teaspoon fresh ground cardamom

Roll out and bake in 5 layers at 350 degrees

Filling

Stew 1 pound of prunes until tender (water to cover prunes). Pit prunes when cooled. Return prunes to juice when cooled. Return prunes to juice and add 1 cup sugar. Boil until thickened. Then spread between layers.

Rannveig Guttormsson, the minister's wife in Minneota for nearly fifty years made *Vinarterta* and it passes muster. The variation, pried out of her grandson's wife, Gail Perrizo, a French Canadian *Vinarterta* cook, is to add cinnamon to the mashed prunes when you boil them. Note the great gulf in recipes. Sour cream in Mrs. Jokull's, sweet milk in Mrs. Guttormsson's. Presumably these two august Icelandic ladies are still debating this vexing question in the next world. May the angels enjoy the leftover crumbs. The idea of the heavenly hosts serenading one another with cardamom breath pleases me.

Whatever the dangers to international harmony, I am now going to give you a piece of the devil's work to caution you against it. Having this *Vinarterta* in your house might once have been cause of investigation by The House Un-American Activities Committee. It is surely as rational or legal as any means they invented to persecute and terrorize Americans for the sin of behaving like Americans. Or that during the Cultural Revolution the Chinese used to summon their neighbors to "struggle meetings" and beat them to death. If you missed H.U.A.C. or the Cultural Revolution, bide your time. They are coming again. Faster than you think. Trust me. Under no circumstances should you try this recipe in your house. Hide it from children in case the TV is broken and they should read this page and be seduced by it. It is wrong. It courts the wrath of the gods. It is the Canadian Icelandic version of *Vinarterta*. Every deviation from Minneota *Vinarterta* is a mistake, a blasphemy. Here it is as it appears in David Arnason's book *The New Icelanders*.

Vinarterta

Vinarterta is a Viennese torte that was popular first in Denmark, then in Iceland in the 1860s and 70s. The fad soon ended in Iceland, but the immigrants who came to Canada continued to make it. It is the national dish of New Icelanders, though it is rarely seen in Iceland itself.

To make:
Cream 1 cup of butter well. Add 1½ cups sugar gradually. Add 3 eggs, one at a time. Beat after each addition. Add 1 teaspoon almond extract, 1 cup light cream. Add 4 cups sifted all purpose flour with 3 teaspoons baking powder

and ¼ teaspoon salt. Work in the four as much as possible. Turn out on a pastry board. Divide into seven equal parts, roll thin and bake in a rather quick oven. Spread the following prune filling between layers.

Prune filling:
Soak ½ cup pitted prunes and cook until tender. Add 2½ cups sugar and bring to a boil. Cook until tender. Remove from stove and add 1 tablespoon vanilla and 1 teaspoon crushed cardamom. Let filling cool before spreading between layers. Ice with thin butter icing with almond flavour. There is some dispute as to whether the authentic recipe calls for six layers or seven. We belong to the group of seven, but acknowledge that there may be some virtue to six.

There it is! Don't you dare make it! (In fact, it's splendid stuff, but quite different from Mrs. Jokull's version.)

Now we have brown bread and *Vinarterta* on the table, maybe some homemade rhubarb jam and a *rullupylsa* — a pickled mutton sausage. We need coffee. Since, like so many immigrants to the midwest, the Icelanders settled above the foulest well-water in North America, fragrant with iron, sulfur, and various bilious salts, we need a recipe. Fill a large white enamel coffee pot with whatever water you have. While it comes to a boil at the back of the stove, break an egg into a glass bowl and stir it around until it froths a bit. Add coffee grounds sufficient for the pot, remembering always that your grandfather left Iceland (or wherever) because the Danish merchants imposed a monopoly on the import of coffee, gouging the poor farmers so mercilessly that they emigrated first to Brazil and afterwards here to North America. Make a brown pasty goop out of egg and grounds. Break the shell into it if you like. When the water boils vigorously, empty the bowl of goop into the pot. It will froth maniacally. Throw a cup of cold water over the top so that the grounds congeal and sink. Bring the coffee just back to the boil and dowse it again. Let it steep and settle for a while.

Now you have coffee fit for *Vinarterta* or brown bread, mild, clear coffee with no bitterness but plenty of memory.

Nine years ago I went to China to teach for a year, a "foreign expert" on a university exchange. I arrived, like so many others, a cultural virgin and came home not quite deflowered, but having a small sense of what defloration might be. I had never traveled to or lived in a third-world country before, a place where the poverty and misery of daily life couldn't be disguised as "exotic, colorful peasant life in a wise and ancient civilization." If an American actually lives somewhere else for as little as a year, simple sanity requires that you step outside the world of travel brochures and received ideas. I saw, if not quite from inside, at least a close-range view of what it meant to be truly poor and simultaneously conscious of that poverty. That insight affected the life and opinions of every American I met who went through the experience, feeling the hot breath of a quite un-American world on his face. Furthermore, it had an effect on the notion of what eating meant—of what food, in fact, stood for in a human life.

When I came home, genuinely thin for the first time in a quarter century, people asked endless questions that seemed to me at the time silly, but as I think twice seem now to be the only questions they had it in their power to ask: not real questions at all, but not-quite-clicked-in still foggy metaphors for what they really wanted to know. Do they eat dog? Indeed they do. Delicious. Snake? Yup, but I couldn't afford it. Eels? Ambrosial! Cat, monkey, buffalo cartilage, pig nose, dried squid, rubbery sea cucumbers, straight infusions of whole garlic cloves, bean curd aged to an astonishing rottenness, fried chunks of straight belly fat, bottom feeding rough fish, dried insects, all of it, all. Whatever walked, crawled, slithered, flew, or swam through nature or grew out of the thin soil between two rocks had a democratic chance of appearing in a Chinese wok and finally at table.

The Chinese use food to a much greater degree than

Americans can begin to imagine for ends beyond eating, mere staying alive, beyond even what Clarice might have done. She cooked as a gesture of affection, doing her just business to make a communal life, living up to what she thought her duty, though it often mingled with her pleasure. She cooked because that's what you did if you were Clarice, or Pauline or my mother Jona or Auntie Dora or Runa or Augustine or ten other people probably now dead you can name out of your own life. But neither did they eat to get ahead in the world (or get ahead in the world to up the ante of what and where you ate) nor did they use a table as a place to quash political questions and pacify foreigners or strangers. Remember Nixon's banquets in China: the endless dishes, the endless toasting, the endless empty chit-chat. Every teacher or businessman in China endures these banquets, given by officials who have some use they intend to make of you. Every time a subject comes into table talk that might veer into the general neighborhood of content, more dishes arrive, more toasts, more blathering about weather and the food itself. You quickly discover that these very officials have clawed their way up the ladder of ambition to be precisely where they are—at an endless succession of rich tables, sampling choice delicacies on the Party budget, humoring foreigners and each other. Important people eat important food. When you are stuffed like a boiled sausage ready to burst, groggy from rice liquor and too many eels, it's time to talk business over tea and fruit. It was beyond Auntie Clarice to imagine food as a weapon or an opening move in negotiations. She, of course, used her table as a way of manipulating those who sat down to it, but in slightly more benign ways.

When I first moved to China, my students christened my Minneota marsupial paunch "the landlord's belly." They imagined that anyone who stored that many spare meals behind their stretched belt must be a rich and important person. They meant the description half whimsically, but only half. To be fat in China—or any poor country—required money and high position. The poor, a billion strong in China and many billions on the planet, have little use for Nordic Track or NutriSystem.

Every American I know who arrived home after a long stretch in China found himself shocked by the sheer blubber of his fellow citizens. The shock began at the first American airport where you landed and continued for months until your mental picture of what a human being ought to look like clicked back into American sync. Presumably by this time, pizza, Kentucky fried, tube time, your Chevy, and "Welcome Home" dinners served by your equivalent of Auntie Clarice have clicked your own midsection back into sync, too. You've put your old China Levi's into the "tomorrow" pile and bought an elastic waist or two.

Yet here it is the poor who wallow in blubber, the rich and successful whose skin is stretched tautly over their visible ribs. Americans spend enough on diets and exercise contraptions and hypnosis and stomach stapling to feed a whole Chinese province grandly for years. The slums are full of landlord's bellies without a dime to pay rent to a thin and bony landlord.

The meat and potatoes look prevails in Minneota, as in any farm town. Past the first litheness of youth, we grow steadily out over our big silver country-western belt buckles; we fill out our stretch slacks. Only in the nursing home do we shrink down again to sparrowy lightness, a little dried out and finally leached of fat for our flight into the next world of glorified bodies.

The true glory of Chinese eating comes not in banqueting halls or behind discreet screens, but in shabby food stalls in the streets or in the Chinese equivalent of Auntie Clarice's kitchen, a room full of generosity, ingenuity, and good smells. The genius of Chinese cooking lies not in opulence, but in thrift—using everything, making something out of nothing, improvising, making poetry out of making do. In that regard, it resembles the cooking of farm women like Clarice who survived the Depression from beginning to end and learned spontaneity from that stern task master—necessity. I ate fifteen-course meals in a cramped room, dishes cooked on a five-gallon pail stove of charcoal topped with chicken wire for a wok to sit on. The hosts probably went into debt for a month to feed an overweight foreigner who had done them some small favor or whom they either fancied or pitied: so far from home, so lonesome, so hungry. What might have been compost in a Minneota kitchen became high art in the hands of a Chinese Aunt or Uncle Clarice. Cooking is a unisex art (which explains a little of its sexiness). At a table full of astonishingly thin people laughing and noisily smacking their lips, chopsticks flying around the fish-flavored pork, the chili eels, the golden needle mushrooms, the white fungus soup. These occasions needed only brown bread and *Vinarterta,* and if I had stayed in China long enough, I might have been able to make a few converts.

After China, I never again looked at a table in Minnesota with quite the same eyes. Lutefisk was not a joke but a metaphor of ancestral solidarity, of eating your way into history. *Vinarterta* was not only a pleasure, but a gift of love and intelligence, true soul food, the Icelander's sweet potato pie. Women like Clarice were not kitchen drudges, but the genuine cement inside a community's sense of itself and its work on this planet. Fat was not a disgrace, not even a health problem, but a sign that we had been lucky in America but hadn't yet figured out how to make intelligent use of that luck or be sufficiently conscious in our gratitude for it. State dinners in Saint Paul or in Washington honoring something or other, or catered nouvelle cuisine in the dining salons of the suburban rich seemed as loathsome and comic as they really were— the Midwest equivalents of Great-Hall-of-the-People-Festive-Banquets-for-Foreign-Friends. Julia Child seemed a better friend to American civilization than Bob Dole, Bill Clinton, the Hug Doctor, the Stock Exchange, David Letterman, the

Council of Bishops, or Amway. To love and respect food is only to be human, to honor desire as it deserves in our too short span of bodily life in this often sweet world.

I'll close by taking you to lunch twice at two of my favorite cafes, one in China and one in Ghent. Neither are fancy. You won't have to "dress." Old Levi's and muddy boots will do very nicely. Neither costs much. You can leave your surplus cash at home or give it to the poor. Both places will please you and fill you, not only with human food, but with fun, adventure, the warmth and battiness of your fellow higher mammals. If you don't fancy these cafes, then I'm not sure that our friendship will have a future; but I am a hopeful man, always open to the possibility that human beings will come to their senses.

It's a muddy street in Wuhan, a few blocks away from the college where I teach. Spring has been cold, raw, damp, indoors and out, skies slate gray and dripping. The scratchy loudspeakers trumpet cheery propaganda at all hours; the students look gloomy and morose, still sunk in 1992 by their 1989 Tiananmen hangovers. The bureaucrats are a cut below average which means Dante would sink them deep in the ice. The foreigner food in the screened room at the college is overpriced grease and overaged fish. Cheer up. It's lunch time. My students first discovered the Shanghai *hun-dun* stand in a nondescript row of street food stalls. It looked even shabbier than its neighbors, but they assured me that the *hun-duns* were very delicious and cheap. So they were.

It's a sort of lean-to, half-outdoors and half-in, the interior roofed with leaky sheet-metal sections. Customers sit under umbrellas eating or sandwiched in a corner next to a pot positioned to catch the cold drips. The cook, the waitress, and all the customers are bundled in multiple layers against the stiff wind off the Yangtze. Come in, sit down, find a dry stool. Summon your best Wuchang pigeon Chinese and order a *pijiu* (beer) and a large bowl of *hun-dun*. A mammoth black iron pot steams and bubbles over an open fire. The smell coming at you is a sort of olfactory incantation. Two young girls sit folding raw *hun-dun* onto a board, their hands half-gloved against the wind. They grab a *hun-dun* skin, stuff it with a chopstick full of meat, shrimp, and mysteries, fold it neatly and efficiently into itself, and set it in an orderly row on the floury board. Now and then, a fresh infusion of *hun-dun* plop into the steaming pot and another little cloud of aromatic fog engulfs the place. The waitress dusts the quart beer bottle and opens it with the house church key. She sets down a bowl of hot pepper sauce for the adventurous and the Sichaunese, then brings you a brimming bowl of *hun-dun* in soup with a recently rewiped porcelain spoon. A new leak develops in the tin roof so you move slightly to keep rain out of your *hun-dun*. Bon appetit! The *hun-dun* are plump and juicy, swelled up in the ambrosial stock. The proprietor comes over to greet you. He is a handsome man in his forties, Shanghai-nese, a P.L.A. veteran, trying to make a few *renminbi* in the *hun-dun* business, one of the "New China" capitalists. "How are the *hun-dun*," he asks. *"Hen Hao!"* (very good!) you say, because language sufficient to their quality lives in you only in English. Maybe your face tells him the rest of the story, and he gets the point that you are mightily pleased so he is pleased, too. "Tell other foreigners," he says. You are tempted to lick the bottom of the bowl, so piquant and lovely was the stock. You don't, though. Manners. . . . You ask what is the secret of the flavor. "I am from Shanghai," he says. "We like a little sweetness, a little fish flavor." The stock is a masterpiece in any language. The tab? Three *kwai* or somewhere in the neighborhood of a half-dollar. I'll buy in Wuhan. You just get there. That soggy stall is my happiest memory of that unhappy city.

Now on to Ghent, five miles east of Minneota, population 300 or so, site of Belgian-American Days every August and Rolle Bolle tournaments every frost-free Thursday night. Ghent boasts a Catholic Church, a Catholic school, a grain elevator or two, a big farm-supply store, a body shop, a co-op

garage, a post office, a legion hall, a ballroom, two fine bars—
Ted's and Minnesota's oldest legal bar, the Silver Dollar—a
handful of retired priests, the largest colony of Flemish speakers in Minnesota, the retirement houses of local farmers
adorned in summer with enormous meticulously weeded gar-
dens. There's a little skating rink, a ball diamond, the ghost of
a road house, and the M&M Cafe, formerly the Copper
Penny—site of our lunch. It's a blustery Thursday in February,
five-below with a stiff Alberta clipper blowing from the northwest, shimmying the stop signs and trying to bite anything
alive in the neck. Get your butt in here—if we don't get there
by noon, the special will be gone. Business has been booming
since the *Mascot* came out last week with the story that Lyon
County Pork Producers gave Brenda their big award for "ex-
cellence in pork promotion." The plaque hangs right there on
the wall next to the church picture. The place is already filling
up, old wood booths along the side, three big kitchen tables in
the middle. The front one has got a "no smoking" sign on it
next to an ashtray with a couple of butts in it. Don't worry.
This is Ghent, not the Cities. The back table where Mark and
Marian, Brenda's parents (and the M&M of the name), sit
when business is slow is adorned with an eternal cribbage
board, a couple of decks, a scratch pad, and a pencil stub. After
the rush, the retired, the help, the relatives, and any other
stray, live bodies come in for a leisurely game of afternoon
whist, 500, buck euchre. There's a leather dice cup on the
counter, but nobody shakes for lunch, only morning coffee.
We're in luck! Look at the blackboard—*Gentse Hutspot,*
Belgian boiled-dinner today—$4.00 with soup or salad and
rolls, coffee extra. There's Earl, the U.P.S. man on his daily
rounds. No *Hutspot* for him. He's regular as a Swiss watch—
peanut butter and jelly sandwich, banana cream pie, 7-Up, a
pack of Tareytons, a minute to scan the Marshall papers before
firing up the truck. A man who can't be tempted by *Hutspot!*
Now there's discipline! Not me. I'll have the special, wild-rice

soup, coffee, maybe bread pudding afterwards. We'll see how
full we get. Bring the brown mustard, too, maybe the homemade horseradish. Sit down, we can squeeze another chair
here. Cold enough for you then? Been a pretty nice winter so
far; guess we've got it coming. Have they turned on that rural
water from South Dakota yet? Tuesday. Heard it blew out
pipes all over town. Johnsons got a basement full of water.
Here's the soup. Pass the pepper. Got an extra napkin? What
do you mean, I'm not drinking coffee fast enough? Oh, this
Hutspot is good! Sticks to the ribs on a cold day. Isn't this a
parsnip? Don't see those much anymore. I like 'em. I don't like
'em. Eat your damn parsnip—it's good for you.

If you're not having a good time by now, you never will.
You have consciously chosen the pinched abstemious life of
the thin-lipped anchorite, and I can't help you. These are your
fellow human beings crowded together in a smoky cafe, eating
food they like, jostling playfully, talking smart, praising what
deserves praise. I ask Brenda, too busy now to make chit-chat,
for the recipe and she gives it to me while she piles plates. It's
simple—like the universe from one angle. Just throw a big
chunk of pork in the bottom of the pot. Brown it first, her
mother Marian interrupts. Yah, you brown it, throw some salt
and pepper on it, then pile on layers of any available vegetable
in the root family: rutabagas, parsnips, turnips, then make another layer of potatoes, carrots, onions. Celery, too, adds
Marian, wanting to do her motherly duty and get the recipe
right. Oh, celery's a nothing, says Brenda; if you've got it,
throw it in, if not, don't worry. Put it all in the pot, cover it
with cabbage, and cook the hell out of it. No juice or stock, I
ask? No can of beer? Mark chimes in: all that pork and those
vegetables make their own juice. Why waste the can of beer? It
just cooks off. Drink the beer and eat the *hutspot*.

Got room for bread pudding? It's made out of yesterday's
caramel rolls, but we'll nuke it a little and there's half-and-half
to top it off. I think I saved just enough room.

That's what eating is like in civilization among human beings. If you can think of a better way to stay alive on this planet, try it. You probably shouldn't include me. I like this world. Pass the *Vinarterta*, please.

In case your kitchen library is lightly stocked, I'll add a bibliography of my favorites. This small list will improve not only your table, but your prose. I'm on the side of whoever was asked whether they thought long-hair music superior to short—Beethoven to Jelly Roll Morton or Glen Gould to Art Tatum—and gave the answer, just and correct, that there is only good music and bad music, a distinction of quality, not of kind. The same is true of literature, of whatever is superior in the written language of an age. I prefer these food books to vast numbers of other kinds: novels, poems, plays, and other essays. Beneath them lives the usual junk, but of what genre is that not true? Is food not a sufficient subject, eating not a substantial enough metaphor to engage our intelligence? Christianity has done pretty well by using food as a base on which to make a theology.

Book List

Julia Child's *Mastering the Art of French Cooking.* One of the crucial books. *The Way to Cook.* The reference to the *Tao De Ching* may be unconscious, but it is perfectly apt. The way to eat is the way to live.

*

The Joy of Cooking. Irma Rombauer and Marion Rombauer Becker. If this classic has not outsold Rush Limbaugh, Robert James Waller, Leo Buscaglia, and probably the Bible, it does not speak well for us as a civilization. It has new gems to discover each day we use it. Try Duckling *Rouennaise* out of your own spattered, binding-cracked personal copy.

> Unless you choke your duck, pluck the down on its breast immediately afterward and cook it within 24 hours, you cannot lay claim to having produced an authentic Rouen duck. The first two steps assure the dark red flesh and the special flavor of this dish. If, as is likely, duck-strangling will bring you into local disrepute, you may waive the sturdy peasant preliminaries and serve a modified version, garnished with quotation marks.

Now those are sentences. Go world-besotted traveler, imitate them, if you dare.

*

M. F. K. Fisher, *The Art of Eating.* And all her other books, too. She is of a piece. I've quoted her already to pique your interest and cannot add to Auden's accurate praise: "I do not know of anyone in the United States today who writes better prose." True then; true now.

*

Robert Farrar Capon, *The Supper of the Lamb.* It's all right for a man to join this list, isn't it? Capon is an Anglican priest, hearty and hungry and wildly orthodox. If C.S. Lewis had been a more enthusiastic and devout eater, he might have written this book. It is a lovely praise of the wonder of food as a divine gift—and the recipes work very nicely too, thank-you.

These are all Americans, our Olympic food squad. You should have *Escoffier* and *Brillet-Savarin* and a good compendium of

Chinese lore on your shelf, too, but of course you already do, don't you?

*

Here are my three favorite stories of dinner, small proof of the power of eating as metaphor:

Babette's Feast by Isak Dinesen. A thin woman with a bad stomach's Dionysian hymn to the power of food and the divine art of cooking.

The Dead, James Joyce. A melancholy Christmas dinner, but a long, lovely hors d'oeuvres to the most delicious concluding sentence in modern prose.

The gargantuan, long, and comic Thanksgiving dinner in Jon Hassler's novel *Dear James.* If you keep your eyes open at your own ghastly ritual family dinners, you will find rich material for literature. Wait patiently for the appearance of the caramel rolls.

*

I will not add to this list Trimalchio's dinner from the *Satyricon* of Petronius Arbiter or several dinners in Rabelais. Put these books over there by the Canadian *Vinarterta* and leave them alone.

*

Note that the titles of several of these books include the words Art and Joy—short, plain English words but heavy and useful. Eat them, get fat on them, and let them bear fruit in your life.

Acknowledgments

This book, maybe more than most, could not exist without the kindness and generous intelligence of others. The courteous cliché turns out, for once, to be true. Thanks first to my friend, Phyllis Yoshida, who has typed, advised, and helped with so many of my books. She understands much more than I how to make technology useful to a Luddite.

And thanks to:

Tom Sand, who knows how to find things

Sandy Mosch and the whole English Department gang at Southwest State University

Jim Phillips for the gift of the photo on page 95

Virgil and Marnie Gislason in whose back room everything arrives

Walt and Raeanna Gislason for a higher view of the planet

The children of Clarice Josephson for recipes, spare rooms, dinner, and political advice: Allen and Marlene, Marilyn and Russ, Chuck and Joan and their son Ken, and Lester and Donna

Frank Josephson, another keeper of stories

My Holm cousins—whether they showed up or not!— Francis, Eileen, Doris, Emmy Lou, Alice Ann, Wally, Roger, Dick, and John David

Perry Lueders for advice on drama, grammar, and recipes

Gail Perrizo and Tom Guttormsson, dear neighbors and partners

The Minneota Library—and Mary Hofteig Buysse

The *Minneota Mascot*—and Jon Guttormsson
and Gail Van Vooren

The Bush Foundation for their generous artist's grant

M.J. Brekken, who can't help giving everything away with love

Bill and Jona Holm, who planted this book deliberately

The dead Minneotans whose lives I have tried to honor, and
the live Minneotans, my neighbors, who accept with calm
wryness the odd fellow who lives among them

Emilie Buchwald and the gang at Milkweed. What luck for a
writer to live close to one of the great editors in America!

To my neighbor, Fred Manfred, who taught me a lot
about living in small places and keeping your eyes open to
history. Fred liked sleeping in Minneota even though
the beds were too short.

David Pichaske, first editor and publisher of the old *Music of
Failure*, who kept the book alive through thick and thin

Ralph Larson for his fine centennial history of Minneota

The South West Regional History Center at Southwest State
University for the magnificent Big Store photographs

Bob Firth and Wayne Gudmundson for trying to
teach me better how to look at pictures

Minnesota Historical Society for "information"

Jeanette Konold for her cooking wisdom
and her brown bread and *Vinarterta*

Brenda, Marian, and Mark Wigness of the M&M Cafe,
Ghent, for hutsepot and good humor

Yu Dingman for teaching me a thing or two about what
Minneota was not, and for tracking down *hun-dun*

Matta and Jon Bjornson for their help with
Icelandic spelling, grammar, and sense

Quoted Works

Material in this book is quoted from the following publications:

Sherwood Anderson, "Death in the Woods," in *Certain Things Last: The Selected Short Stories of Sherwood Anderson*, ed. Charles E. Modlin (New York: Four Walls Eight Windows, 1992), 152, 159, 160.

David Arnason and Vincent Arnason, eds., *The New Icelanders: A North American Community* (Winnipeg: Turnstone Press, 1994), 49. Copyright © 1994 by David Arnason and Vincent Arnason. Reprinted with permission from Turnstone Press.

W. H. Auden, from the back cover of M. F. K. Fisher, *The Art of Eating* (New York: Macmillan, 1937).

The Bhagavad Gita.

William Blake, "The Garden of Love," in *Songs of Innocence and of Experience* (New York: Orion Press, 1967), 43.

William Blake, "The Question Answer'd" and "[The Marriage Ring] The Fairy," in *Blake: Complete Writings,* ed. Geoffrey Keynes (London: Oxford University Press, 1969), 178, 180.

Pat Conroy quote can be found in John Berendt, "The Conroy Saga," *Vanity Fair* (July 1995): 139. Conroy quote taken from the introduction to Conroy's book, *Military Brats.*

David F. Costello, *The Prairie World: Plants and Animals of the Grassland Sea* (New York: Thomas Y. Crowell, 1975), 4.

Father John Doe, "Serenity Prayer" in *Sobriety without End* (Indianapolis: SMT Guild, 1957), 55.

M. F. K. Fisher from *Serve It Forth*. Excerpted with permission of Macmillan General Reference U. S. A., a division of Simon & Schuster Inc., from *The Art of Eating*, by M. F. K. Fisher, 96–99. Copyright 1937, 1954, © 1990 by M. F. K. Fisher.

E. M. Forester, *A Passage to India* (New York: Harcourt, Brace & World, 1924), 51–52.

Epic of Gilgamesh.

Bill Holm, "Old Family Pictures" and "August in Waterton, Alberta," in *The Dead Get By with Everything* (Minneapolis: Milkweed Editions, 1990), 15, 80.

Robert G. Ingersoll, "Mistake of Moses," in *Complete Lectures of Col. R. G. Ingersoll*, vol. 1 (Chicago: Rhodes and McClure, 1896), 276–77.

D. H. Lawrence, *Apocalypse* (New York: Penguin Books, 1931), 124–25.

D. H. Lawrence, "The Gods! The Gods!" in *The Portable D. H. Lawrence*, ed. Diana Trilling (New York: Penguin Books, 1977), 495.

D. H. Lawrence, "Piano," in *The Complete Poems of D. H. Lawrence*, ed. Vivian de Sola Pinto and Warren Roberts (New York: Penguin Books, 1977), 148.

Edward Lucie-Smith, *The Invented Eye* (New York: Paddington Press, 1975), 6–8.

Edmund Baron de Mandat-Grancey, *Cow-Boys and Colonels* (Lincoln: University of Nebraska Press, 1984), 7–11.

C. Austin Miles, "In the Garden," in *Jubilate: A Modern Sunday-School Hymnal*, ed. J. Lincoln Hall, C. Austin Miles, and Adam Geibel (Philadelphia: Hall-Mack, 1917).

Minneota (Minnesota) Mascot, September 8, 1899.

Minneota (Minnesota) Mascot, December 14, 1994, pp. 1, 8.

Flannery O'Connor quote can be found in John Berendt, "The Conroy Saga," *Vanity Fair* (July 1995): 139.

Thomas Paine, *The Age of Reason* (Chicago: Belford, Clarke & Co., 1889), 5–6.

Ole Rölvaag, *Giants in the Earth: A Saga of the Prairie* (New York: Harper Perennial, 1991), 3–4.

Irma S. Rombauer and Marion Rombauer Becker, *The Joy of Cooking* (Indianapolis: Bobbs-Merrill, 1964), 474.

Carl Sandburg, "Gone," in *Chicago Poems* (New York: Henry Holt and Company, 1916), 155.

Robert Service, "The Shooting of Dan McGrew," in *The Spell of the Yukon* (1907; reprint, New York: G. P. Putnam's Sons, 1989), 55. Reprinted by permission of the Putnam Publishing Group from *The Collected Poems of Robert Service* by Robert Service. Copyright © 1940 by Robert Service.

Stephan G. Stephansson from the book, *Stephan G. Stephansson: Selected Prose and Poetry*, trans. Kristjana Gunnars (Red Deer, Alberta: Red Deer College Press, 1988), 30. Translation copyright © 1988 by Kristjana Gunnars.

Wallace Stevens, "Bantams in Pine-Woods," in *Collected Poems* (1923; reprint, New York: Alfred A. Knopf, 1951). Copyright © 1923 and renewed 1951 by Wallace Stevens. Reprinted by permission of Alfred A. Knopf, Inc.

Walt Whitman, "Song of Myself," "Democratic Vistas," and "Songs of Parting," in *The Portable Walt Whitman*, ed. Mark Van Doren, Malcolm Cowley, and Gay Wilson Allen, (New York: Penguin Books, 1977), 86, 325–26, 505–06.

Walt Whitman, "Leaves of Grass," in *Leaves of Grass*, ed. Emory Holloway (Garden City: Doubleday, 1926), 29, 39–40.

Bill Holm was born in 1943, grandson of Icelandic emigrants, on a farm in Swede Prairie Township, north of Minneota. He now lives in town. For thirty years he has taught literature and writing in Lawrence, Kansas, Hampton, Virginia, White Bear Lake, Minnesota, Reykjavík, Iceland, Xi'an, P.R. China, and now at Southwest State University in Marshall, Minnesota, not far from Minneota. In the meantime he has published eight books, both poems and essays, including *Coming Home Crazy* and, most recently, *Eccentric Islands,* a book of travel essays that describes the homeland where so many of the characters in *The Heart Can Be Filled Anywhere on Earth* were born. Holm's dilapidated house is full of books and keyboards—piano, harpsichord, clavichord—on which he practices every day with great love and less skill. Currently he is trying to get to the bottom of Joseph Haydn, whose fifty-odd sonatas show him to be a man who wanted genuinely to please and console his fellow humans with beauty and intelligence. Haydn does this with modesty, calm, humor, and continual invention—not a bad role model for Americans. Holm travels to whatever strange places he can manage, always packing a copy of *Leaves of Grass* next to his socks and underwear.

To order books or for more information, contact Milkweed at
(800) 520-6455 or visit our website (www.milkweed.org).

Eccentric Islands:
Travels Real and Imaginary
Bill Holm

Coming Home Crazy:
An Alphabet of China Essays
Bill Holm

Brown Dog of the Yaak:
Essays on Art and Activism
Rick Bass

Changing the Bully Who Rules the World:
Reading and Thinking about Ethics
Carol Bly

The Passionate, Accurate Story:
Making Your Heart's Truth into Literature
Carol Bly

Swimming with Giants:
My Encounters with Whales, Dolphins, and Seals
Anne Collet

Writing the Sacred into the Real
Alison Hawthorne Deming

The Most Wonderful Books:
Writers on Discovering the Pleasures of Reading
Edited by Michael Dorris and Emilie Buchwald

Boundary Waters:
The Grace of the Wild
Paul Gruchow

Grass Roots:
The Universe of Home
Paul Gruchow

The Necessity of Empty Places
Paul Gruchow

The Art of Writing:
Lu Chi's Wen Fu
Translated from the Chinese by Sam Hamill

Shedding Life:
Disease, Politics, and Other Human Conditions
Miroslav Holub

A Sense of the Morning:
Field Notes of a Born Observer
David Brendan Hopes

Taking Care:
Thoughts on Storytelling and Belief
William Kittredge

Testimony:
Writers of the West Speak On Behalf of Utah Wilderness
Compiled by Stephen Trimble and Terry Tempest Williams

Shaped by Wind and Water:
Reflections of a Naturalist
Ann Haymond Zwinger

Interior design by Will Powers.

Typeset in ITC Galliard by Stanton Publication Services, Inc.

Printed on acid-free Liberty paper
by Sheridan Books.